No Foot, No Horse

Foot Balance:
The Key to Soundness and Performance

To Peter
Best Wishes

Martin

No Foot, No Horse

Foot Balance:
The Key to Soundness and Performance

Gail Williams BA (Hons) PhD
and
Martin Deacon FWCF

KENILWORTH PRESS

First published in Great Britain by
Kenilworth Press Ltd, Addington, Buckingham, MK18 2JR

ISBN 1-872119-15-8

British Library Cataloguing in Publication Data
A catalogue record for this book is available from the British Library.

Layout and typesetting by Kenilworth Press

Colour illustrations by Carole Vincer

Printed in Hong Kong by Midas

Contents

Foreword by Mac Head FWCF

This most useful and long overdue text will have a considerable impact on the welfare of all horses, especially the competition horse, which has to remain sound without the aid of drug therapy. The techniques and information documented are not simply theories that have worked in the odd instance, but are those that have been employed on hundreds of case histories, with a very high percentage resulting in an improvement in the well-being and soundness of the horse. The emphasis on considering the whole horse and its individual conformation and gait, not just the hoof or lower limb when shoeing and trimming, must be strongly encouraged. Virtually all basic tuition of equine anatomy is founded on examples of the 'perfect' horse, which hardly exists. It is only when the student is able to grasp the natural fundamental requirements of the so-called 'imperfect' horse that he or she will start to fully understand proper practice.

There will be some professionals who will have difficulty with the principles of correct foot balance, as what they read is contrary to their present under-standing and previous basic tuition. Even the application of the T-square, which has been in use for over a hundred years, is scorned by some narrow thinkers. Constructive debate is the essence of development but the horse owner and trainer must exercise caution with any practitioner who cannot understand or condemns the main elements of this excellent work.

T. F. M. HEAD, FWCF
Master, The Worshipful Company of Farriers (1998-1999)
JULY 1999

Acknowledgements

We acknowledge with many thanks the following, without whom this book could not have been written:

Chris Colles BVet Med, MRCVS, PhD, Ron Ware FWCF and Mac Head FWCF whose knowledge, thoughts and ideas on the subject of foot balance and farriery have proved such an inspiration.

Ms Jo Hodges Cert Ed, BHSI(SM), LCSP(Assn) for proofreading the chapter on backs.

Carole Vincer for her superb line drawings.

The owners of the many horses who appear in this book, for allowing us to photograph their pride and joy when perhaps he was not looking quite at his best.

Peter Howard and Sue Deacon, our respective spouses, for their encouragement.

Gail Williams and Martin Deacon

Preface

We wanted to write this book so that everyone involved in horse management, from owners and trainers to farriers and veterinary surgeons, would understand the importance of foot balance. Whatever use we put the horse to, his feet form the complete dynamic base upon which he functions. If the feet are imbalanced, then the whole horse is functionally imbalanced and his ability to perform optimally is impaired. The test of whether a horse is 'right' is not simply a question of whether he is sound or lame. In the absence of traumatic injury it can be a long road from sound to lame. Horses have a surprising ability to almost imperceptably alter their locomotor patterns to compensate for functional imbalances. The reverse side of this coin is that in the long term these locomotor compensations lead to injury and/or disease – in the most extreme of situations they could result in a much-loved or talented horse losing his life.

As soon as we apply a shoe to the foot of a horse we are preventing him from undertaking his own natural foot balancing – the normal wear and tear that his feet would be subjected to in the wild. After all, feral horses do not need farriers. Therefore it is important that the foot balance is right before the shoe is applied and the shoe is providing all the necessary support for the horse.

The role of the farrier is of fundamental importance in the management of our horses. Sympathetic farriery, carried out in a professional manner, can make a considerable difference to equine welfare and performance. The promotion of this concept is our whole reason for writing this book. Farriers, vets and owners need to understand this and work together. If we have in some way contributed to this process, we will have achieved our aim.

Gail Williams and Martin Deacon

CHAPTER 1

The Importance of Foot Balance

A good farrier is worth his weight in gold. Poor farriery could cripple your horse for ever. Unfortunately poor farriery is widely available and often encouraged.

Studies carried out on the relationship of foot imbalance to lameness conclude that **up to 95% of all horses have some form of foot imbalance which predisposes them to injury**. Owners therefore need to be able to tell the good from the bad, and to do this they must equip themselves with the knowledge of what constitutes good farriery practice.

In 1752 Jeremiah Bridges wrote an essay entitled 'No Foot, No Horse' and since that time the maxim 'No foot, no horse' has become equine lore. But the concept espoused by Bridges was in no way a new one. In the third century BC the famous Greek general and horsemaster, Xenophon, wrote:

Just as a house would be good for nothing if it were very handsome above but lacked the proper foundations, so too a horse, even if all his other points were fine, would yet be good for nothing if he had bad feet for he could not use a single one of his fine points.

Good foot balance is achieving a foot which is of a shape and strength to support the weight of the horse whilst providing a base for optimum movement. Some of the common problems that might be attributable to faulty foot balance include:

- chip fractures
- navicular disease/syndrome
- arthritis
- bad backs
- shortened striding/stumbling
- bruised heels
- hoof cracks
- sheared heels

in short, a whole host of musculo-skeletal disorders.

In the wild, the equine foot is a success because the feral horse is continually wearing down his hoof in such a way that it provides optimal foot balance for his own individual conformation and limb-loading requirements. As part of our domestication of the horse we have interfered with this process by restricting the horses' freedom to roam and applying shoes, thus preventing the horse from undertaking his own natural foot-balancing process. Without a shoe we could not adapt the horse for our use in agriculture, sport or pleasure, so we must regard shoeing as a something of a 'necessary evil'.

Whilst shoeing certainly is necessary, does it really have to be evil?

If we consider the relationship of foot imbalance and poor farriery to lameness, then evil it is. But it does not have to be like this – if we are genuine in our desire to increase not only our knowledge of the horse but also of his welfare, this is an area which we must consider to be top of our list for investigation and understanding.

The acquisition of this knowledge – especially that regarding foot balance – can prove extremely cost-effective. Lack of it can jeopardise our horses' welfare, which may result in them suffering, becoming ill or lame and requiring veterinary treatment. But if we had sufficient knowledge we could prevent this suffering and save ourselves considerable expense. In this book we will demonstrate that good farriery practice could save you a small fortune in vets' and other health-care professionals' fees.

It is a sad fact that approximately **70% of all sport horses** (certainly in the UK and possibly worldwide) **will sustain at least one musculo-skeletal disorder in any one season,** but it may come as an even greater surprise to know that as many as **threequarters of those injuries are caused or contributed to by imbalances in the feet**. Therefore if your horse is lame you have a three-out-of-four chance of improving or eradicating that lameness simply by paying scrupulous attention to the balance of his feet. Conversely, if your horse is sound his chances of staying that way are substantially improved by carefully monitoring the balance of his feet. In the most extreme of situations you could possibly be saving his life.

The shoeing of horses is an everyday occurrence and something that not many of us give enough thought to. Farriery, however, when properly performed, is an extremely demanding and skilled job. Calling the farrier to our horses is something that we should all do regularly – certainly never longer than every six weeks – but how many of us have looked at our horse and thought, 'It can wait another week'? For some reason horse owners seem to begrudge spending money on what they perceive to be just another expense in the costly business of keeping a horse. If the horse goes lame or pulls off a shoe, the farrier is an easy target for the blame. Few realise that what the farrier does could be the making or breaking of their horse because not many horse owners themselves understand the concepts of foot balance and correct shoeing.

Farriers, on the other hand, seem to regard horse owners as the enemy. They are expected to work miracles for a pittance and – in some cases – are required to trudge across a muddy field, headcollar in hand, to catch the horse before they can even shoe it. Farriers have a reputation, rightly or wrongly, as being bad-tempered and rude. If an owner asks any questions about the shoeing of their horse they are often met with the retort, 'If you think you can shoe it any better, then do it yourself'. What should be a beneficial working partnership for equine welfare turns into a battle, with the horse stuck in the middle.

This book is an attempt to demonstrate that by understanding basic principles concerning the shoeing of our horses, both the owner and the farrier can work in harmony. We will explain how to assess foot balance and how to correct the most commonly encountered farriery-related problems.

Our horses consume a great deal of our money, time and emotions and we therefore owe it to ourselves, as well as to them, to ensure that they have the best that we can possibly give them. We need to change our attitudes and begin to appreciate that what happens at the foot/shoe/surface interface can affect the horse's entire way of going. We need to understand that good farriery really is the key to soundness and performance and that not only could it prolong your horse's active life by many years, but also his entire life will be happier and healthier.

How Foot Imbalances Affect the Moving Horse

Uneven loading of the legs

To begin to understand why there is such a strong relationship between breakdown in the horse and imbalances in his feet, we must first grasp a little of the mechanics by which the horse moves.

The horse can be compared to a Formula 1 racing car in the way that he is designed. In both, the bulk of the mass is located around the centre of mass. The centre of mass is that point in the horse where the clockwise moments equal the anti-clockwise moments or, to put it more simply, that point in the horse where he could be suspended by a tiny hook and be completely in balance in all dimensions. The exact position of the centre of mass in horses is still a matter for debate, but Fig. 1.1 (overleaf) shows where it is believed to be in the standing horse – approximately under the front portion of the saddle.

(Whether the horse can actually move his centre of mass in relation to his body parts during locomotion is a moot point and many dressage, jumping and even farriery texts make bold assertions about the horse shifting his centre of mass backwards or forwards without any scientific basis in fact.)

The horse evolved to run as his major means of defence against predators. To propel the horse during locomotion the major locomotor muscles are sited close to the centre of mass – just as the engine in a racing car is situated close to the centre of mass. The further away from the centre of mass you get, the

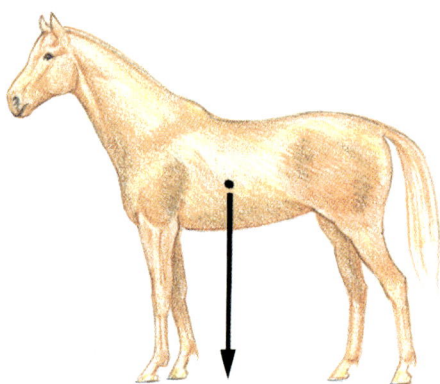

Fig. 1.1 Approximate location of centre of mass in the horse.

lighter the structures must become so that the large locomotor muscles can move the limbs through the air with as much speed as possible. There are no muscles below the knee or hock of the horse. This is because muscles are heavy structures and would become energetically disadvantageous at the extremities of limbs. So the lower limbs are worked by a series of levers and pulleys – tendons and ligaments. The bones in the horse also become lighter towards the extremities. They are small both in terms of their diameter and also in terms of their density. This is again because heavy structures at the extremities are energetically inefficient. We can therefore readily appreciate that the further away from the centre of mass a body part is, the lighter the body part and the more susceptible to injury it becomes because there are no margins for error built into the system.

If Michael Schumacher's Ferrari was sent out to race with imbalanced wheels, he would probably not make it beyond the first chicane. More than likely the wheels would fall off because of the abnormal forces being transmitted through structures which have no margins to deal with those errors. So it is with horses. Equine locomotion involves a series of collisions of the feet with the ground at high velocities, and **unless the feet are balanced, abnormal forces are transmitted up through the limbs and cause breakdown in structures throughout the body**. As it is the structures in the lower limb that have the least margin for error it is usually these structures that are primarily affected, but depending upon the nature and degree of the abnormal forces, breakdown can occur anywhere in the body.

Tendon and related problems

A further factor to be considered is a facet of equine locomotion known as 'elastic recoil energy'. As mentioned earlier, the horse's prime defence mechanism from a predator is to outrun it. We have seen that the major groups of locomotor muscles are located close to the centre of mass and it is these muscles that have one end attached to the trunk and the other end attached to

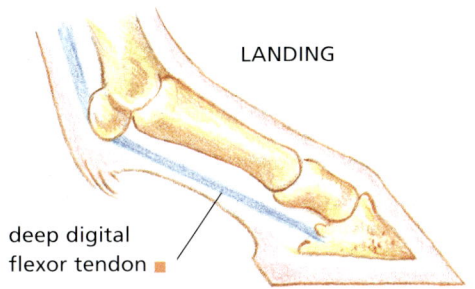

LANDING

deep digital
flexor tendon ■

Fig. 1.2 The orientation of the foot as it lands. Note how the fetlock begins to bend as the limb takes weight.

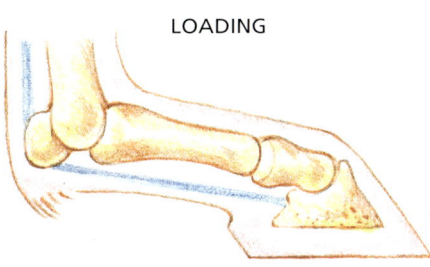

LOADING

Fig. 1.3 Orientation of the foot during maximum weightbearing. Note how the tendon has to stretch. It is during this time that the tendon is storing elastic energy.

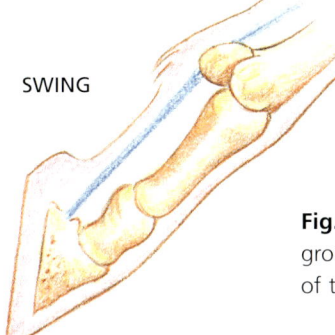

SWING

Fig. 1.4 Lifting of the foot from the ground is aided by the elastic recoil of the tendon.

various positions at the top of the legs. These muscles are primarily used for swinging the legs backwards and forwards (retraction and protraction) and – to a limited extent – inward and outward (adduction and abduction). Another group of locomotor muscles are known as flexors and extensors. It is these muscles which bend and straighten the leg and do not, in the majority of cases, have an attachment to the trunk. Because these muscles are in the upper legs and work to change the angles of joints in the legs, they are not very large. Those that work to flex and extend the lower leg have lengthy tendons attaching the muscle to the lower leg. Those tendons have 'elastic properties', i.e. they can be stretched and ping back into their original shape like an elastic band. This happens because when the tendon is loaded as the horse first puts his foot to the ground, the tendon stores elastic energy which is released when the foot is lifted from the ground.

Equine tendons have a strain rate of about 21% before the whole tendon fails. This means that a 100mm-long tendon can stretch to about 121mm before the tendon fibres break. When you consider that in the galloping horse the superficial digital flexor tendon in the forelimb undergoes a strain rate of 17% you can appreciate how little margin for error there is. Consider then that on top of all of this we put, say, 12 stone on his back and ask him to jump 6ft fences!

Figure 1.2 shows the orientation of the foot as it lands. Note how, as the fetlock begins to bend, the tendon at the back of the leg is being stretched. In this case the deep digital flexor tendon is shown but the effect is similar in the superficial digital flexor tendon and the suspensory ligament. Figure 1.3 shows the deep digital flexor tendon at the point in the stance phase where the leg is taking the greatest amount of weight – see how much more the tendon is stretched.

Figure 1.4 demonstrates how, when the foot is lifted off the ground, the elastic tendon releases its stored energy and allows the foot to be raised without any large energetic cost to the muscles. If the foot is imbalanced and the limb is not being correctly loaded, this interferes with the elastic rebound of the tendons, which in turn affects locomotion. It is one of the reasons why tendon injuries are so often associated with imbalanced feet.

So purely in terms of mechanics we begin to understand the relationship of foot imbalance to equine injury. Let's now look more closely at the mysteries of the equine foot and how it works...

CHAPTER 2

Anatomy and Biomechanics

Basic anatomy of the foot

In order to understand the mechanics of the foot it is necessary to appreciate a little of its structure. Fig. 2.1 shows very simply the bones from the fetlock down.

Figure 2.2 shows a cross-section through the lower limb. This illustration makes it easy to appreciate the extent of the pulley system of tendons and ligaments referred to in Chapter 1.

The foot, together with that part of the lower limb which comprises the pastern, are collectively known as the equine digit. The bones of the equine

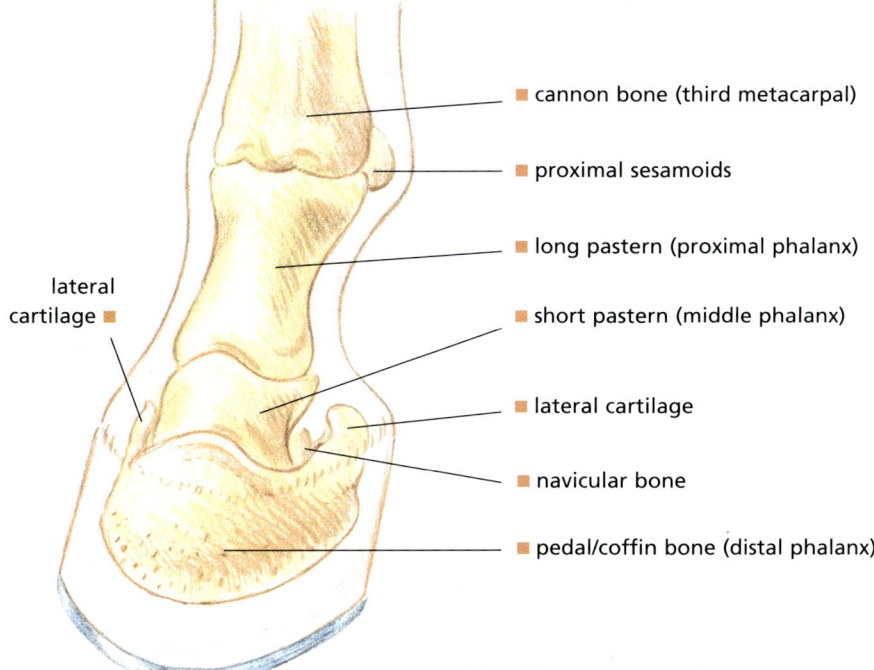

■ cannon bone (third metacarpal)

■ proximal sesamoids

■ long pastern (proximal phalanx)

■ short pastern (middle phalanx)

■ lateral cartilage

■ navicular bone

■ pedal/coffin bone (distal phalanx)

lateral cartilage ■

Fig. 2.1 Simplified diagram of the bones of the equine foot.

digit commence with the long pastern bone (the proximal phalanx) which articulates with the cannon (third metacarpal) bone and the proximal sesamoid bones at the fetlock joint. The fetlock joint is what is known as a ginglymus joint (i.e. one that permits movement in one plane only) because its structure allows it only to flex and extend. This is so because a bony ridge at the base of the cannon bone slots into a corresponding groove in the top of the long pastern, thus preventing the joint from rotating from side to side and from left to right (see Fig. 2.1).

To a certain extent the ginglymus joints which comprise the horse's lower limb account for the horse's inability to adequately compensate for foot imbalance because they do not allow a complete range of joint movement which could adapt to uneven loading.

The short pastern bone (middle phalanx) articulates at the top end with the long pastern and at the bottom end with the pedal bone. The joint between the long and short pasterns (the proximal interphalangeal joint) is another ginglymus joint but it also has little movement in a flexion/extension capacity. In terms of mechanics, therefore, the long and short pasterns can be considered to be one functional unit.

Fig. 2.2 The lower limb cut through the mid-line section.

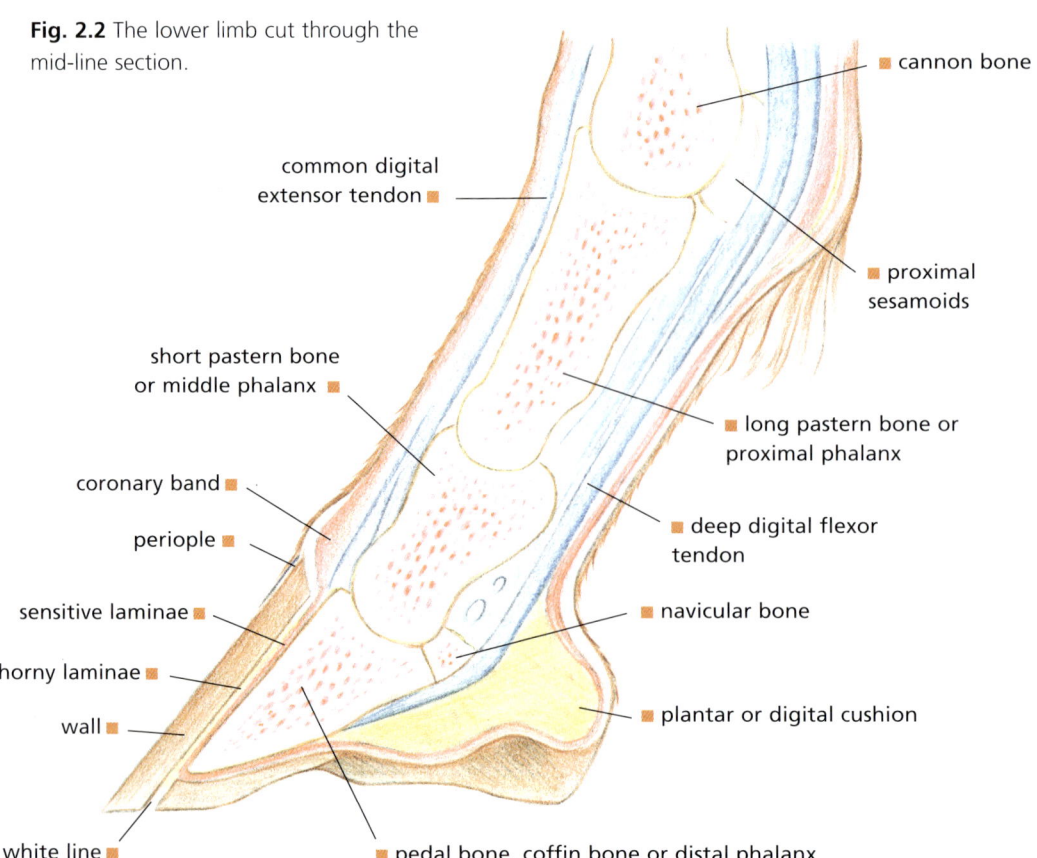

- cannon bone
- common digital extensor tendon
- proximal sesamoids
- short pastern bone or middle phalanx
- long pastern bone or proximal phalanx
- coronary band
- periople
- deep digital flexor tendon
- sensitive laminae
- navicular bone
- horny laminae
- wall
- plantar or digital cushion
- white line
- pedal bone, coffin bone or distal phalanx

ANATOMICAL NOMENCLATURE

Anatomical nomenclature is generally related to positional adjectives – words which describe whereabouts on the body a particular body part can be found. These can be very confusing to the everyday horseman, more used to terms such as 'near', 'off', 'front', 'back', etc.

Given below is a small glossary of terms which can be read in conjunction with the diagrams.

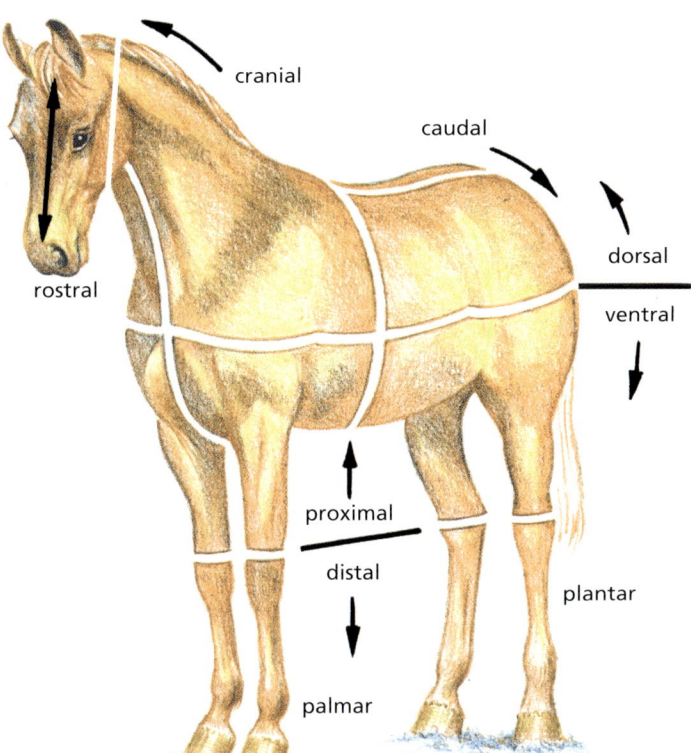

LOOKING FROM IN FRONT OF THE HORSE

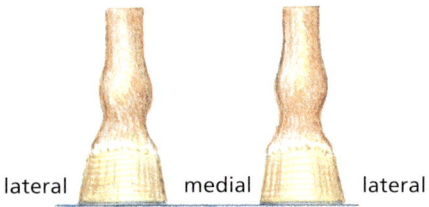

lateral   medial   lateral

The term **'medio-lateral'** describes the orientation across both planes. Therefore medio-lateral foot balance means the balance between the inside and the outside of the foot.

LOOKING FROM THE SIDE

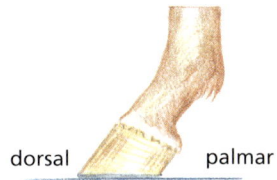

dorsal   palmar

The term **'dorso-palmar'** describes the orientation across both planes. Thus dorso-palmar foot balance means the balance between the front and the back of the foot.

COMMON TERMS

Some terms are common to all areas of the body. **Deep** and **superficial** indicate relative distances from the outside of the body; **medial** and **lateral** give the position nearer to or farther away from the midline of the body.

LIMBS

Proximal – that part of the limb towards the topline
Distal – that part of the limb towards the hoof
The terms proximal and distal have no anatomical points as such. For example, the distal sesamoid is another name for the navicular bone, whereas the proximal sesamoids are behind the fetlock joint. They are so named because the proximal sesamoid bones are closer to the topline of the horse than the distal sesamoid bone.
Dorsal – that part of the limb (below the knee or hock) towards the front of the horse
Palmar – that part of the front limb (below the knee) towards the rear of the horse

Plantar – that part of the hind limb (below the hock) towards the rear of the horse
For example, in the front limb the deep digital flexor tendon is dorsal to the superficial digital flexor tendon but is palmar to the cannon bone – it is in front of the superficial digital flexor tendon but is behind the cannon bone.
Cranial (or **rostral** if referring to the head) – relates to those parts of the body towards the front of the horse
Caudal – the equivalent of palmar/plantar save that it applies above the knee and hock

BODY

Dorsal – positions nearer to the topline (from the tip of the horse's nose to the tip of his tail)
Ventral – positions nearer to the floor of the thorax
Cranial – positions nearer the head
Caudal – positions nearer the tail
Many texts will talk about anterior and posterior as a substitute for cranial and caudal, but these terms are incorrect in quadrupeds.

The pedal bone (distal phalanx) is also known as the coffin bone because it is completely 'buried' inside the hoof capsule. It articulates with the short pastern bone by way of a ginglymus joint (the distal interphalangeal joint). Attached to the medial and lateral aspects of the coffin bone are the lateral cartilages (see Fig. 2.1)

One further bone completes the bones of the equine digit and that is the relatively small but, in terms of foot balance and equine locomotion, vitally important navicular bone – the distal sesamoid. Almost everything to do with this bone is controversial, not the least being its function. It functions either as a true sesamoid, providing the deep digital flexor tendon with a constant angle of insertion onto the underside of the coffin bone (see Figs. 1.2, 1.3. and 1.4 in Chapter 1) or it acts like a shock absorber. Fig. 2.3 shows the equine foot cut through a section from the top of the pastern down through the navicular bone, the sole of the foot and the frog. This photograph demonstrates the 'boat' shape of the bone – hence the name navicular. Underneath the navicular bone can be seen the deep digital flexor tendon. With the bone shown in this orientation the potential shock-absorbance capacity can be appreciated.

All the bones in the lower limbs are held together by a complex series of ligaments that also possess the ability to store and release elastic recoil energy. This is an important issue because foot imbalances create abnormal loading of these ligaments, which result in altered limb flight.

The weight of the horse is suspended from the inside of the hoof capsule –

Fig. 2.3 Section through pastern and foot.

extensor tendon ◾

short pastern ◾

lateral cartilage ◾

navicular bone ◾

deep digital flexor tendon ◾

hoof wall ◾

frog ◾

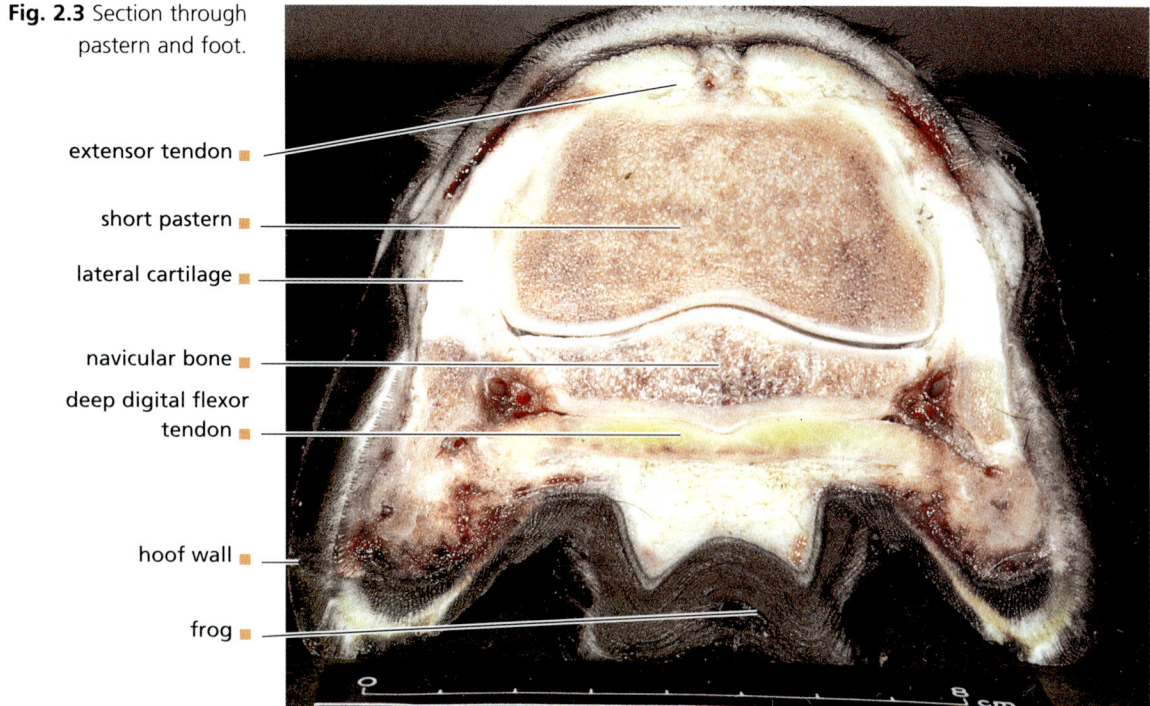

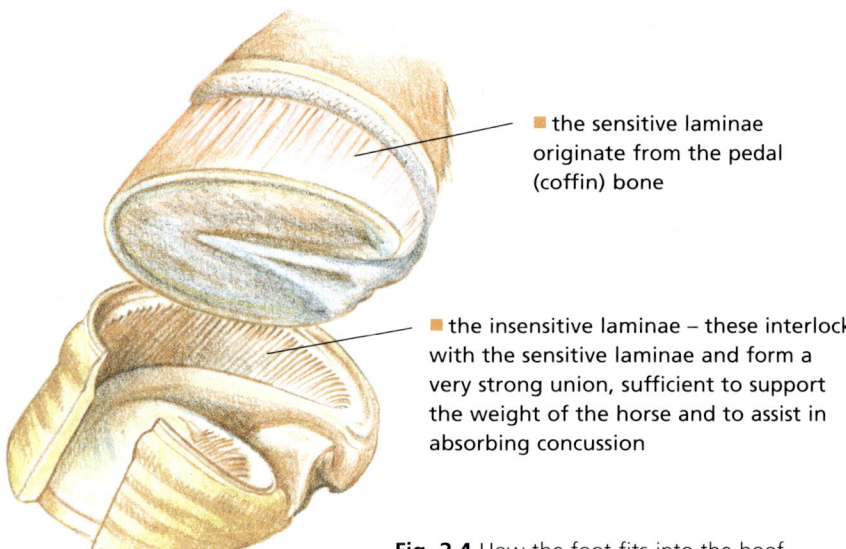

■ the sensitive laminae originate from the pedal (coffin) bone

■ the insensitive laminae – these interlock with the sensitive laminae and form a very strong union, sufficient to support the weight of the horse and to assist in absorbing concussion

Fig. 2.4 How the foot fits into the hoof.

no weight is taken directly onto the sole of the foot. This is achieved via an interlinking network of fibres or laminae. Fig. 2.4 demonstrates how the hoof fits over the foot almost like a glove. On the inside of the hoof are the insensitive (epidermal) laminae and these interlink with the sensitive (dermal) laminae which are attached via the laminar corium to the pedal bone. Thus the weight of the horse is taken by the interlocking of these microscopic structures

Fig. 2.5 Microscopic view of a cross-section of hoof. Note how the epidermal laminae (**e**) interlink with the dermal laminae (**d**).

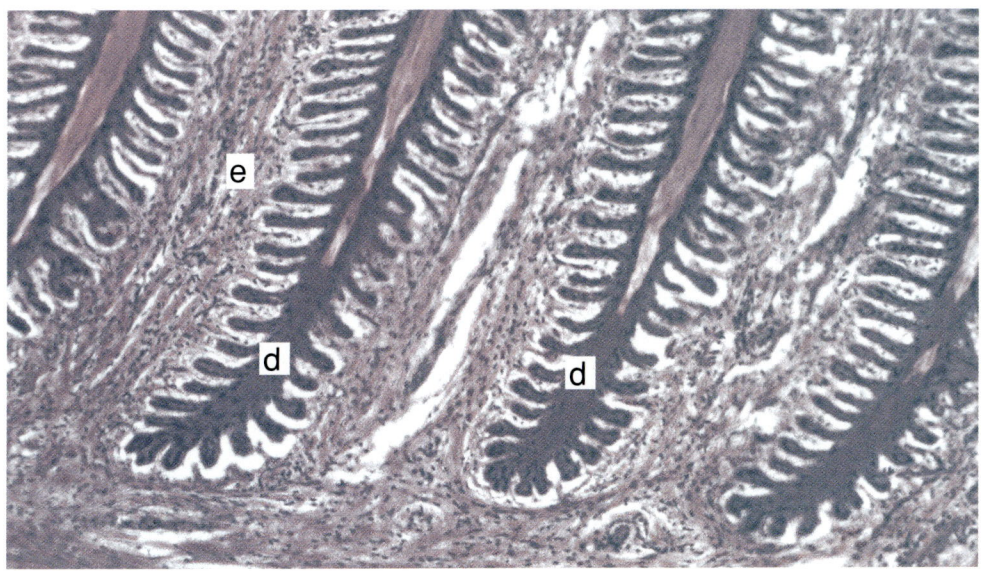

(Fig. 2.5). Despite the fact that these structures look very frail, they are more than able, when in good health, to bear the weight of the horse.

As the hoof grows, the epidermal laminae 'slide' down the dermal laminae.

The hoof wall is made of a type of collagen known as keratin and extends from the coronet band to the ground surface. The hoof is continuous with the outer layer of skin (epidermis). The inner layer of skin (dermis) is continuous with the dermis (corium) of the hoof (see Fig. 2.4).

The horn itself is structured by millions of tightly packed tubes oriented longitudinally from the coronet band to the ground surface. These horn tubules arise from secretion of keratin at the periople by tiny structures known papillae – Fig. 2.6.

In mechanical terms, think of holding together a large number of drinking straws. An individual straw would not be a very strong structure but when

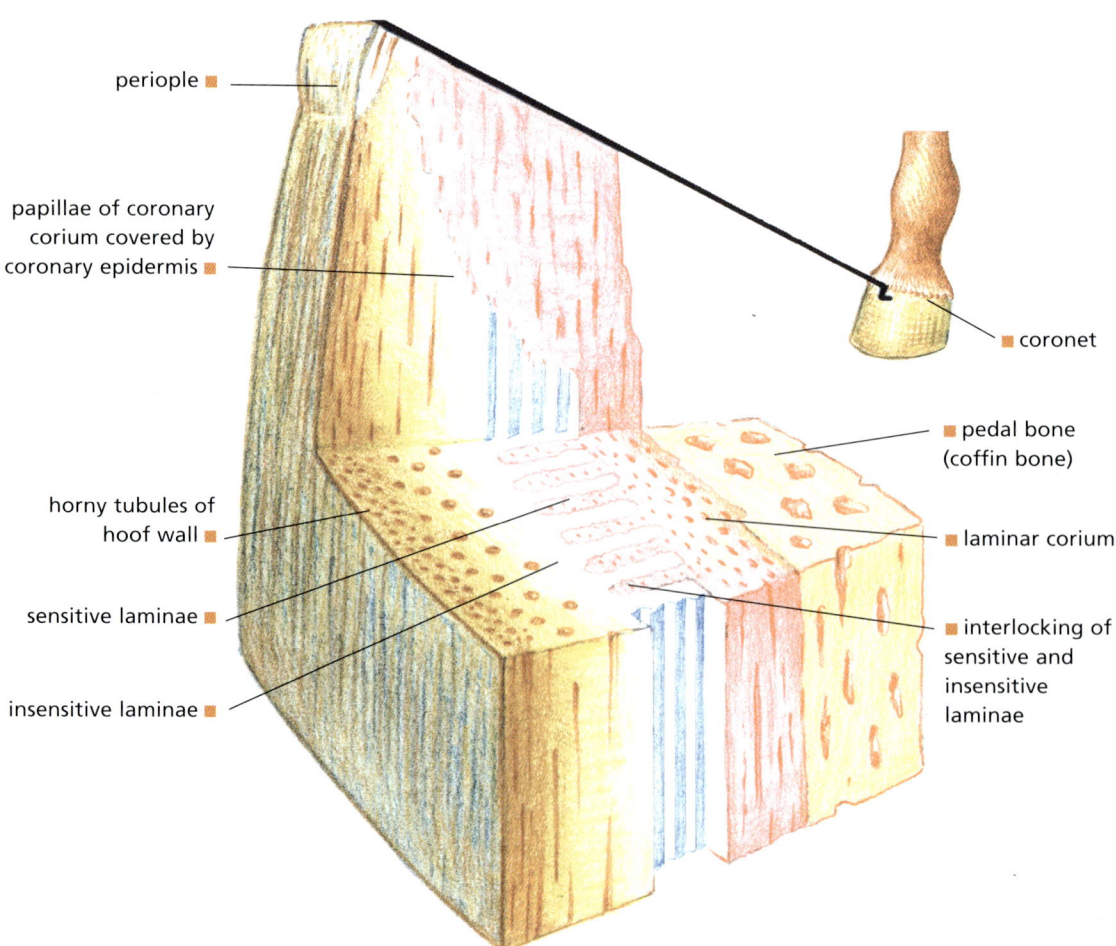

Fig. 2.6 Three-dimensional dissection of the coronary region and the hoof wall.

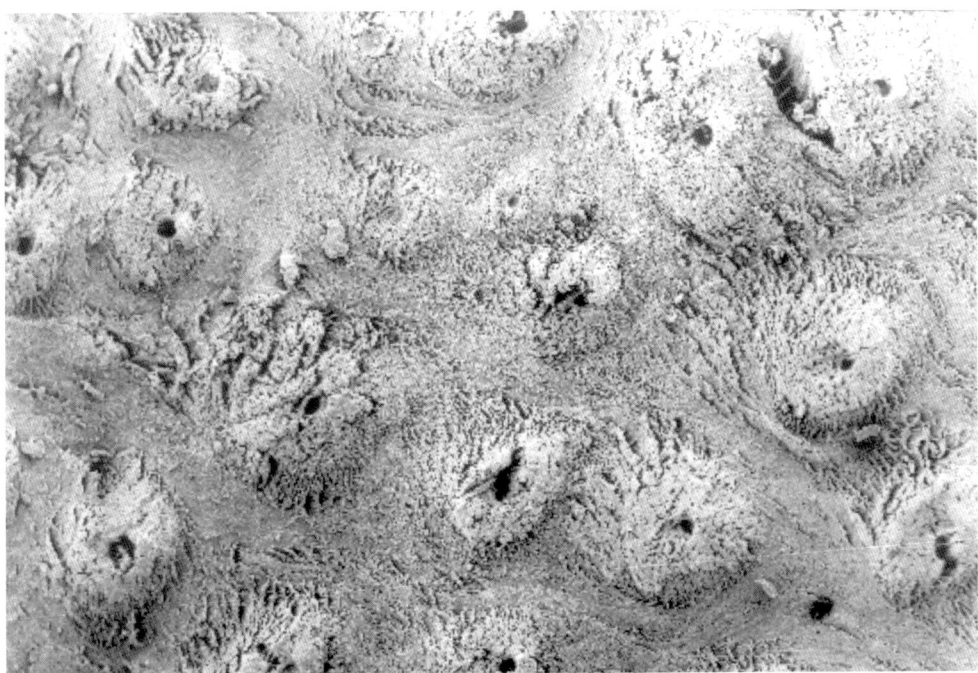

Fig. 2.7 Scanning electron micrograph of a cross-section of equine hoof (courtesy of the Faculty of Applied Science, De Montfort University, Leicester).

bundled together a mass of straws can support a significant amount of weight.

Fig. 2.7 shows a scanning electron micrograph of a cross-section of hoof in which the structure of the horn tubules can clearly be seen.

It is perhaps as well to point out at this stage that the keratin of the hoof can either be pigmented (the hoof is dark) or non-pigmented (the hoof is pale) or indeed a mixture of both. Many people believe that darker hooves are stronger, but this is not the case. Pigmentation of the hoof bears no relation to its strength.

The horn tubules grow by approximately a quarter of an inch (6mm) per month. This means that it can take anything up to twelve months for the toe to grow out. Temperature and humidity can affect hoof growth – e.g. growth can be accelerated in warm, humid environments.

The gross anatomy of the ground surface of the hoof is shown in Fig. 2.8. The sole of the foot should be concave and not touch the floor at any part except near its junction with the white line. In a freshly trimmed foot, the white line should be visible where the wall of the hoof meets the sole. The white line marks the location of the sensitive corium and, as such, determines where the farrier can drive safely his nails. The structure of the sole is similar to that of the horn in that it is made up of vertical tubules of keratin secreted by papillae in the corium of the sole. The sole is, however, softer than the horn as it has a higher moisture content – roughly one third of the sole is composed of water.

Fig. 2.8 The ground surface of the foot.

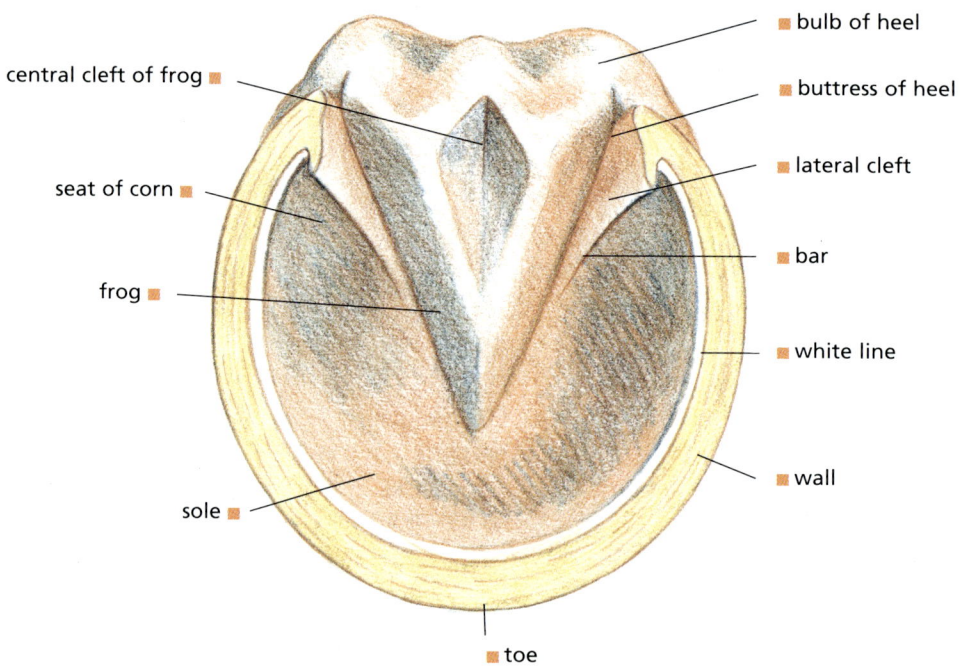

central cleft of frog ■

seat of corn ■

frog ■

sole ■

toe ■

bulb of heel

buttress of heel

lateral cleft

bar

white line

wall

The periople, bulbs and frog form a collar around the wall and sole. The frog is a wedge of keratinised tissue with a greater than 50% water content, making it softer than the walls or sole.

The shape of the front foot is wider across the quarter than the hind foot, whilst the hind foot is longer than the front foot. This is a reflection of the disparate biomechanical functions between front and hind limbs – the hind feet being more pointed to allow for increased propulsive ability.

Biomechanics

As in all running quadrupeds, generally the front limbs act to support the weight of the animal whilst the hind limbs act to propel the animal forwards. Obviously it is not quite so cut and dried as that because the hind limbs do play some role in supporting the weight of the horse and the front limbs do help propel the horse forwards. However, approximately 60% of the horse's weight is taken by his front limbs and 40% of his weight on his hind limbs. So the horse is naturally 'on his forehand'. An average-size warmblood will weigh approximately 600kg so will carry 180kg on each front foot and 120kg on each hind foot whilst he is standing still. The weightbearing portion of each foot covers an area of approximately 70cm^2. We can then calculate that, without moving, the horse is bearing 2.6kg/cm^2 on his front feet, which does not appear, at first sight, to be a lot (except of course when he stands on your foot). However, there are two important factors to take into consideration. As the horse starts to move, not all four feet are on the ground at the same time – at the gallop there are times when only one foot is on the ground at any one time. Also as the horse begins to move, the forces on his feet become greater – remember your school physics:

$$Force = Mass \times Acceleration$$

The greater the acceleration, the higher the forces that the equine foot has to deal with. In fact, in the gallop each foot may have to withstand forces equating to a weight of 1000kg, or approximately 14.3kg/cm^2.

During locomotion these concussive forces acting through the forelimb must ultimately be resisted by the foot and in particular by the hoof wall. The properly conformed and functioning equine foot changes shape during weight-bearing as the sole loses its concavity and the hoof wall deforms outward. In the unshod foot, the heels, quarters and toes all spread outward. The heels are able to spread out by the greatest amount because the hoof wall is thinner at the heels than at the toe and because the hoof is open at the back.

This change in shape of the foot is believed to result from a compromise between complex force changes occurring internally within the epidermal hoof capsule and external compressive forces acting against the foot from the ground. Many factors can influence the natural functioning of the hoof wall, for example:

• The mechanical properties of the hoof wall can be changed by such factors as poor diet, cold and dry environments, wet environments, poor foot balance and many other factors.

• Hoof capsule shape can also affect the mechanical properties. Upright, boxy feet do not allow for appropriate concussion absorption. Conversely flat, splayed feet cannot expand during weightbearing and increase the concussive forces. Deformation of horn tubules can alter weightbearing characteristics. Remember how we likened the hoof structure to a bunch of drinking straws? Imagine then how strength would be lost if some of those straws became crushed.

• Shoeing alters the natural functioning of the hoof wall. A metal shoe nailed onto the foot prevents expansion of the hoof wall at the toe and quarters. Metal shoes increase the concussive forces transmitted from the hoof to the bones inside the hoof. They are also known to decrease the hoof's natural shock-absorption. This leads to a 'double-whammy' effect – the shoes increase the concussion and at the same time decrease the foot's ability to absorb that concussion.

• The ground surface plays a part. If a horse is continually being worked on an artificial sand surface this also restricts the expansion of the hoof wall. If a horse is continually engaged on road work then the concussive forces are increased. Invariably horses doing high levels of road work are shod – the road surface increases the concussion, the shoe amplifies that concussion and the shoe restricts the concussion absorbency of the foot – a 'triple-whammy'.

The structures of the unshod foot are particularly well adapted to absorb energy as the horn of the hoof undergoes visco-elastic deformation. This simply means that the deformation is time and rate dependent. How the foot actually achieves this time-and-rate dependent change is quite complex. It had, for some time, been thought that as the limb took weight the frog was compressed, resulting in pressure on the bars, and the resultant pressure within the digital cushion forced open the lateral cartilages and expanded the hoof (Fig. 2.9).

We now know that during weightbearing the pressure within the digital cushion actually decreases so that this long-held theory cannot be correct, despite what is said in many farriery and veterinary texts. When the horse puts his foot to the floor at the beginning of the stance phase, his weight is transmitted down the limb to the coffin joint. The pedal bone is attached to the

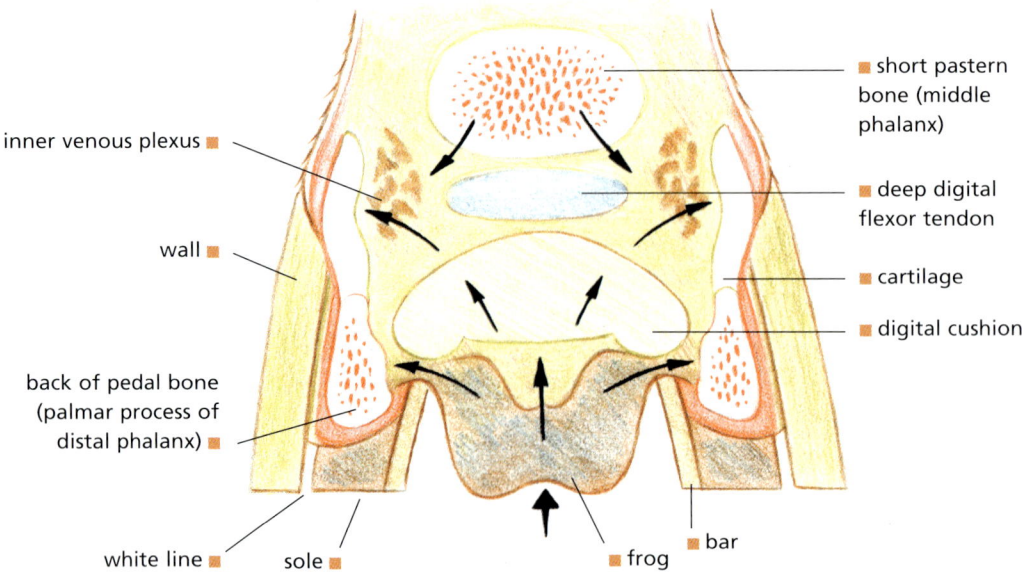

Fig. 2.9 The long-held, but erroneous theory as to how the hoof expanded upon weightbearing. It was thought that as the frog compressed the digital cushion from the bottom, the digital cushion was compressed, which forced open the lateral cartilages, which in turn caused the hoof to deform outward. The correct theory is shown in Fig. 2.10.

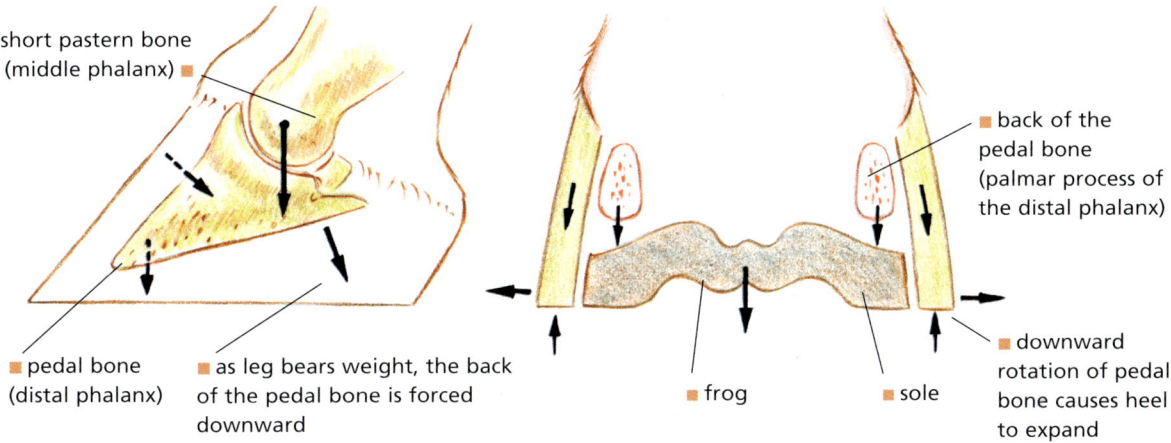

Fig. 2.10 The current theory as to how weightbearing affects the foot. The pedal bone (distal phalanx) is unsupported at the rear and so it rotates backwards when the foot bears weight. This forces the heels outward.

inside of the hoof by the laminae, and the weight bearing down from the coffin joint pushes the pedal bone downward towards the floor. Because the laminar attachments are to the front and the side of the pedal bone, the back of the pedal bone is largely unsupported. This means that the back of the pedal bone can be pushed down further than the front, and it rotates backwards.

This creates a greater force at the heels and because of the relatively flexible attachment of the hoof at the heels, they can spread out more than the hoof can at the toe. This expansion of the hoof allows some of the concussive forces to be absorbed. As the heels spread out, the sole loses its concavity, allowing the soft tissues within the foot to spread out. The frog drops with the sole until it contacts the ground, where its function is to act as a cushion to prevent the total drop of the sole and, as a result, restrict the spread of the heels.

Thus it can be seen that, contrary to popular belief, pressure against the frog during the stance phase is not a pre-requisite for hoof expansion.

Using this latest biomechanical model for hoof expansion it can be appreciated that if the loadbearing is unequal on any particular aspect of the hoof, it will cause unequal widening of the foot. For example, if the outside wall of a hoof is longer than the inside wall, greater compressive forces will act upon the outside wall forcing it out further than the inside wall. Over a period of time this foot imbalance will result in a flaring out of the outside wall and a contraction of the inside wall (Fig. 2.11).

We also know from the very latest in scientific research that force does not travel directly up through the centre of the bony column of the horse's limb. In fact the medial aspect of the bones is subjected to the greatest loading factors. For this reason bone in the leg is more dense on its inside aspect and the joints are thicker on their inside aspect. Any changes to the transmission of forces throughout the limb can create injuries such as chip fractures of the

Fig. 2.11 Foot conformation resulting from unequal loadbearing. Note how the outside wall has flared out whilst the inside wall has become upright.

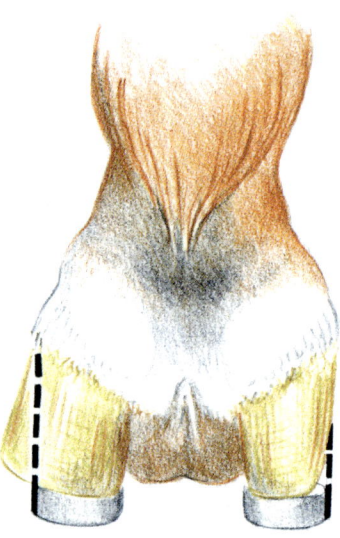

joints. We have seen that the joints in the equine digit are ginglymus joints, which restrict sideways and rotational movements. This restriction is not a total one as very slight movements in these planes are possible. Consider, however, that if the foot is imbalanced – for example, if the outside wall of the hoof is longer than the inside – the joint spaces on the outside of the leg are going to be closed up. Thus it can be seen that any further attempt to compensate for imbalance (for example, uneven ground) can create abnormal forces with which the joint cannot cope. In extreme circumstances this can lead to chip fractures in these joints. See Fig. 2.12.

When the foot accepts weight, the fetlock extends. This sinking of the fetlock

Fig. 2.12 Ginglymus joints restrict rotational and sideways movement. A foot imbalance creates misalignment of these joints and predisposes them to injury.

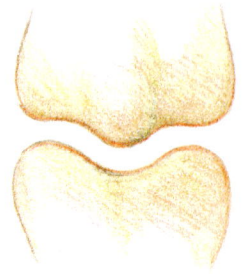

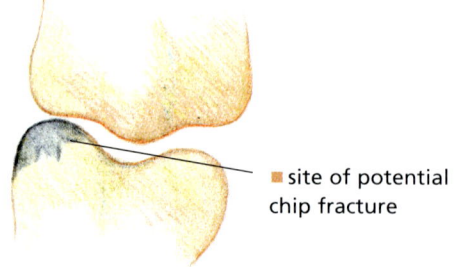

■ site of potential chip fracture

■ a ginglymus joint in normal position when the leg is straight and the feet are balanced

■ if the foot is not balanced – i.e. one side of the hoof is longer than the other – this affects the orientation of all the joints above it in the leg: therefore there is no further room for error and if the horse meets uneven ground he is in grave danger of acquiring a 'chip' fracture

has to be resisted if it is not to hit the ground. The extension of the fetlock is resisted firstly by the suspensory ligament and almost simultaneously by the superficial digital flexor tendon, followed closely by the deep digital flexor tendon. Remember how during this phase these tendons are storing energy. In the slower gaits the horse should land flat-footed and it has been noted during slow-motion study of equine locomotion that the foot does not necessarily 'grip' immediately it hits the floor and, more often than not, it can move very slightly forwards by a matter of a very few millimetres.

In humans we know that there are some athletes who, whilst running, place their feet down harder than other athletes. These heavy-footed individuals are known as 'macro-clumpers', whilst their more dainty-footed peers are known as 'micro-clumpers'. Human sports scientists have known for many years that macro-clumpers are more prone to injury than micro-clumpers because over months of training their limbs are subjected to greater concussive forces. There is no reason to suppose that horses are any different, which may account for why some horses are more prone to concussion-related injuries than others. Macro-clumpers, therefore, need to have their feet in optimum balance even more so than other horses, as uneven concussive forces will affect them more acutely.

You should by now have an appreciation of the complex nature of the structure and function of the equine foot and an understanding as to why a significant amount of your care and attention should be directed towards ensuring that your horse has the best feet that can possibly be achieved for his conformation. We know that elite performance horses have an ability to move more efficiently and economically than their less-gifted peers. This locomotor efficiency commences with the horse being able to cope with the forces of locomotion. There is absolutely no point in subjecting your horse to the most scientifically evaluated training programme and feeding him the most expensive feed and dietary supplements if he is not putting one foot in front of the other with the most effective ergonomics.

CHAPTER 3

Assessing the Horse

For those of you with the close-to-perfect horse, this chapter will demonstrate just how simple it can be to ensure that your pride and joy is functioning to the best of his ability in locomotor terms. Despite what many will tell you, there is little mystery to the art of foot balance in horses with reasonably good conformation.

Hoof/pastern axis and dorso-palmar balance

One of the most important, but extremely simple, things to ensure is that your horse has a straight hoof/pastern axis. Fig. 3.1 demonstrates how this is observed. When you are assessing this on your horse it is vital to remember the following:

- First, make sure he is standing on a level surface, squarely on all four feet.

- Second, it is important to find the actual centre of rotation of the fetlock joint itself and not the space between the proximal sesamoid bones and the fetlock joint. To do this run your fingers down the widest part of the cannon bone (from inside to outside of the leg) until you reach the fetlock joint. This is the approximate centre of rotation of that joint.

- Third, the coffin joint cannot be palpated because it is inside the hoof capsule and in practice this measurement (marked **x** on Fig. 3.1) can only been made on a radiograph (x-ray).

In mechanical terms the importance of correct hoof/pastern axis and heel support can be explained as follows. Because of the structure and function of the equine digit, the weight of the horse (looking from this side view) is transmitted directly down the centre of the cannon bone and from the centre of the fetlock joint perpendicularly to the ground. The heel has to be directly under this line of weightbearing to be able to adequately support the horse.

Think of the structure of a Bauhaus chair (Fig. 3.2). If the ground rail of the

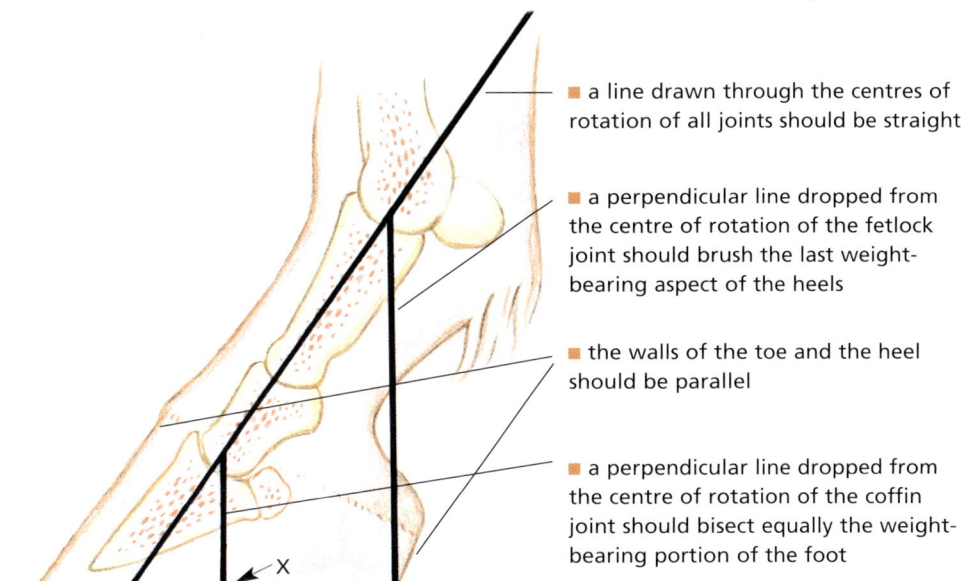

■ a line drawn through the centres of rotation of all joints should be straight

■ a perpendicular line dropped from the centre of rotation of the fetlock joint should brush the last weight-bearing aspect of the heels

■ the walls of the toe and the heel should be parallel

■ a perpendicular line dropped from the centre of rotation of the coffin joint should bisect equally the weight-bearing portion of the foot

Fig. 3.1 Diagrammatic representation of dorso-palmar foot balance.

chair did not extend back well under the weight of the seated person, the chair would simply topple backwards. In mechanical terms the same thing applies to the horse. If the last weightbearing aspect of the heels is not under the vertical force line then the horse immediately becomes imbalanced and has to alter the way he stands and the way he moves because of it.

A further problem is additionally created because if the heel is not playing a full role in supporting the fetlock then some other structure(s) in the horse has to support it. In the horse this other structure is generally the superficial digital flexor tendon, but the suspensory ligament and deep digital flexor tendon also play a part. It does not take a great leap of intellect, therefore, to see why imbalances in this plane can cause damage to tendons simply because they are having to take on a greater role in supporting the weight of the horse.

weight of seated person

Fig. 3.2 Bauhaus chair. If the ground rail did not extend beyond the weight of the seated person, the whole chair would topple backwards.

Fig. 3.3 Horse with broken back hoof/pastern axis. The heels have collapsed and are not supporting the fetlock.

broken back hoof/pastern axis ■

perpendicular line from fetlock ■

last weightbearing aspect of shoe ■

Fig. 3.3 shows a horse with a severe broken back hoof/pastern axis, and Fig. 3.4 shows the same horse immediately after he was correctly shod.

Fig. 3.5 shows a radiograph of a horse with a broken back hoof/pastern axis. You can see from this x-ray how clearly the coffin joint is bent backwards and that there is very little weightbearing area behind the line dropped from the coffin joint. This creates a number of problems for the horse.

First, as we have seen, it throws the whole horse into a state of imbalance which creates long-term locomotor problems (see Chapter 4). Second, however, and, just as important, is the fact that it actually causes the horse pain. Because so much of the horse's weight is concentrated towards the back of the foot the effect is to interfere with the blood supply to that area. You know how painful it feels when you are wearing something so tight – perhaps a ring or even a new pair of shoes – that it is stopping the blood from flowing properly. The same happens to horses with this type of foot conformation. In fact, the horse shown in the radiograph had been lame for several months but as soon as his foot balance was corrected so that he did not have a broken back hoof/pastern axis he was immediately sound.

Third, one of the locomotor compensations that the horse makes with this long toe/low heel conformation is a tendency to land toe first. This is because the horse has no sense of feeling on the outside of the hoof or sole but afferent nerves within the hoof capsule relay messages to the brain telling it how the

Fig. 3.4 The horse in Fig. 3.3 immediately after he was correctly shod. Note the hoof/pastern axis is now straight and the heels of the shoe are supporting the fetlock.

■ straight hoof/pastern axis

■ line from centre of rotation of fetlock brushes last weight-bearing aspect of shoe. In this horse the heels were collapsing so it was necessary to extend the shoe to where the heel should be

Fig. 3.5 Radiograph of a horse with a broken-back hoof/pastern axis. Note the uneven proportions of weightbearing surface in front of and behind the centre of rotation of the coffin joint.

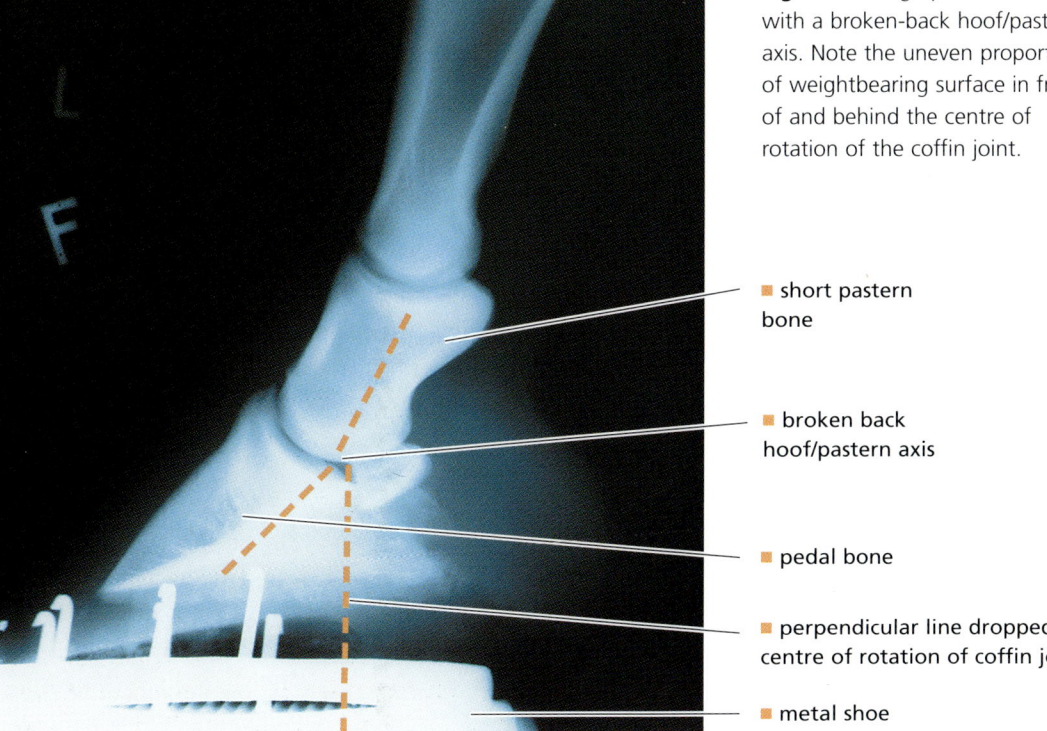

■ short pastern bone

■ broken back hoof/pastern axis

■ pedal bone

■ perpendicular line dropped from centre of rotation of coffin joint

■ metal shoe

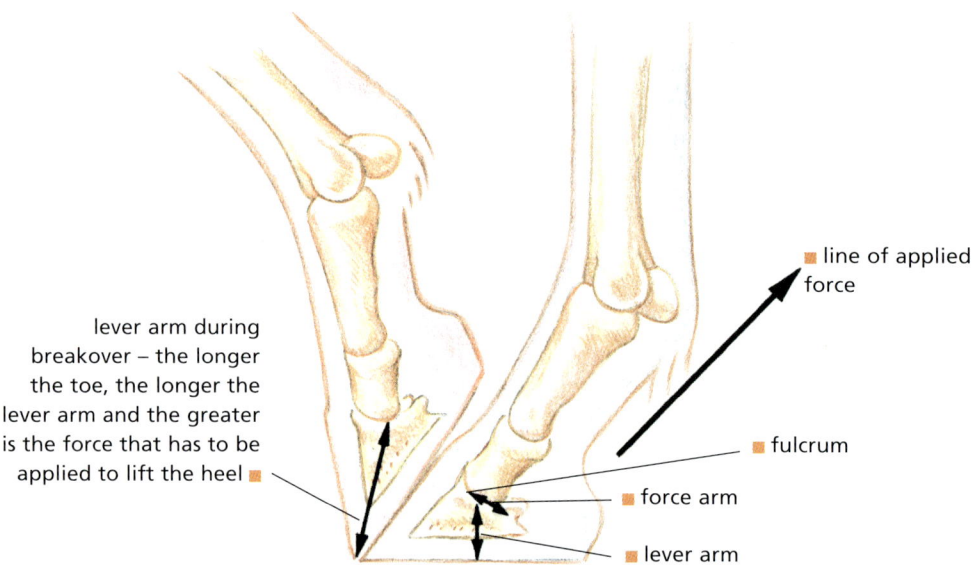

lever arm during breakover – the longer the toe, the longer the lever arm and the greater is the force that has to be applied to lift the heel ■

■ **line of applied force**

■ **fulcrum**

■ **force arm**

■ **lever arm**

Fig. 3.6 The mechanical leverage involved in breakover. If the toe is allowed to become too long the resistance to breakover increases, leading to potentially serious injury. Long toes have been implicated as a predisposing factor in navicular disease.

bones of the digit are orientated in space and time. Because the horse naturally seeks a straight hoof/pastern axis he automatically orientates the bones so that they will land in this conformation. By doing this, the long-toed horse will unknowingly be pointing his foot towards the ground just before the foot lands, causing the toe to come into contact with the ground first rather than landing flat footed. This may cause the horse to stumble at worst, but even at best will create abnormal forces for the rest of the foot to try to deal with.

Fourth, in mechanical terms during breakover (the rotation of the heels around the toe at the end of the stance phase) the foot acts as a lever with the fulcrum being the coffin joint. The force for the lifting of the heel is provided by the deep digital flexor muscle acting through its tendon inserted onto the underside of the pedal bone. The distance from the insertion of the deep digital flexor tendon to the fulcrum is the length of the force arm. The resistance to the flexion of the coffin joint is due to the ground-reaction force with the lever arm being the distance from the point of application of the ground-reaction force to the fulcrum (Fig. 3.6).

Because the lever arm is longer than the force arm, the lever is one of Third Class. These types of levers are common in equine extremities as they convey speed of movement rather than a mechanical advantage. However, by increasing the length of the toe the length of the lever arm is greatly increased and the force required to lift the heel must consequently be significantly greater. As the force for lifting the heel is provided via the deep digital flexor tendon, then this tendon compresses the navicular bone against the back of the

Fig. 3.7 Horse with a broken forwards hoof/pastern axis.

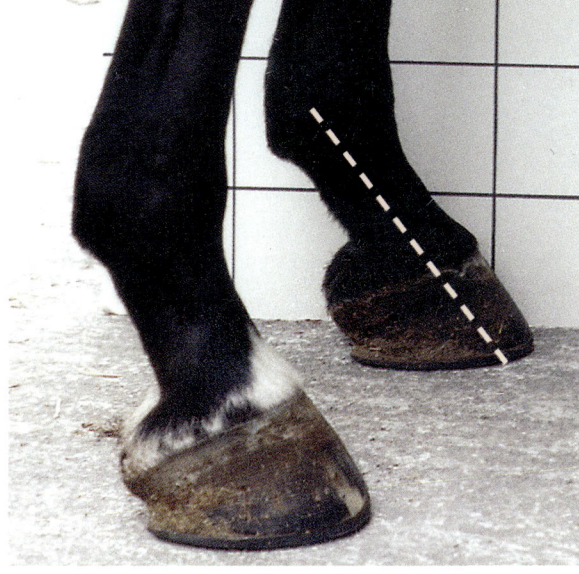

Fig. 3.8 The horse in Fig. 3.7 after correct trimming and shoeing. Note the straight hoof/pastern axis.

coffin joint with even greater severity. It is mooted by many researchers that this additional compressive force against the navicular bone also interferes with the blood flow to the navicular bone and is causative for navicular disease.

It was thought for many years, particularly in the United States, that this long toe/low heel conformation increased stride length because the lengthened lever arm retarded breakover. For this reason many horses were deliberately trimmed to have this foot conformation. We now know that long toes do not increase stride length but endow the horse with all of the locomotor problems described above.

Despite all of this knowledge, however, it is still one of the most common foot imbalances seen in horses today. In major studies carried out all over the world it has been noted that a broken back hoof/pastern axis was one of the biggest single contributors to forelimb injury in the racehorse and that up to 77% of all racehorses displayed this foot imbalance.

Fig. 3.7 shows a horse with a broken forwards hoof/pastern axis. Although this type of foot imbalance is not as serious in terms of locomotor problems as the broken back hoof/pastern axis, it does have the effect of concentrating the horse's weight towards the front of the foot because there is a small weight-bearing area in that region. This can lead to long-term problems such as pedal osteitis. It can, in extreme cases, lead to injury to the suspensory ligament, as long heels and low toes create a greater strain within that ligament. Fig. 3.8 shows the same horse after he had been correctly shod.

Exactly the same method of assessment can be used for the hind feet.

Medio-lateral balance

Medio-lateral balance – the balance from the inside aspect of the foot to the outside aspect of the foot – is essential for the prevention of injury. Those injuries thought to be mainly associated with medio-lateral imbalances include degenerative joint disease, chip fractures in joints, fractures of the sesamoid bones and sesamoiditis.

Medio-lateral imbalances are particularly difficult for the horse to deal with because of the ginglymus nature of the joints in his extremities. Unfortunately it is also true that the majority of horses in the UK have medio-lateral imbalances in that they are 'outside high' – the outside wall of the foot being longer than the inside wall. The reasons for this are many and varied and some of them will be dealt with in subsequent chapters of this book.

Fig. 3.9 shows a generalised structure of the horse's front limbs looking from the front. However, in practice it is difficult to be absolutely precise with these types of measurements – particularly to ensure that the weightbearing surface of the foot is at right angles to the centre of the cannon bone – and for the practical horse owner a system needs to be devised to ensure that you can gauge that measurement. To all intents and purposes it is this particular measurement that is the key to medio-lateral balance. In the reasonably well-conformed horse, however, there is nothing so simple as to determine whether your horse has medio-lateral balance. All you need is a farrier's 'T-square' (Fig. 3.10).

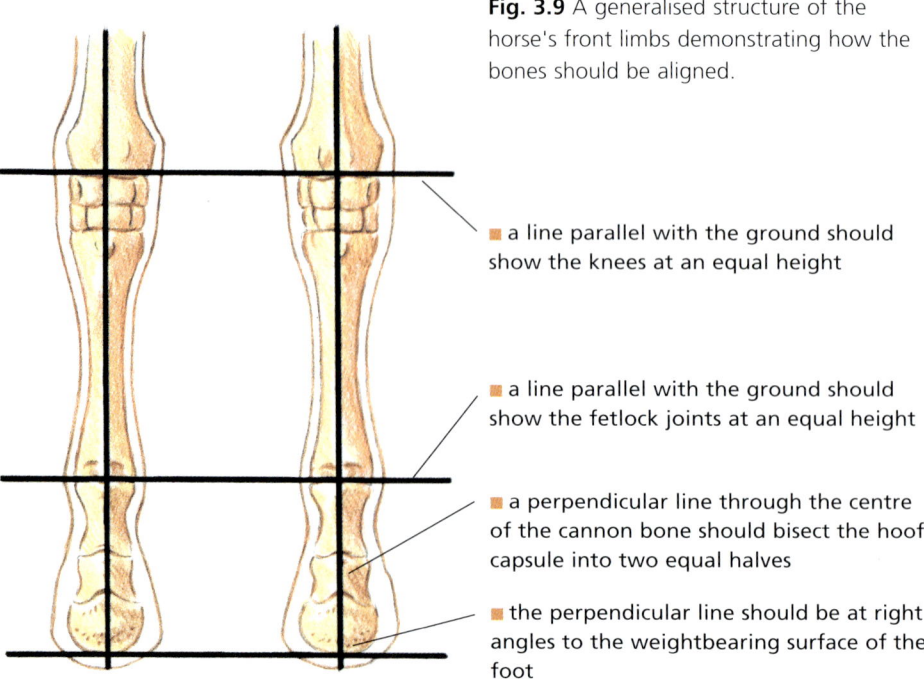

Fig. 3.9 A generalised structure of the horse's front limbs demonstrating how the bones should be aligned.

■ a line parallel with the ground should show the knees at an equal height

■ a line parallel with the ground should show the fetlock joints at an equal height

■ a perpendicular line through the centre of the cannon bone should bisect the hoof capsule into two equal halves

■ the perpendicular line should be at right angles to the weightbearing surface of the foot

How to use the T-square

- Lift your horse's foot as if you were going to pick his foot out.

- Make sure that you do not pull the leg away from the body and that you let it hang in a natural position under his body.

- Hold the limb by the middle part of the cannon bone (do not hold it by the pastern or fetlock) and apply the T-square with the long arm lying directly along the back of the superficial digital flexor tendon.

- The right-angle bar of the T-square should be close to the weightbearing surface of the foot, and the weightbearing surface of the foot should be level with the bar.

- If the foot is not level with the bar then you have a medio-lateral imbalance.

The reason why so many horse owners have horses which are 'outside high' is because when the farrier is shoeing the horse and assessing his medio-lateral balance, unfortunately the foot is not being held in a natural position underneath the horse. Because of the way the farrier stands when he is trimming the hoof, the horse's foot is pulled away from the side of the horse so that the farrier can place the foot between his legs. This means that the leg is twisted

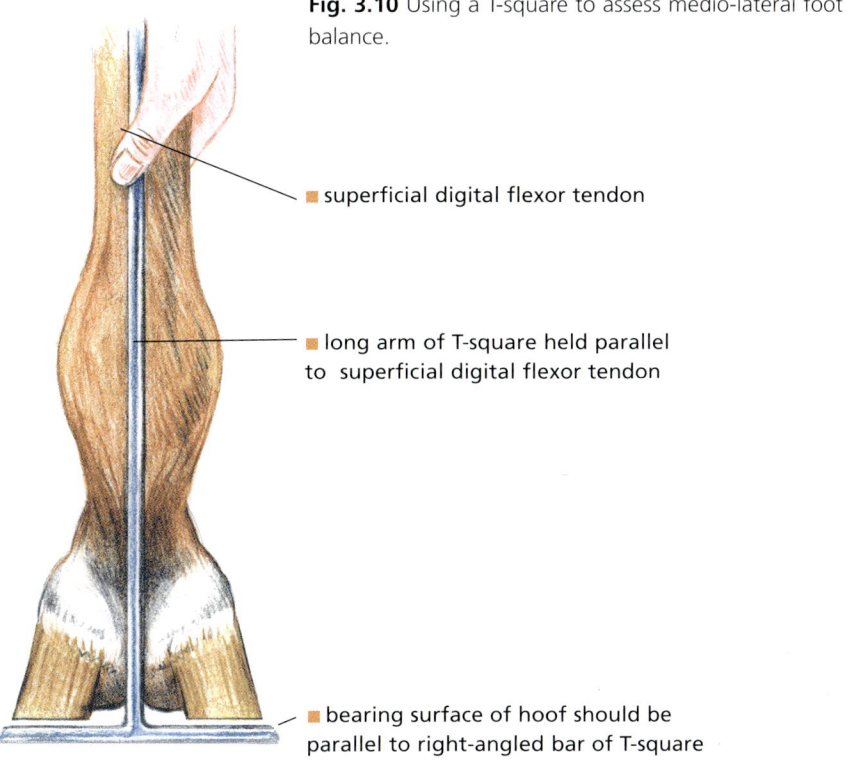

Fig. 3.10 Using a T-square to assess medio-lateral foot balance.

■ superficial digital flexor tendon

■ long arm of T-square held parallel to superficial digital flexor tendon

■ bearing surface of hoof should be parallel to right-angled bar of T-square

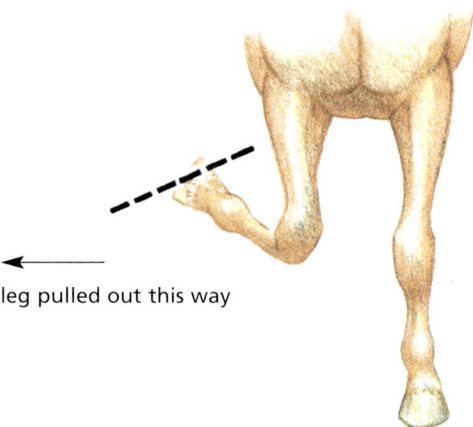

leg pulled out this way

Fig. 3.11 When the farrier places the horse's foot between his legs, he pulls the foot away from the side of the horse. This can result in the leg being twisted whilst the farrier is assessing the foot, leading him to trim the foot on an incorrect line.

when the farrier is assessing medio-lateral balance and he trims it on an incorrect line (Fig. 3.11) resulting in the horse being 'outside high'.

It is also important to ensure that there is an equal amount of hoof on either side of the imaginary line running down the front of the cannon bone. The hoof shape should be equivalent to an upside down ice-cream cone with the inside wall being at the same angle as the outside wall (Fig. 3.12).

Fig. 3.13 shows diagrammatically a distorted hoof capsule so that there is

Fig. 3.12 Ideal foot shape with equal amount of weightbearing on either side of the central line. The medial and lateral walls have the same angle and the hoof is shaped liked an upside-down ice-cream cone.

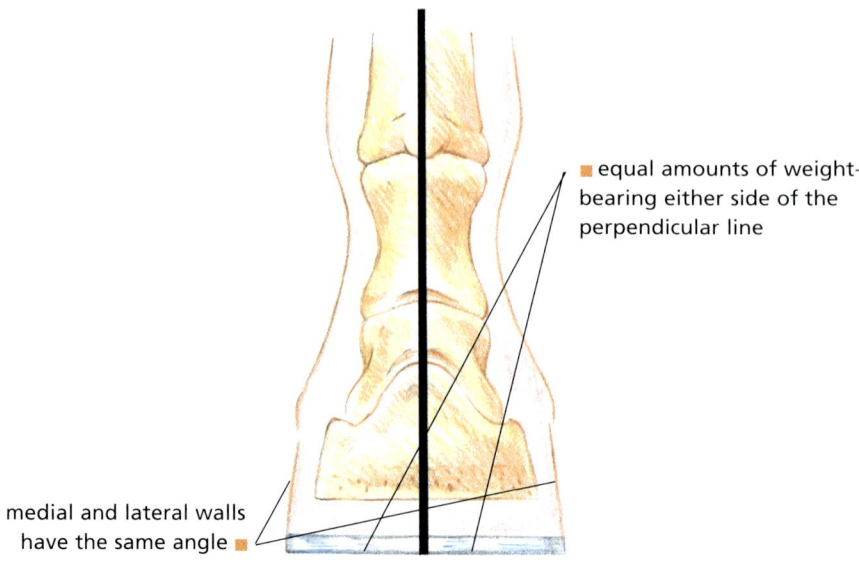

■ equal amounts of weight-bearing either side of the perpendicular line

medial and lateral walls have the same angle ■

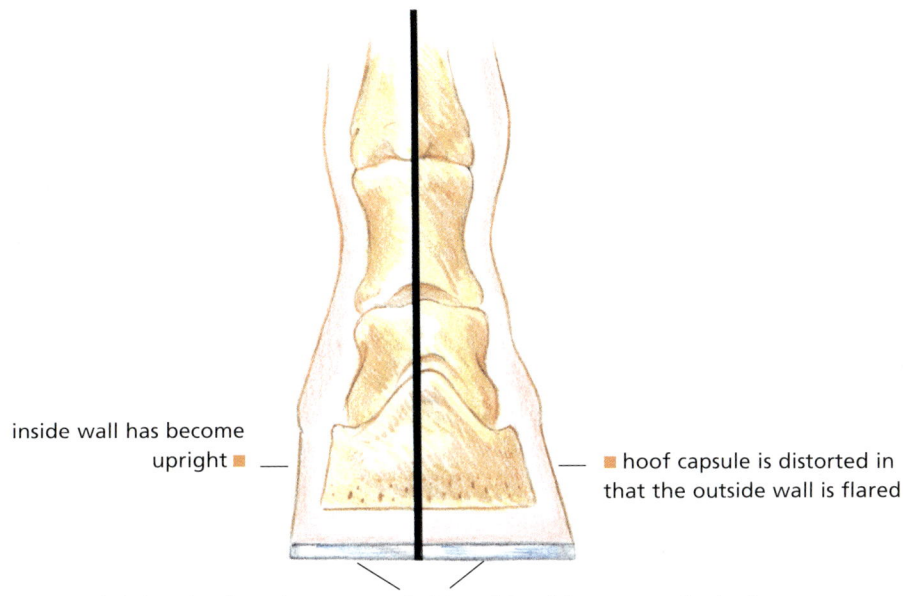

inside wall has become
upright ■ ——

—— ■ hoof capsule is distorted in
that the outside wall is flared

weightbearing is no longer equal either side of the perpendicular line

Fig. 3.13 A distorted hoof capsule leading to unequal weightbearing either side of the central line. This results in one side of the hoof flaring out whilst the other side becomes upright.

unequal weightbearing either side of the imaginary perpendicular line, whilst Fig. 3.14 is a photograph of a horse in which this hoof capsule distortion has become a reality.

Fig. 3.14 Hoof capsule distortion in the horse (shown diagrammatically in Fig. 3.13).

■ outside wall flared

■ inside wall upright

■ unequal weight-bearing surfaces

Further, as we have already seen, the hind limb functions differently to the front limb.

All horsemastership texts will tell you that the horse must move on two tracks and that the hind limbs should be perfectly straight with the toes pointing directly forwards when the horse is standing still (see Fig. 3.15). In our opinion, especially in the speed horse, this is not natural. If you watch a horse from behind moving away from you, you will note that as he gets into the faster gaits – particularly the gallop – he will place his feet more widely apart. This is to prevent the hind feet from coming into contact with the front feet. In other words the horse is no longer moving on two tracks. To enable the horse to place his feet wider apart he rotates the whole hind limb out from the hip joint (at the acetabulum) – this means that his hocks are pushed out and his lower limb rotates inward (Fig. 3.16). If he began with feet pointing straight to the front then at the gallop his feet would be pointing inward – pigeon-toed.

In our opinion it is far more natural for a horse to stand slightly cow-hocked with his hind toes pointing in a 'five-to-one' position – as shown by the horse in Fig. 3.16. This will mean that when he rotates the hind limb outward at the gallop his feet will be pointing straight forwards, thus enabling him to attain optimum biomechanical function.

Fig. 3.15 The generally accepted ideal of hind-limb conformation showing the feet pointing straight forward.

Fig. 3.16 As the horse moves faster, his hind feet have to be placed further apart to prevent contact with the front feet. To do this the horse rotates the limbs out from the hip joint (acetabulum) and the hocks are pushed out. In turn the distal limb rotates inward.

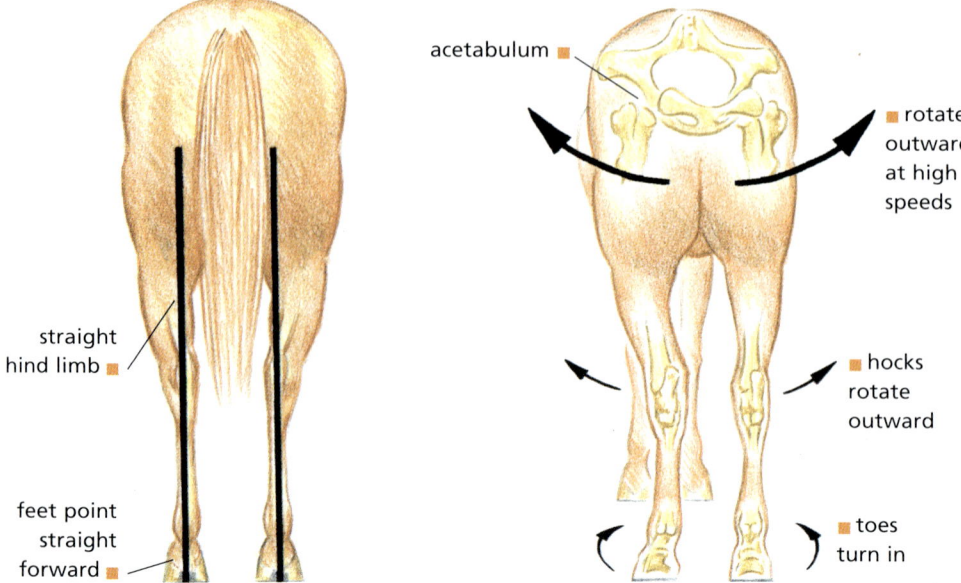

straight hind limb ■

feet point straight forward ■

acetabulum ■

■ rotates outward at high speeds

■ hocks rotate outward

■ toes turn in

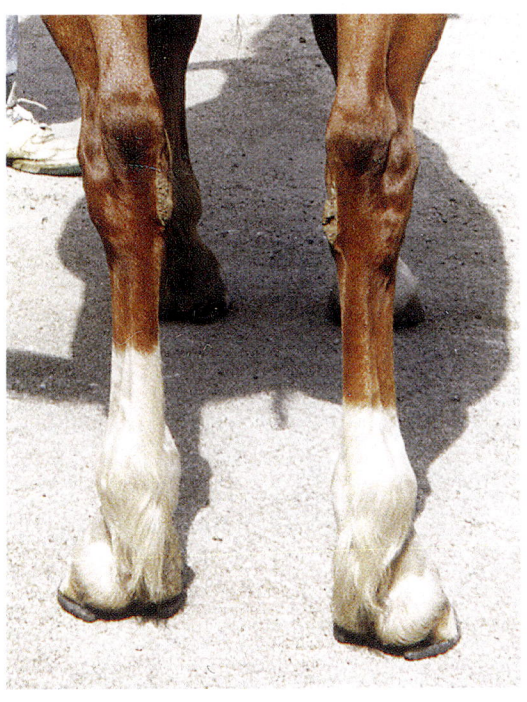

Fig. 3.17 A more natural hind limb conformation with the toes pointing at a 'five to one' position. At speed, when the hocks are pushed outward, the feet will point to the front thereby giving optimum performance.

Assessment of medio-lateral balance in the hind feet is a more complex task because the T-square cannot be used in the same way in the hind foot. It can only be done with the T-square when the foot is on the ground – see Fig. 3.18. The long arm of the T-square should bisect the cannon bone.

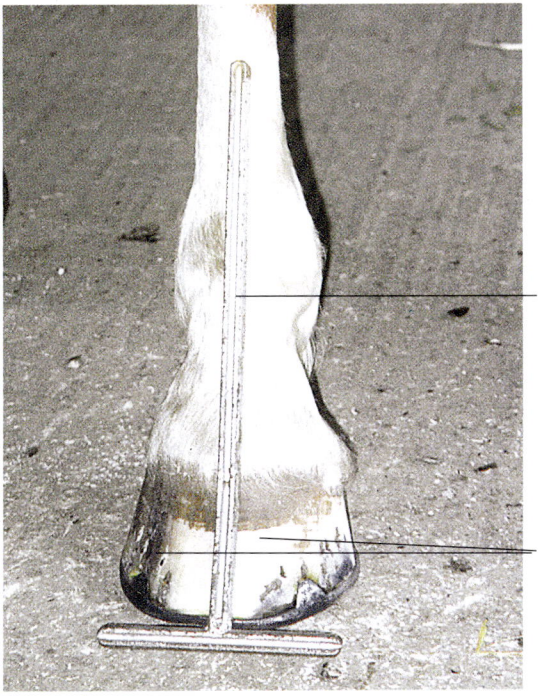

Fig. 3.18 Assessing hind foot medio-lateral balance.

■ long arm of T-square bisects cannon bone

■ each side of the foot is equal – a mirror image

Ground surface of the foot

The next assessment to make concerns how the foot looks on the solar surface – i.e. what the underside looks like when you pick up the foot. Fig. 3.19 shows the ideal shape of the foot from this aspect.

Fig. 3.20 shows a common problem that occurs when these measurements are not adhered to. Note how the shoe is wider than it is long.

In Fig. 3.21 you can easily differentiate between the shoe taken off a horse which had been similarly shod and the more correct shoe with which it was replaced.

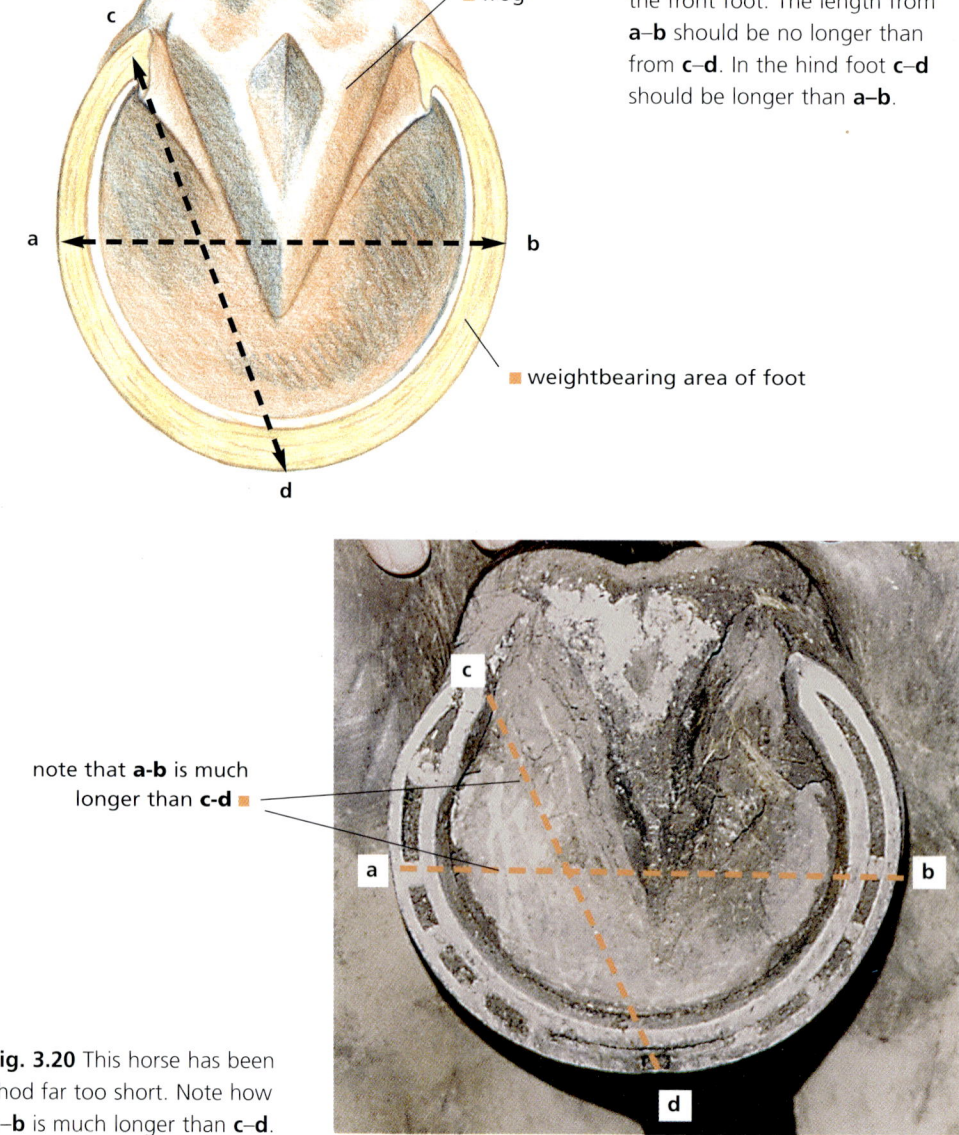

■ frog

■ weightbearing area of foot

Fig. 3.19 Ideal ground surface of the front foot. The length from **a–b** should be no longer than from **c–d**. In the hind foot **c–d** should be longer than **a–b**.

note that **a-b** is much longer than **c-d** ■

Fig. 3.20 This horse has been shod far too short. Note how **a–b** is much longer than **c–d**.

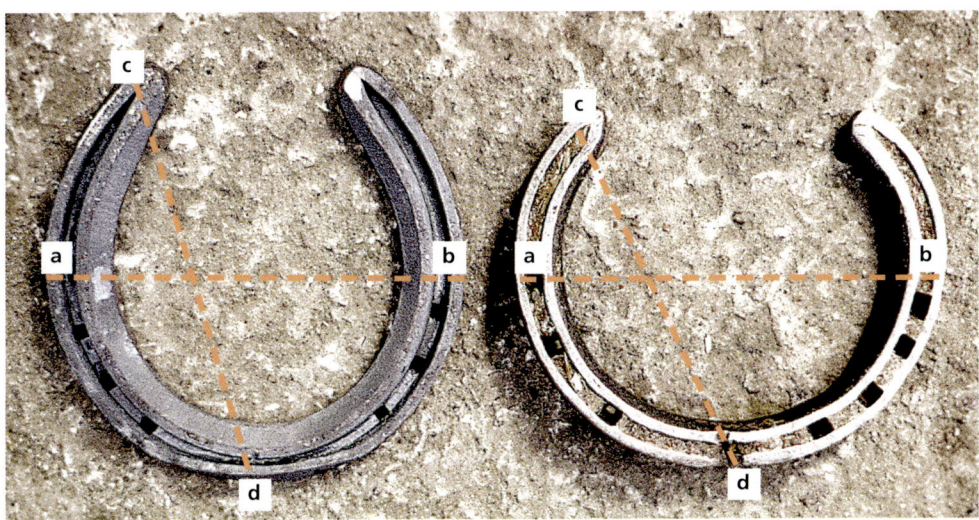

Fig. 3.21 The shoe on the right was removed from a forefoot and replaced by the one on the left. See how the length of the new shoe is more appropriate in that **a–b** is the same length as **c–d**.

As a graphic example of how short shoe number one was, Fig. 3.22 shows a side view of the horse wearing the old shoes. Note where the last weight-bearing aspect of the shoe is compared with the imaginary perpendicular line from the centre of the fetlock joint.

When looking at Fig. 3.22 it is perhaps easy to think that you could not

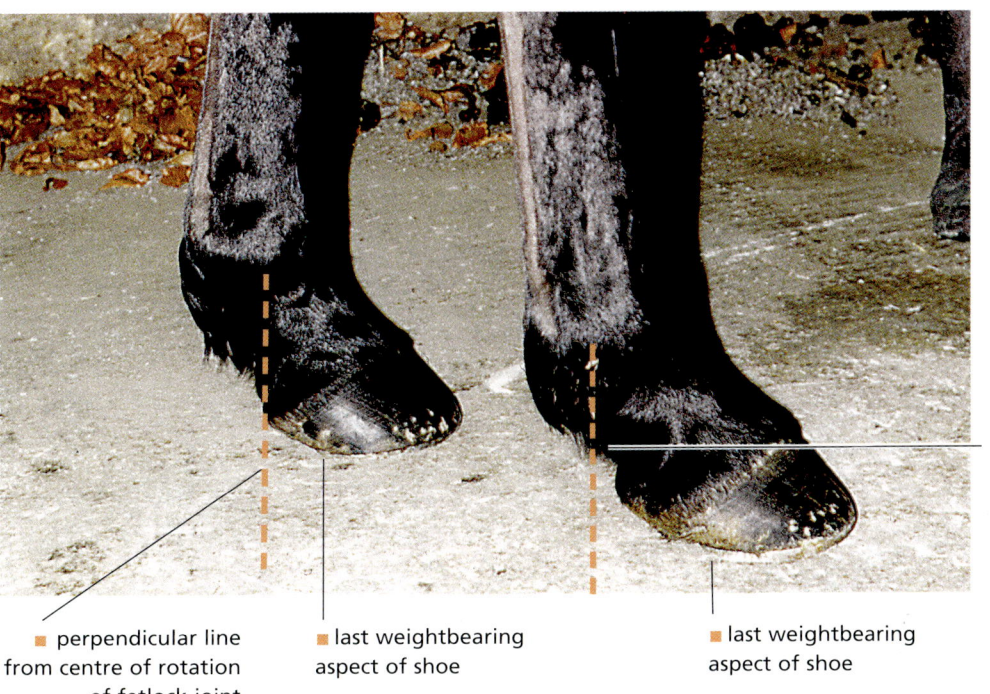

Fig. 3.22 This horse has been shod much too short. See how he has no support for the fetlocks.

■ perpendicular line from centre of rotation of fetlock joint

■ perpendicular line from centre of rotation of fetlock joint

■ last weightbearing aspect of shoe

■ last weightbearing aspect of shoe

possibly extend the shoe back to underneath the fetlock joint because as soon as the horse started to move, his hind feet would tread on the back of the front shoes and pull them off. The point to remember here is that because the heels are not supporting the fetlock as they should be, the fetlock is sagging down, being held in the 'sling' of the tendons and creating an optical illusion. As soon as the heels of the shoe are in the correct place the horse will be able to stand up properly. This was particularly well demonstrated in Figs. 3.3 and 3.4 earlier in this chapter.

When looking at the sole, it is important to bear in mind that (to use a football analogy) it should be one of two halves: a line drawn through the central groove of the frog should divide the foot equally in half, whilst the point of the frog should be in direct line with the centre of the toe.

In the hind foot, because it is a longer, thinner foot than the front one, the shoe must always be longer than it is wide.

Pair symmetry of hooves and limbs

The next point to consider is whether your horse's left and right legs are mirror images. We have seen from Fig. 3.9 that each knee and fetlock should be the same height from the ground as its partner, and this can be relatively easily measured.

In the perfect horse the front feet should be an identical pair and the hind feet should be an identical pair. You will recall that in a previous chapter we mentioned that the hind feet are generally longer and narrower than the front

broken forwards
hoof/pastern axis ■

broken back
hoof/pastern axis ■

Fig. 3.23 Mismatched feet. The left foot has a broken back hoof/pastern axis whilst the right foot has a broken forwards hoof/pastern axis.

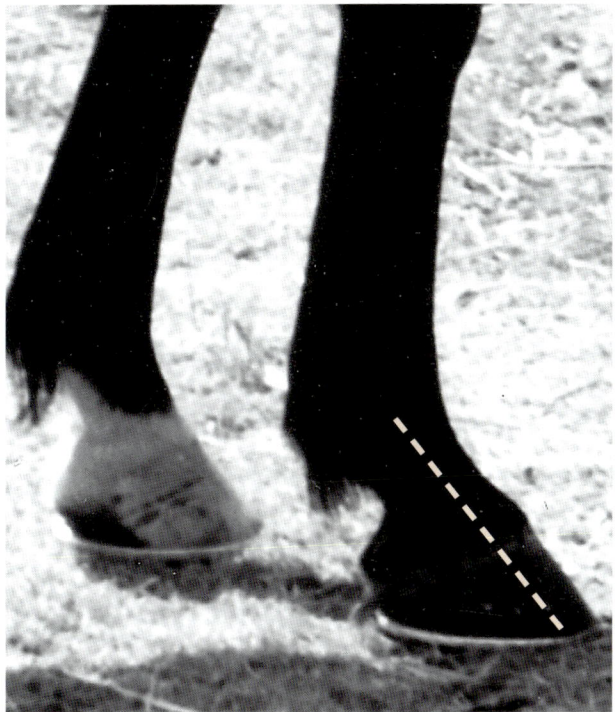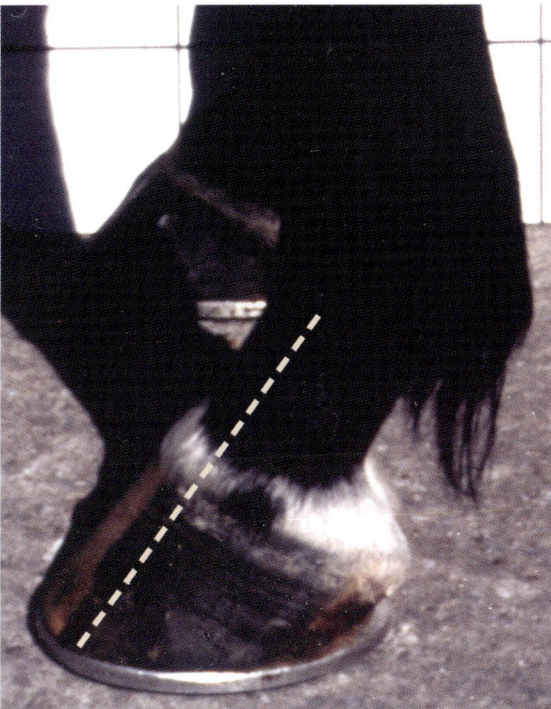

Figs. 3.24–25 The same horse as in Fig. 3.23 after correct trimming and shoeing. Note how both feet are now correct.

feet. The reason for this is that the horse is carrying more of his weight on the front feet and they will therefore need a greater weightbearing surface. The hind legs are generally acting to propel the horse forwards and the longer, narrower hind feet are more efficient for this purpose.

It is vitally important in terms of mechanics for each of these pairs of feet to be identical to the other. If they are not, they are experiencing different forces which will affect the individual limbs in individual ways. If each limb is experiencing different forces then normal locomotion will be disrupted.

Fig. 3.23 shows a horse displaying two different front feet: the right foot has a broken forwards hoof/pastern axis and the left foot has a broken back hoof/pastern axis. Figs. 3.24 and 3.25 demonstrate how this was corrected in one trimming and shoeing.

Non-contact of hooves and limbs

The perfect horse will move on two tracks when trotted up in a straight line (Fig. 3.26). By moving in this way the horse ensures that his left and right front feet do not make contact with each other and that his left and right hind feet do not make contact with each other. This is vitally important for the horse, as any contact between the limbs, especially at the faster gaits, will injure him.

Fig. 3.26 Horses should move on two tracks.

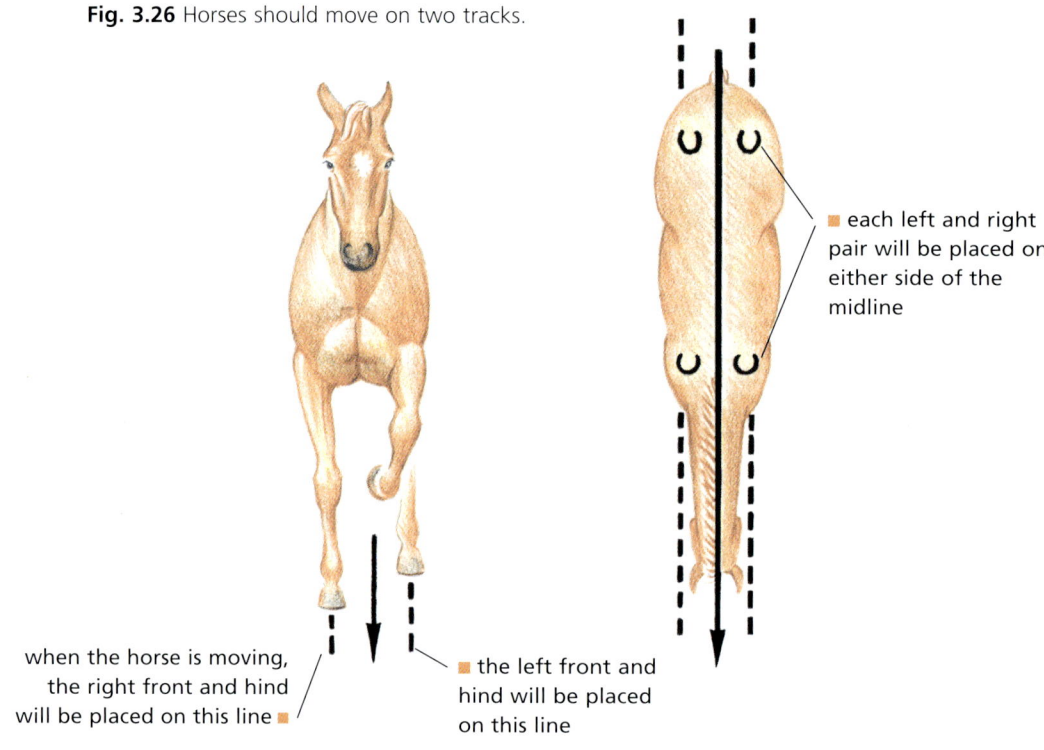

■ each left and right pair will be placed on either side of the midline

when the horse is moving, the right front and hind will be placed on this line ■

■ the left front and hind will be placed on this line

Fig. 3.27 This horse with good foot conformation is breaking over the centre of the toe and the left hind foot is being placed in the same line as the left front foot, indicating movement on two tracks.

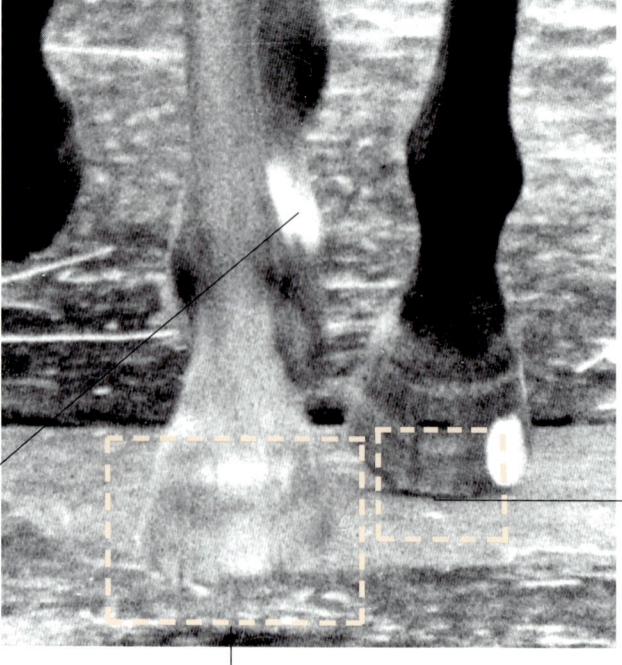

left hind foot about to be placed on same line as front foot, indicating movement on two tracks ■

■ horse breaks over centre of toe

■ hoof capsule demonstrating medial and lateral walls with same angle

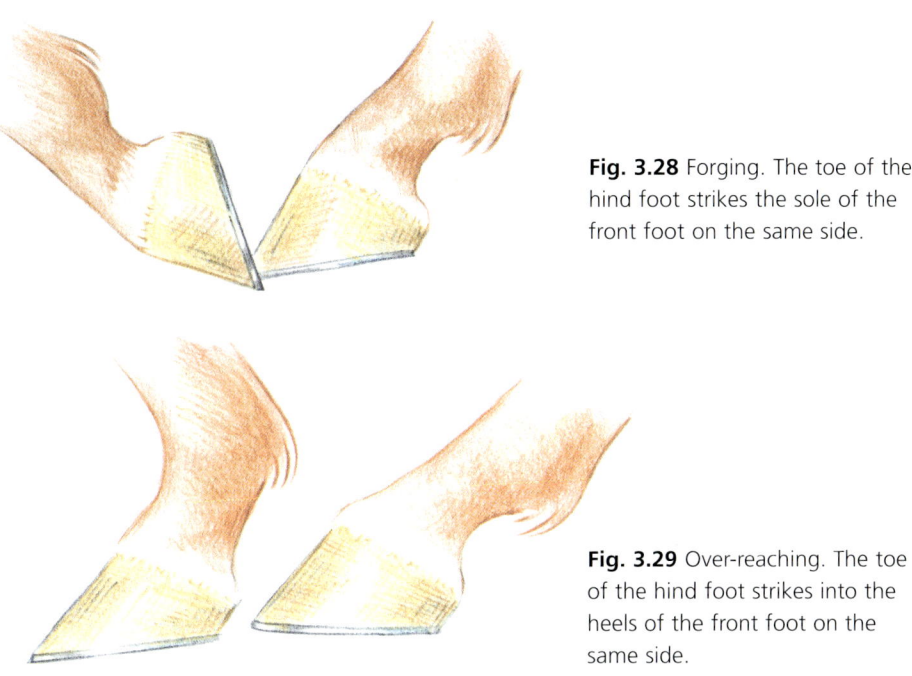

Fig. 3.28 Forging. The toe of the hind foot strikes the sole of the front foot on the same side.

Fig. 3.29 Over-reaching. The toe of the hind foot strikes into the heels of the front foot on the same side.

One of the things that enables the horse to move on two tracks in this way is the fact that during breakover the toe of the front foot is pointed towards the front and he breaks over the centre of the toe (Fig. 3.27).

The horse shown in Fig. 3.27 is an excellent example of a horse with good limb conformation and foot balance, moving freely on two tracks.

Of course it is not just interference between front and hind pairs that is important when considering non-contact of hooves. It is also vitally important that the hind feet do not come into contact with front feet. Figs 3.28 and 3.29 show two common examples of hind/fore interference – forging and over-reaching. Forging involves hitting the sole of the shoe or the front foot with the hind toe on the same side. Its causes are varied ranging from conformation (short-backed/long-legged horses), through to tiredness or toes being too long.

Over-reaching is similar to forging save that the hind foot strikes either into the bulbs of the heels on the front foot or into the heels themselves, often causing lost shoes. Again, the causes are similar to those of forging.

There are locomotor problems when the front foot makes contact with the hind limb causing injury. The names given to them depend upon where on the hind limb the front foot makes contact (Fig. 3.30, overleaf).

So now you should be in a position to assess your horse to ascertain any problems he may have. To a certain extent this is the easy part – what do you do now? A horse's locomotor patterns may change over time, not just as a

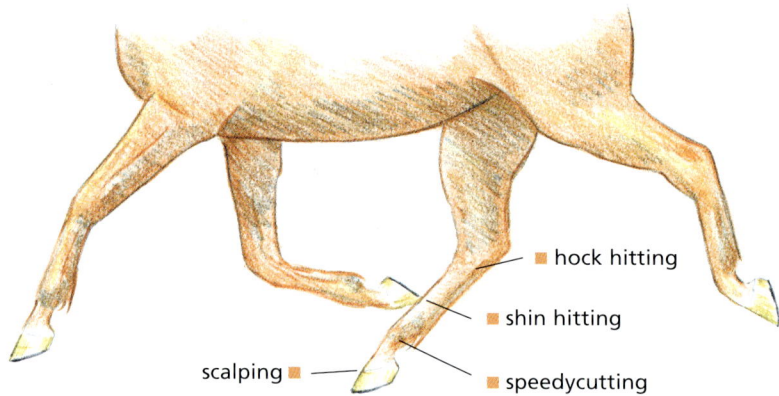

hock hitting

shin hitting

scalping

speedycutting

Fig. 3.30 Various types of hind-limb contact.

result of training but in an attempt to compensate for any abnormal forces which are being generated by imbalances in his feet. It is vitally important that you assess your horse's way of going at regular intervals. When was the last time you stood and watched your horse move whilst someone else trotted him up for you?

Changes in his locomotor patterns are the only way that your horse can let you know about the forces he is experiencing. Just because a horse is not lame does not mean that he is not suffering some disruption to normal locomotion, which may eventually lead to some form of lameness. Every horse is a book – all you need to do is learn to read it.

CHAPTER 4

Remedial Bar Shoes

Myriad shoe constructions have been designed and fitted to horses throughout the centuries. However, we will confine ourselves to describing the most common types of remedial shoe – the various 'bar' shoes – since it is these shoes, along with the normal open-heeled fullered, concave shoe, that will be used in the case studies throughout this book.

Fig. 4.1 shows the five types of bar shoe. They are so called because they have an additional bar either joining both heels or supporting the frog in some way.

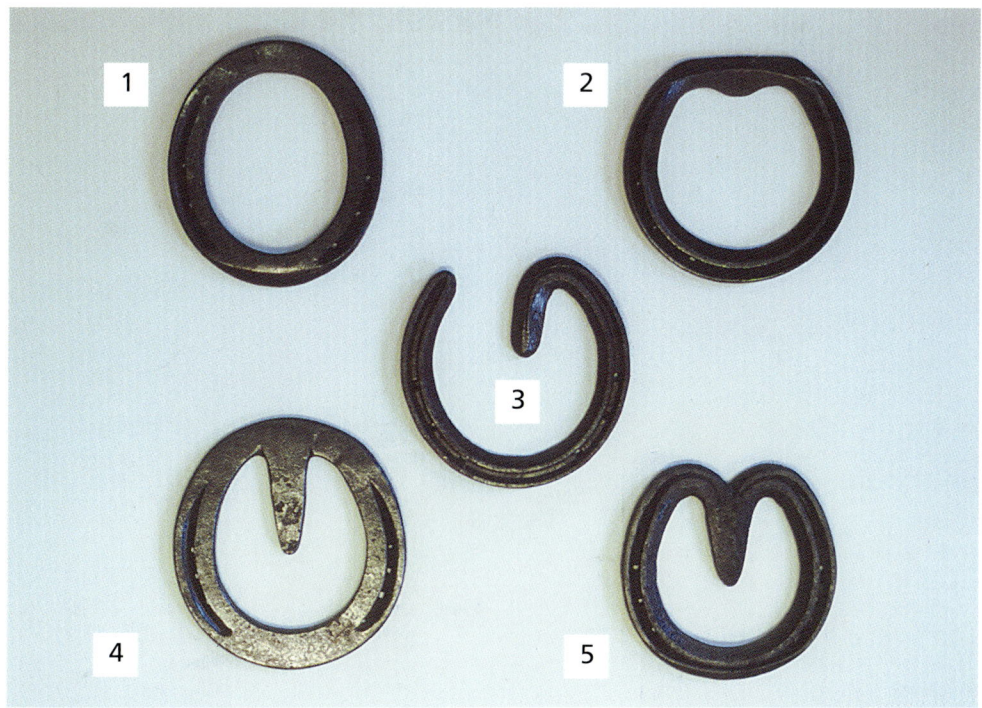

Fig. 4.1 The five types of bar shoe. **1** – egg-bar; **2** – straight-bar; **3** – half-bar; **4** – combination egg-bar/heart-bar; **5** – heart-bar.

The egg-bar shoe

As its name suggests, the egg-bar shoe is shaped rather like an egg. This is perhaps one of the most commonly used remedial shoes and one which most will recognise. It is also the most widely misused shoe!

There are good reasons why some horses should be shod in egg-bar shoes and generally, contrary to popular opinion, they do not affect a horse's performance capacity if properly fitted and the horse properly managed. Indeed eighteen horses competed at the Los Angeles Olympics in 1984 wearing egg-bar shoes, and in the 1986 World Championships the entire Dutch dressage team horses were shod in egg-bars.

They are commonly associated with the treatment of navicular disease and are wrongly applied to horses with that condition, regardless of the foot shape or the horse's conformation. Indeed, there is no real biomechanical reason why egg-bar shoes should be effective in the alleviation of pain caused by navicular disease. The reasons for this statement will be discussed in Chapter 9.

The egg-bar shoe adds approximately 25% more ground-bearing surface to the foot. Because of the shape of the shoe, this extra ground-bearing surface is concentrated around the heels. This conveys a greater amount of support to the heel area and therefore it is a shoe which can be used when the heels are collapsed (Fig. 4.2).

note how these heels have completely collapsed (rolled under) the foot ■

egg-bar shoe supporting collapsed heels ■

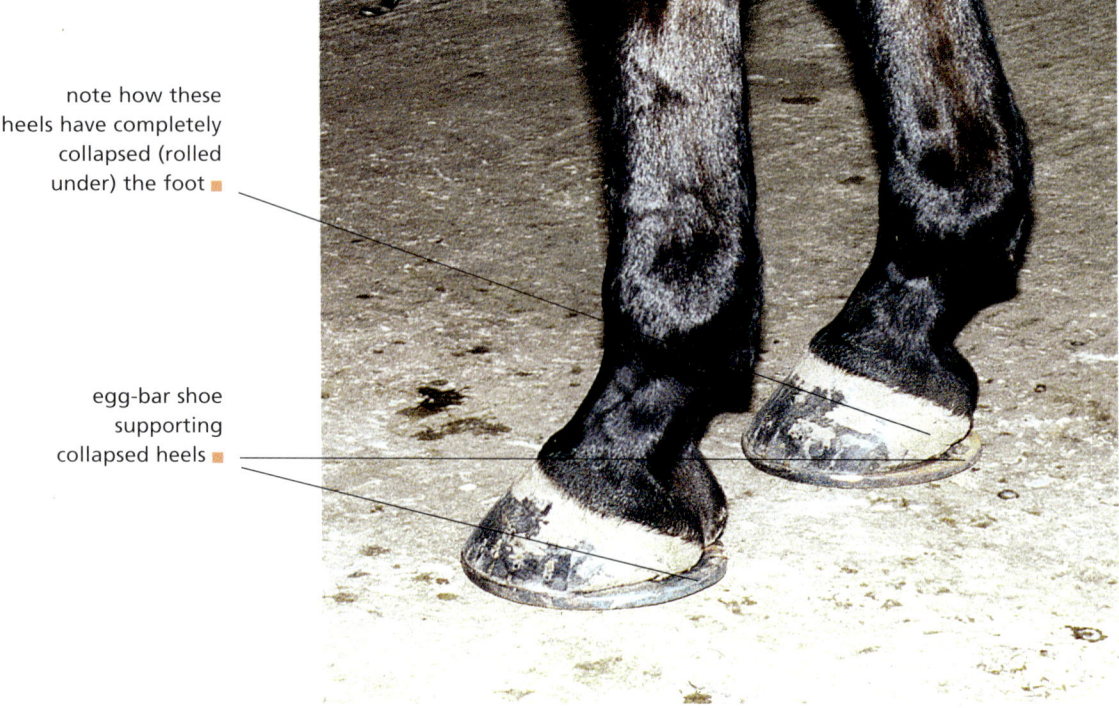

Fig. 4.2 Egg-bar shoes fitted to a horse with collapsed heels.

It is also a shoe that should be used where there is an abnormal force bearing down on the heels. Such a situation arises in the horse with long, sloping pasterns (Fig. 4.3).

Fig. 4.3 Horse with long, sloping pasterns. Egg-bar shoes are the shoe of choice for the horse with long, sloping pasterns as they give much needed support.

In such a horse there is no way that the heels can support the fetlock (refer back to Fig. 3.3, page 32) and the farrier cannot extend the branches of the shoe back that far – such a shoe would be pulled off almost immediately. In these circumstances the egg-bar shoe is the shoe of choice because it can give horses with long, sloping pasterns as much support as possible.

Occasionally egg-bar shoes can cause a horse to land heel-first. In these circumstances the deleterious effects of landing heel-first outweigh the benefits of the egg-bar shoe and their application should cease.

The straight-bar shoe

Like in the egg-bar, the heels are joined together, but whereas the egg-bar is rounded, the bar on this shoe is straight. In functionally correct horses the bulbs of the heels are held in line with each other by dense connective tissue.

In the horse with a medio-lateral foot imbalance this connective tissue can be broken down, because the horse is landing on one side of the foot (more often than not the outside aspect) rather than flat-footed as he should. The abnormal stresses result in a condition known as 'sheared heels,' which is the descriptive term for the breakdown of the tissue in between the bulbs of the heels. Sheared heels can also occur in the hind feet through imbalances caused by road studs, which create a disproportionate amount of force on the outside heel.

The signs of sheared heels are fairly obvious. When looking from the rear of the horse the bulbs of the heels will not be at the same height (Fig. 4.4). When the foot is picked up you can actually move the heels against each other because the foot has become mobile and the central cleft is split through to the hair line(Fig. 4.5).

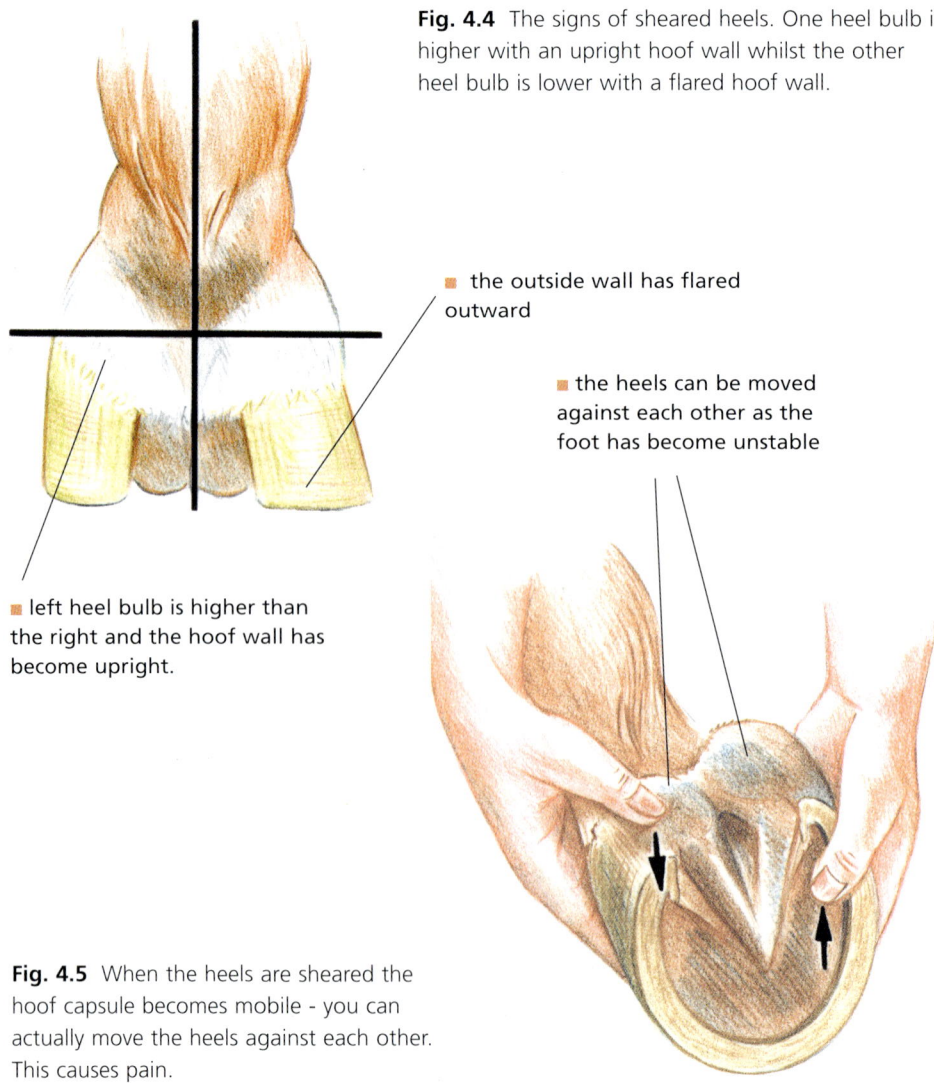

Fig. 4.4 The signs of sheared heels. One heel bulb is higher with an upright hoof wall whilst the other heel bulb is lower with a flared hoof wall.

■ the outside wall has flared outward

■ the heels can be moved against each other as the foot has become unstable

■ left heel bulb is higher than the right and the hoof wall has become upright.

Fig. 4.5 When the heels are sheared the hoof capsule becomes mobile - you can actually move the heels against each other. This causes pain.

To allow the sheared heels to repair, the foot has to be put into balance, and a straight-bar shoe applied (Fig. 4.6) to prevent the heels moving against each other.

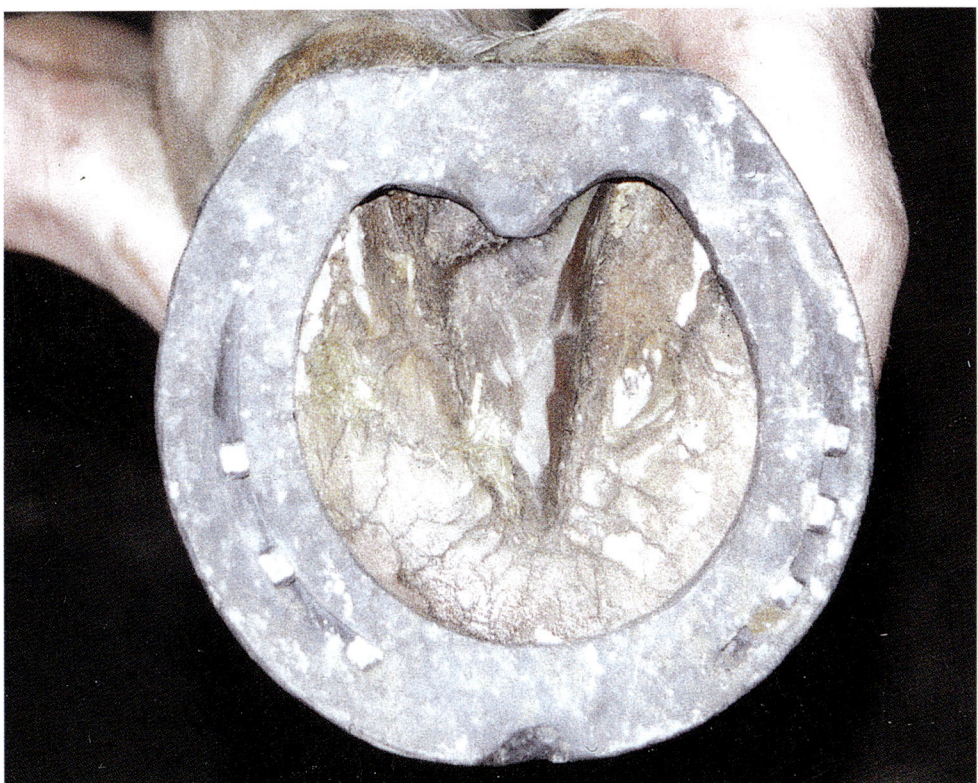

Fig. 4.6 A straight bar shoe.

The half-bar shoe

On a half-bar shoe the bar is attached to only one half of the shoe. The bar itself rests lightly on the underside of one half of the frog and is a unilateral support shoe. This means that when the horse weightbears, the weight is taken not only on the wall but also on that side of the frog on which the foot needs the most support. This effectively doubles the area of support on one particular side of the foot – usually the medial side.

If the circumstances are such that the heel cannot take any weight, the heel can be trimmed down so that it does not come into contact with the heel of the shoe and all the weight on that side of the foot will be transmitted down through the one half of the frog and taken on the bar.

This shoe is used in cases where either one half of the foot needs more support than the other, or weight needs to be taken off one heel altogether.

This can occur when the hoof capsule becomes so distorted that it has begun to spiral around the foot as shown in Fig. 4.7. In these circumstances the only way in which to allow the hoof capsule to return to normal is to either substantially reduce the amount of weight it is taking or to remove the weightbearing from it altogether. Fig. 4.8 shows the application of the half-bar shoe to such a foot.

Fig 4.7 The hoof capsule can become distorted in cases of chronic imbalance and can spiral around the foot. In such cases the application of a half-bar shoe is appropriate.

outside wall has flared out ■

hoof capsule

■ inside quarter has gone beyond the upright and is actually on the inside of a line dropped from the coronet band

hoof capsule has spiralled around

Fig 4.8 A half-bar shoe fitted to a foot whose hoof capsule has begun to spiral around.

The heart-bar shoe

The heart-bar shoe has a bar that looks like the top part of a heart, hence the name. It is similar to the half-bar but the bar is attached to both heels. This shoe has commonly been associated with the laminitic horse as it was believed to support the pedal bone and prevent it from rotating, but its application in that respect is now considered to be controversial at best, requiring expert application by a farrier and a vet working together. This shoe is now more often used in horses where effectively the 'ground has to be brought up to meet the foot'.

For this reason the shoe is generally applied to horses who have flat feet – i.e. the sole has no concavity. Mechanically, in the normal foot as the weight bears down the limb, the sole loses some of its concavity. In the flat foot this weight causes the foot to become almost convex, the effect of which is to tear the sole from the wall. This type of foot conformation generally arises in weak feet.

Another effect is that flat feet allow the lower border of the hoof to expand excessively, which in turn increases the amount of spreading. This leads to very poor structured horn because it deteriorates as a result of the movement across the ground surface. The sole also deteriorates and loses its structure. These weak, splayed, flat feet invariably also have collapsed heels. As explained in Chapter 3, this leads to problems with the blood supply to the foot. Lack of appropriate nutrients being brought to the sole by the blood supply results in a deterioration in sole structure and the sole loses its chalky appearance. Further, as the foot is so flat the sole comes into contact with the ground surface and affects its quality.

The heart bar reduces the amount of downward movement of the sole by supporting the foot under the line of vertical force, thus preventing any convexity. As a result the blood vessels do not become so compressed. This allows for a better blood supply and restores the balance of mechanical function of the foot.

Horses shod with heart-bar shoes need careful management as thrush can develop under the frogplate, and in some cases a low-grade necrosis of the frog tissue can result. If horses are to be shod in heart bars for any length of time it is sometimes wise to give the feet an occasional 'rest' by shoeing them in a straight-bar shoe for one shoeing period. It is sensible to apply an antibacterial/dehydrating foot dressing between the frogplate and foot.

When applying this shoe the frog must be trimmed back to infantile tissue – i.e. clean, healthy frog tissue. The frogplate should lie flat on the frog with no space between it and the frog itself. There are many theories as to how tightly against the frog the frogplate should rest. As a rule of thumb, to establish whether the pressure is acceptable to the animal, apply the shoe with two heel nails only, pick the opposite foot up and hold it with just one or two fingers. If the horse stands comfortably on the applied heart-bar shoe then the pressure is acceptable.

The heart-bar shoe is the shoe of choice in the horse with heel pain in both heels where there is a combination of the foot being wider than it is long, with a flat sole and collapsed heels and bars. The effect is to remove some of the force being applied to the back third of the foot.

The combination egg-bar/heart-bar shoe

The final shoe in this section is the combination egg-bar/heart-bar shoe. This is the shoe for a horse evincing all of the problems requiring a heart bar *plus* long sloping pasterns which require the support of the egg-bar.

Extensions

One final point about remedial shoeing involves what are known as 'extensions'. These can form part of a bar shoe or any ordinary open-heeled shoe and are used where the hoof capsule is distorted and there is an unequal amount of weightbearing surface on either side of the foot. Fig. 4.9 demonstrates how this works.

Fig 4.9 This horse needed an extension fitting to the shoe so that he had equal weightbearing either side of the central line.

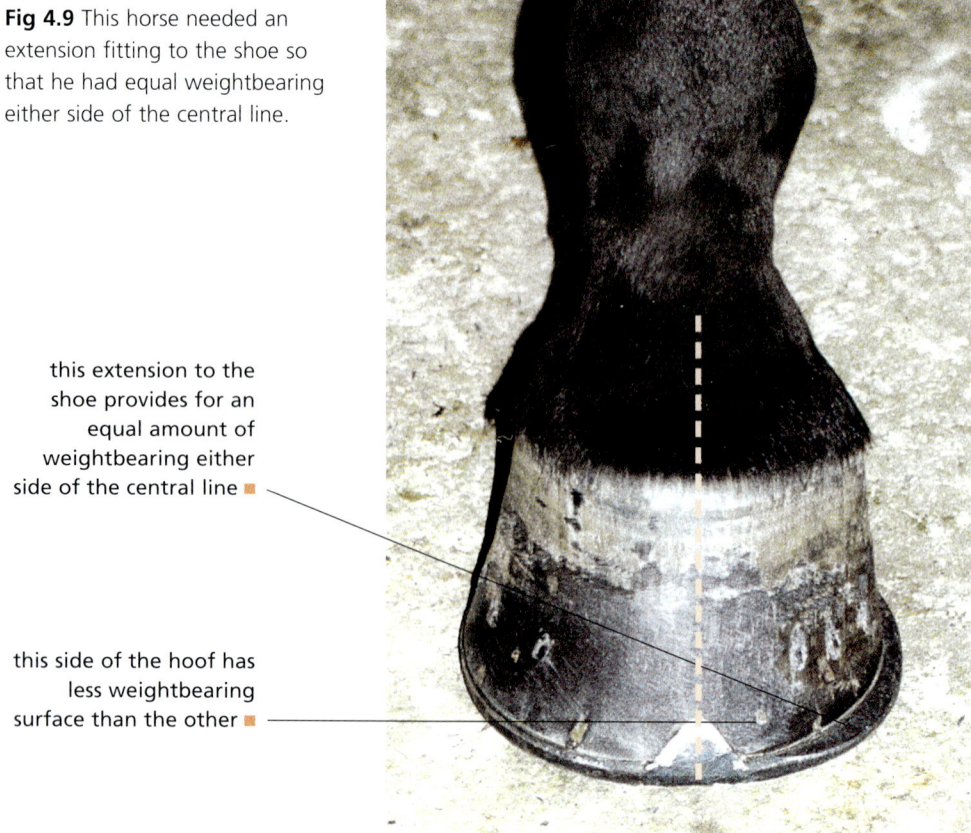

this extension to the shoe provides for an equal amount of weightbearing either side of the central line ■

this side of the hoof has less weightbearing surface than the other ■

In this chapter we have described the different types of shoe that are generally used in remedial work, and explained how each one differs in its capacity to restore normal hoof shape and function and to assist the poorly conformed horse to deal with the challenges that nature has thrust upon him in terms of mechanics. All of these shoes require the knowledge, care and expertise in their forging and application that can only come from the most skilful of remedial farriers. Unfortunately these are rare creatures and if you find one, look after him well.

CHAPTER 5

Poor Feet and Bad Backs

There is an interesting story about a famous British middle-distance runner who for many years suffered recurring injuries which prevented him from becoming the best in the world. Then one day a specialist in human locomotion discovered that this runner had one leg very fractionally longer than the other. From then on the athlete competed with a folded page from a telephone directory placed in one of his running shoes – his injury problems became a thing of the past and he attained athletic stardom.

There is no reason to think that similar problems do not exist in horses and that adjusting their foot balance, even in a minute way, can have positive or negative effects upon their performance and soundness. Think what would happen if, for example, you placed a small wedge on the outside edge of your shoes and walked around in them for a few weeks. Initially you would not have any particular problems but after a day or so you would notice that your ankle was beginning to ache; then after a few more days perhaps your knee would start to play up. After some time your hips and eventually your back would begin to hurt. This is because in order to accommodate the effects of the shoe wedge, you have had to alter the way you move very slightly and this has completely unbalanced all your locomotor systems. The joints have been put under stress – they are dealing with abnormal forces – and pain commences. Another effect of these changes to your movement patterns is that your locomotor muscles have to work in slightly different ways.

In the horse, as we have seen in Chapter 1, the majority of his locomotor muscles are situated along the shoulder, back and quarters – his topline. Changes in the action of muscles which protract and retract the hind limbs create abnormal forces acting against the pelvis, which can cause rotation and strain in both the lumbo-sacral and sacroiliac joints and also in the long muscles of the back. Muscle spasm occasioned by injury or abnormal locomotor forces has the same effect. As there is very rarely just one muscle responsible for moving a body part, any muscular dysfunction can have a domino effect by either forcing another muscle to work harder than it should or by preventing it from working at all. Thus a vicious spiral is created and this is why, in our view, back pain in horses should not be viewed in isolation: there is a possibility that the cause of the pain may stem from dysfunction in other systems. After all, there is no point in patching up the roof if the cause of the problem is crumbling foundations.

The relationship between bad backs and bad feet has long been mooted. After all, any problems in the back will create abnormal locomotor patterns, which will affect the way the feet are placed on the ground and will eventually lead to hoof-capsule distortion and improper balance. Conversely, imbalances in the feet will cause abnormal locomotor patterns which, eventually, will lead to problems in the topline.

This chapter is not meant to be a definitive view of the effects of faulty foot balance on backs – there is so little hard evidence on the subject that it would be foolish to attempt such a task. All we know is that because of the way the horse is put together and how he moves, there can be little doubt that sore backs and incorrectly balanced feet have a causal relationship with each other. Women readers will know that standing up all day wearing high-heeled shoes takes its toll on their backs as well as their feet. They will also know that they can run substantially faster in flat-heeled shoes than in high heels.

There is something else to be borne in mind. If a horse has had to alter the way he moves (for whatever reason) and has been moving abnormally for a long time – as in the case of chronic foot imbalance or chronic back discomfort – to a certain extent his locomotor muscles will have adapted to that way of moving. This means that you cannot expect an overnight, miracle cure. In a lot of cases of chronic foot imbalance, putting the feet back in balance and making the horse move 'normally' can cause pain in muscles that have atrophied through lack of use. Many horses can appear to move rather clumsily at first until muscles that have either been over-used or under-used settle down into a normal pattern. Therefore it is not uncommon to see a horse initially move badly even though his feet have been put into correct balance. It is in these cases that your farrier, veterinary surgeon and physiotherapist, osteopath or chiropractor can work together to return the horse to normal locomotor function.

If a horse has experienced chronic locomotor dysfunction the results of his abnormal movement can be seen in abnormal muscle development. The evidence of his discomfort will be visible for all to see – like reading words on the pages of a book. All you have to do is learn how to read this particular language.

Fig. 5.1 (overleaf) demonstrates how, for example, the long toe/low heel (broken back hoof/pastern axis) abnormally affects the forces acting on joints throughout the horse's body, thus completely unbalancing his whole locomotor system.

We can see how this imbalance in the locomotor system has affected the

Fig. 5.1a

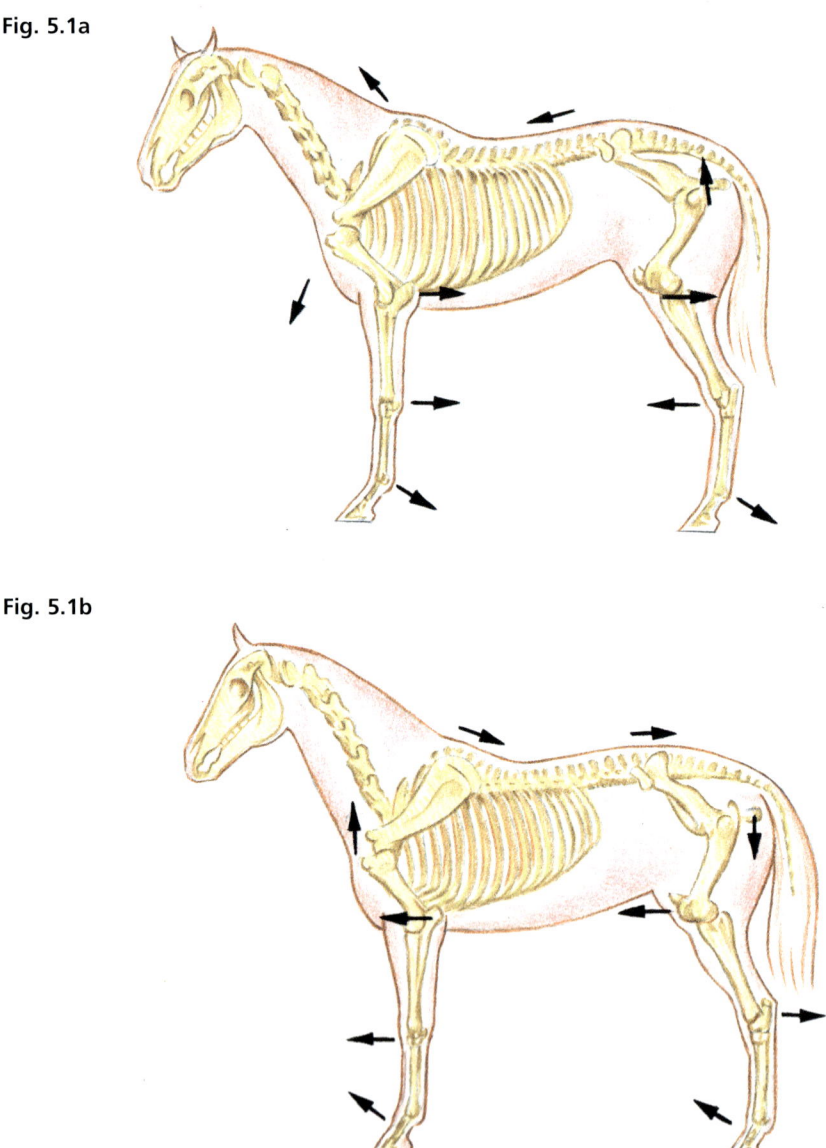

Fig. 5.1b

Fig. 5.1 (a) Long toe/low heel conformation. This throws the horse completely out of balance. **(b)** Balancing the feet brings the whole horse back into balance.

horse in Fig. 5.2. This is a horse in his late teens in full work at a riding school. The first thing that becomes obvious when you look at this photograph is the lack of muscle in his hindquarters, back and top of neck, whereas the muscles around his shoulder are large and over-developed. The same scenario can be observed in the younger horse shown in Fig. 5.3. In this horse you can also observe the over-developed pectoral and sternocephalic muscles, and you can

■ lack of muscle in back, quarters and top of neck

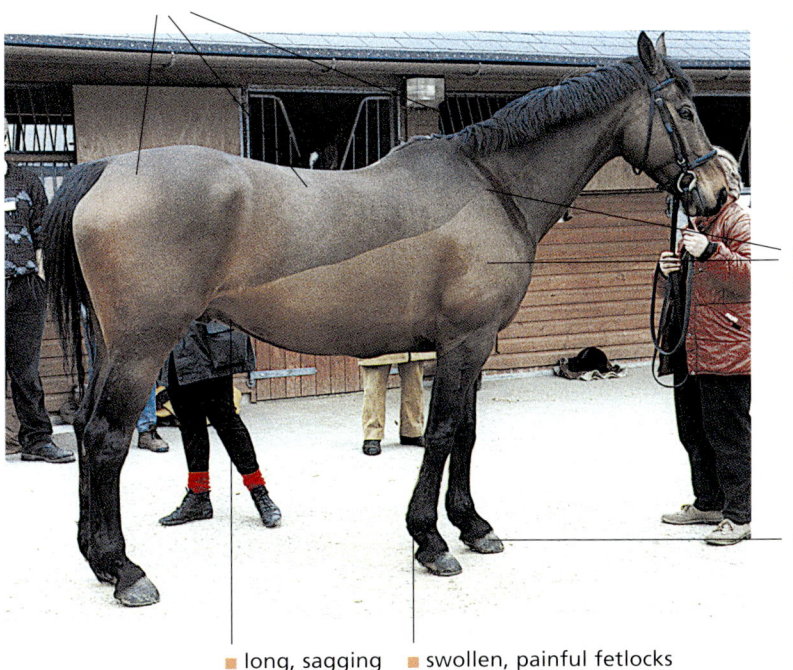

Fig. 5.2 This is a very sore horse. Abnormal muscle development tells you that this horse has problems. In many cases (such as this) years of faulty foot balance have contributed to his poor development.

■ over-developed shoulder muscles

■ feet overlong and shod far too short

■ long, sagging underline   ■ swollen, painful fetlocks

lack of muscle in back, quarters and top of neck ■

obvious tension and spasm at base of neck in cervical serratus ■

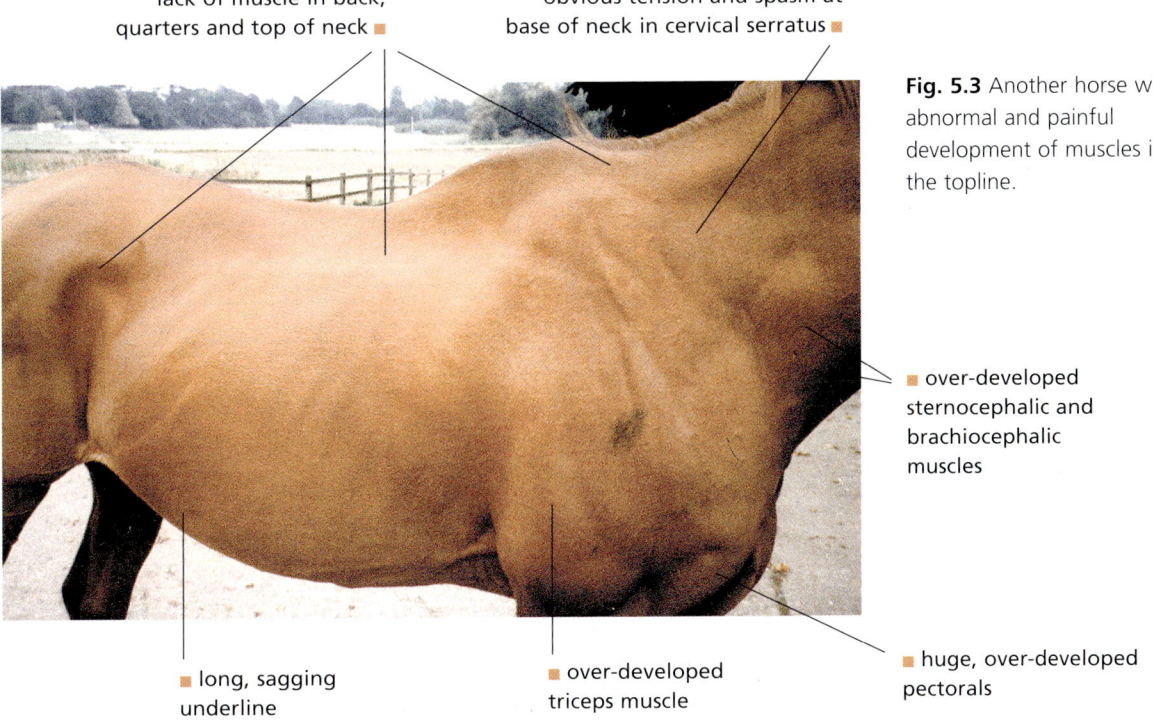

Fig. 5.3 Another horse with abnormal and painful development of muscles in the topline.

■ over-developed sternocephalic and brachiocephalic muscles

■ long, sagging underline   ■ over-developed triceps muscle   ■ huge, over-developed pectorals

almost feel the tension in the base of the neck just by looking at it.

Both these horses demonstrate abnormal muscle development resulting from a type of locomotor dysfunction known as 'having the engine at the wrong end', and certainly in the case of the horse in Fig. 5.2, this abnormal locomotion was greatly contributed to by poor foot balance and shoeing. In terms of biomechanics what has happened to this horse is likely to be as follows. Because he has been poorly shod and managed, his feet being too long with collapsing heels and no support under the fetlocks, the superficial digital flexor tendon has had to assist in supporting the fetlocks. The fetlocks have become sore and swollen because of the abnormal forces upon them (see Fig. 5.1) and the superficial digital flexor tendons have become painful. To try and relieve the pain felt in his front legs, the horse tries to take more weight through his hind legs. Remember that in normal circumstances 60% of the horse's weight is carried on his front feet whilst the hind legs are used to propel the horse forwards. In these abnormal circumstances, the biomechanical roles of the legs are reversed and, because the hind limbs are now supporting more of the weight of the horse, their role in propulsion becomes seriously hampered. But the rider will still insist that the horse goes forwards.

In Fig. 5.1 (a) we can see that the elbow is being pushed backwards and the shoulder is being forced downwards. The triceps and the pectorals therefore have to assume a 'weightlifting' role to resist this. Further, because the rider is still insisting that the horse works and the hindquarter muscles cannot propel the horse forwards adequately, the triceps and pectorals also have to assist in pulling the horse along. As a result they become over-developed (hypertrophied) and painful. In fact if you prodded the horses in Figs. 5.2 and 5.3 in those muscle areas they would almost go into orbit.

To help prevent the shoulder from collapsing and to support the head, the brachiocephalic and sternocephalic muscles also have to work overly hard and become hypertrophied.

Finally, because the horse cannot work through the back, the longissimus dorsi muscles waste and go into spasm, leading to pain. Therefore, in an attempt to support the weight of the rider, the cervical serratus at the base of the neck contracts tightly to pull the scapula forwards. This abnormal action leads eventually to spasm in this muscle which can be felt – just like corrugated cardboard – by running your fingers over it. The knock-on effect of this is that the trapezius muscle (on the top of the neck in front of the withers) cannot function properly and atrophies, leaving an observable dip in front of the withers.

Unhappily, it is only horses with the most saintly of temperaments who ever get to this chronic state of locomotor dysfunction, because they continue to try and work for the rider despite the fact that they are in pain. Many horses will at best have resisted and at worst deposited their riders on the floor long before they get to this stage, thus giving themselves the reputation for being difficult

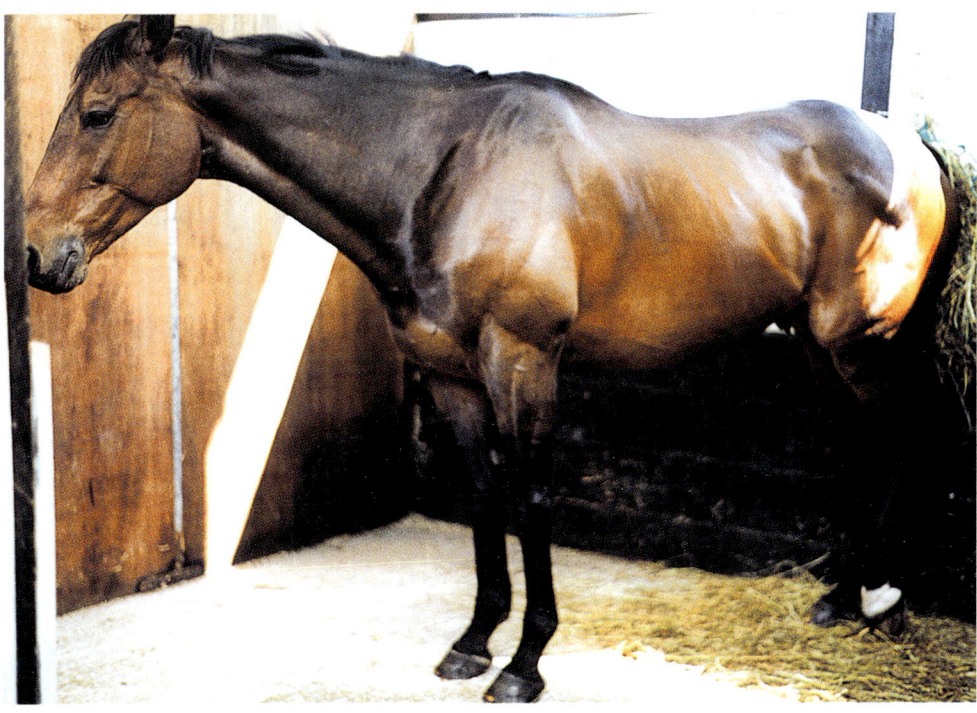

Fig. 5.4 This was a top three-day event horse whose flat, splayed feet with poor medio-lateral balance have contributed to his poor topline development and subsequent loss of performance.

or dangerous and being discarded through no fault of their own. Most horses will work willingly and happily so long as they are not in any discomfort.

You may think that only the novice owner/trainer could be guilty of allowing a horse to develop chronic locomotor dysfunction in this way. Unfortunately you would be wrong. Take, for example, the advanced three-day event horse shown in Fig. 5.4. In the previous season this Thoroughbred horse had been placed at Blenheim three-day event and was due, in less than two weeks, to go at Badminton. Yet he displays all of the 'engine at the wrong end' signs and his back is so sore that to relieve the pain he is forced to 'sit' on his haynet. The majority of this horse's problems stem from his flat, splayed feet with collapsed heels. This horse was not sound to compete at Badminton that year.

The young warmblood horse in Fig. 5.5 (overleaf) is still occasionally winning in the dressage arena despite the fact that he also displays signs of abnormal locomotion. It makes you wonder what this horse's potential could be if he were moving properly!

As we said at the start of this chapter, sore backs and foot imbalances are intrinsically linked; which comes first does not necessarily matter. What is important is that you do not look at these things in isolation. 'Holistic treatment' is a much over-used phrase but in terms of overcoming locomotor problems an holistic approach is fundamental to success. Many things need to

Fig. 5.5 This young warmblood is showing the early signs of 'engine at the wrong end' syndrome.

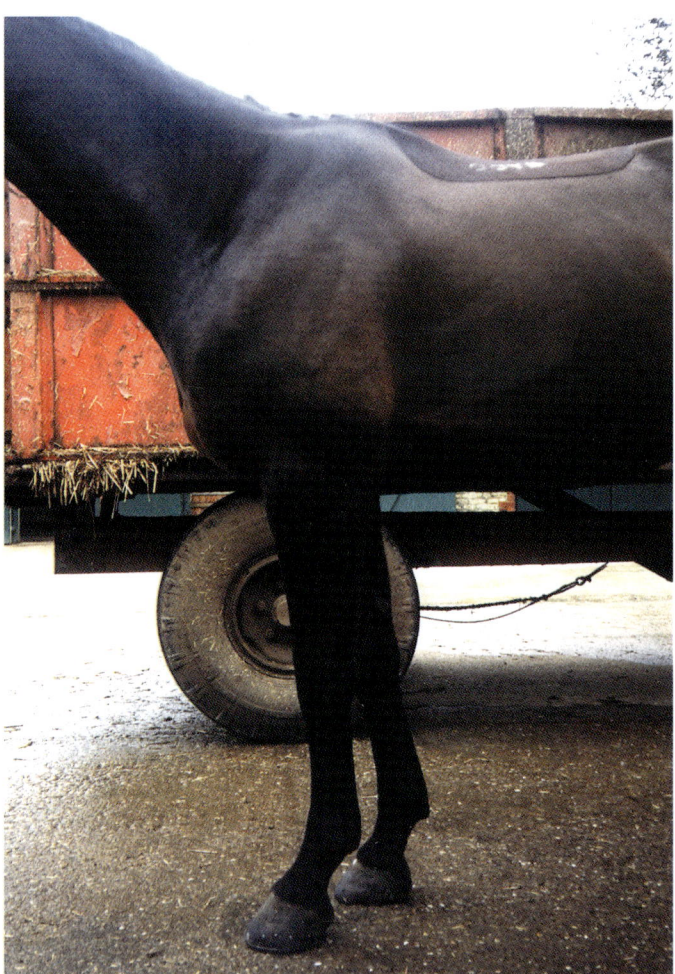

be taken into consideration – for example, farriery, veterinary investigation, physiotherapy, manipulation techniques, massage, tack (particularly saddles), the effects of the rider and the riding surface. The simple fact remains that it does not matter how extensive your training programme, or how many expensive feed supplements you use or what kind of dust-free bedding you invest in, if your horse is not putting one foot in front of the other as efficiently as possible he is never going to attain his athletic potential and is always likely to be subject to injury.

CHAPTER 6

Hoof Capsule Deviations

In cases of chronic foot imbalance, the hoof capsule itself very often becomes distorted. Unless you apply the criteria set out in Chapter 3, the imbalance will be perpetuated and become worse. Once a hoof capsule is seriously distorted it can take years to restore it to a natural shape. Most horsemastership texts will tell you that the shoe must be made to fit the foot. That is all well and good if the foot is strong, well proportioned and a natural shape, but if the foot is distorted any shoe made to fit that foot will not be providing adequate support and weightbearing and will only serve to make a bad situation even worse. It is better to try not to think of making a shoe fit the foot but rather of making it fit the whole horse.

Take, for example, a hoof capsule distorted by chronic medio-lateral imbalance such as is shown in Fig. 3.14 (page 39). This type of distortion is created when a medio-lateral imbalance (in this case the horse was being trimmed so that the outside wall was always longer than the inside) prevents the horse from placing his foot down flat. When a horse is trimmed 'outside high', the outside (lateral) wall makes contact with the ground fractionally before the inside (medial) wall. This causes the foot to rotate outwards around the point of contact until the inside part of the foot lands heavily with a secondary concussion. Over a period of months the abnormal forces created by this secondary concussion start to break down the connective tissue between the bulbs of the heels, and results in the inside heel migrating proximally (up the leg) whilst the outside wall flares outwards. Eventually this will lead to completely sheared heels.

Fig. 6.1 shows the solar view of the right forefoot of a horse who has been remedially shod for such a hoof capsule distortion. The first thing to notice about this foot is how much higher the inside bulb of the heel appears to be when compared to the outer bulb. A very common mistake to make when assessing hoof conformation is to assume that to achieve good medio-lateral balance the length of the heel – as measured from the coronet band – should be equal on both sides. Unfortunately this can create serious problems because

Fig. 6.1 Note how the inside heel looks longer than the outside heel. This is a result of chronic medio-lateral imbalance (the horse has been trimmed outside high), forcing the inside heel to move up the leg. Also you can see that this medial wall is much more upright than the lateral wall. This type of foot required a half-bar shoe.

inside heel looks higher than outside heel ■

note how the bar portion of the shoe rests lightly against the inside part of the frog ■

the coronet is not a fixed structure and can deform as a result of foot imbalance, invariably by the inside heel moving up the leg.

It is vitally important, therefore, to use a T-square to assist in obtaining medio-lateral balance. Most farriers, when picking up this foot, would believe it to be 'inside high' because they use the coronet band as their point of reference, and immediately trim down the medial wall. But this would compound an already serious medio-lateral imbalance by making this horse very much more 'outside high'. But if they used a T-square they would find that this foot is now in perfect medio-lateral balance, despite the fact that the heels are of odd length.

Because the heels of the front feet of the horse in Fig. 6.1 were beginning to shear (but fortunately the foot had not got to the stage where it was completely sheared and mobile), this was causing pain and the horse became lame. Therefore skilled farriery was needed not only to return the horse to soundness in the short term, but also to correct the distortion of the hoof capsule in the long term. In this instance a half-bar shoe was applied after ensuring that the medio-lateral balance of the horse was correct by using a T-square.

The half-bar shoe works by taking the weight of the horse off the medial heel and transferring that weight through the medial aspect of the frog instead. Note how in Fig. 6.2 the medial heel of the horse does not come into contact with

Fig. 6.2 Note how the medial heel is not in contact with the shoe at all. All the weight that should have been taken by this part of the foot is now being transferred to the medial part of the frog to allow this 'jammed-up' heel to return to a normal position. Also note how the horn tubules at the heel are not parallel to those at the toe, indicative of collapsing heels.

the shoe at all. This allows the medial heel to return to its correct position, the connective tissue to repair and for the foot to return to a more natural confor-mation.

A very extreme example of what can happen in chronic cases of medio-lateral imbalance is shown in Fig. 6.3. This is the left forefoot of an interna-tional Grand Prix dressage horse! Not surprisingly this very valuable horse was lame because the heels were completely sheared, the medial heel was migrating up the leg and interfering with the pastern when the horse moved.

How this horse came to be in this state is not surprising when you look at

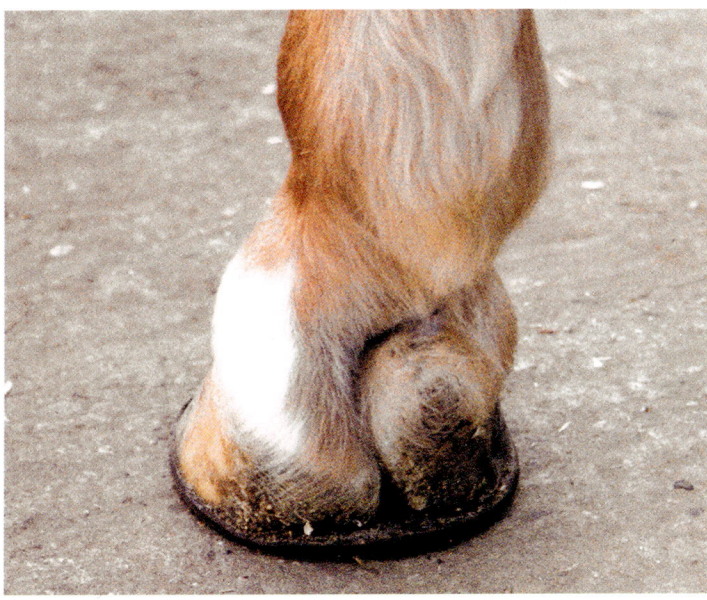

Fig. 6.3 The inside heel of this horse has completely sheared and is migrating proximally to the extent that when the horse moves and the fetlock drops, the pastern comes into contact with the heel.

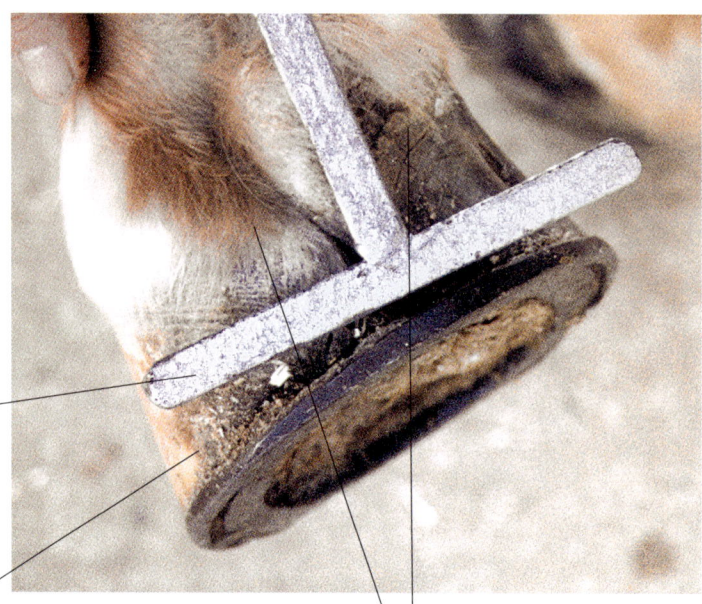

Fig. 6.4 A significant medio-lateral imbalance created this horse's problem. Use of the T-square shows how much excess hoof there is on the outside wall despite the fact that the length of horn at the heels appears to be equal.

in order to have good medio-lateral balance this base of the foot should have been level with the bar ■

see how much excess hoof there is on this lateral wall and you begin to understand how this condition developed ■

■ note that the length of the horn from the coronet band is very similar

Fig. 6.4 and see how much higher the outside wall of his hoof was when his medio-lateral balance was assessed – and yet the length of the heels measured from the coronary band were the same. Fig. 6.5 shows the same horse after remedial farriery and demonstrates that medio-lateral balance could be attained from the first session. Note how, although the weightbearing surface

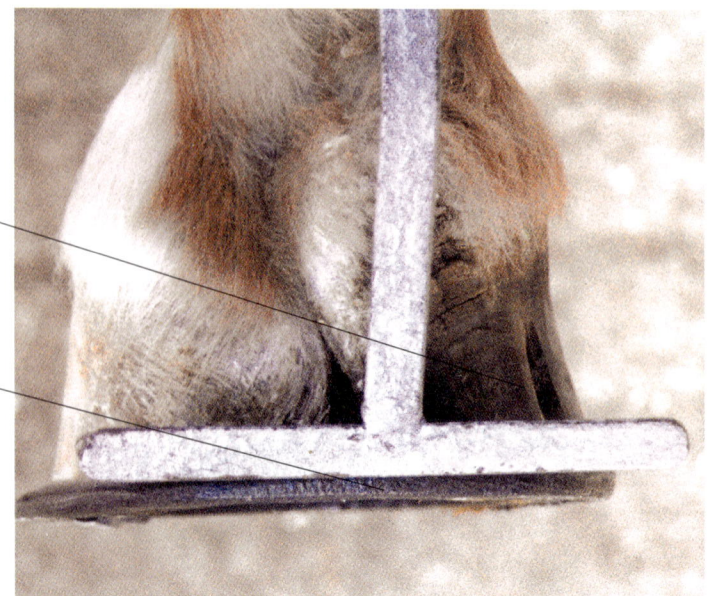

the inside heel now looks longer than the outside one, despite the fact that the foot is in balance ■

the weightbearing portion of the foot is in line with the bar ■

Fig. 6.5 Post remedial farriery, this horse now has good medio-lateral balance, despite the unequal length of horn at the heel.

of the foot is in line with the bar, the heels are now completely different lengths. This particular horse was shod with a straight-bar shoe because the heels were completely sheared and the entire foot was unstable. In these cases a straight-bar shoe is required to stabilise the foot.

When assessing horses for hoof capsule deviations it is important to ascertain how much symmetry or otherwise there is in the ground contact portion of the foot. Remember from Chapter 3 (Figs. 3.9 and 3.12 – pages 36 and 38) that there should be an equal amount of weightbearing on either side of a midline drawn down the centre of the cannon bone. This is not easy to assess when the hoof is distorted or if the horse has a lower limb deviation.

The severely distorted hoof capsule of the Grand Prix dressage horse in Figs 6.3-6.5 is a good case in point but there is a simple way of assessing what the horse needs in terms of weightbearing support.

Assessing weightbearing requirements

- Stand close to the side of your horse, facing in the same direction and slightly in advance of his front legs.

- Place your hand just above and behind the knee and lift the leg upwards and forwards (see Fig. 6.6). It is important to get the horse to relax and hang the lower leg freely from the knee.

Fig. 6.6 Hanging the leg forwards and sighting down the front of the leg can give you a good impression of the inequality of weightbearing surface to the foot. In this horse there is an appearance of some hoof wall medially, but none laterally. This indicates that the horse will require some lateral support from the shoe.

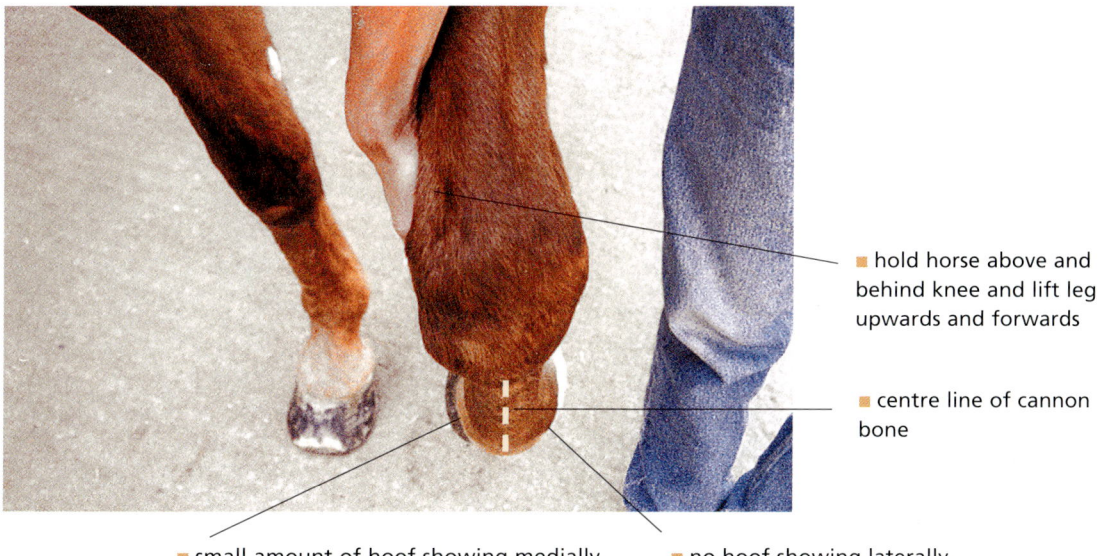

■ hold horse above and behind knee and lift leg upwards and forwards

■ centre line of cannon bone

■ small amount of hoof showing medially   ■ no hoof showing laterally

• Sight down the centre of the lower leg and look to see how much of the weightbearing portion of the hoof is showing either side of the midline. Remember that there should be equal amounts of weightbearing either side of the midline.

Notice how in Fig. 6.6 you can see a small amount of hoof showing on the inside but all you can see on the outside is the white hair on the coronet band and no hoof. This immediately indicates that this horse has no adequate lateral support on this foot, which must be corrected.

Fig. 6.7 shows the same foot after remedial farriery. You can immediately appreciate the difference between this and Fig. 6.6, now that the horse has been given a shoe with a lateral extension to provide the appropriate lateral weightbearing support.

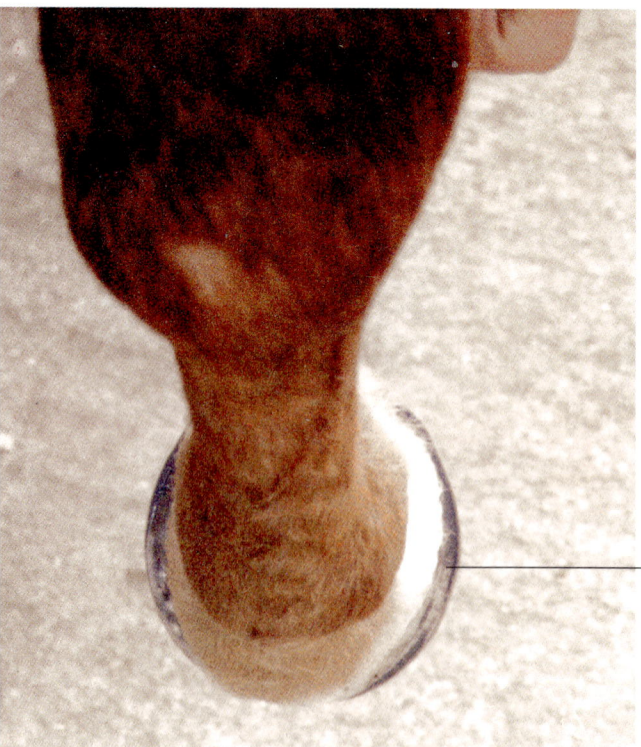

Fig. 6.7 After remedial shoeing, the lateral extension creates symmetry and balance to the foot.

■ lateral extension to shoe to provide lateral support; note how the shoe gives the foot much more symmetry, despite the hoof capsule deviation

This horse now has complete medio-lateral balance in that the weightbearing surface is at right angles to the cannon bone and it has equal weightbearing, both medially and laterally, to the centre of the cannon bone.

Figs 6.6 and 6.7 are very interesting in another aspect with regards to this horse. When you are sighting down a horse's limb in this way you can immedi-

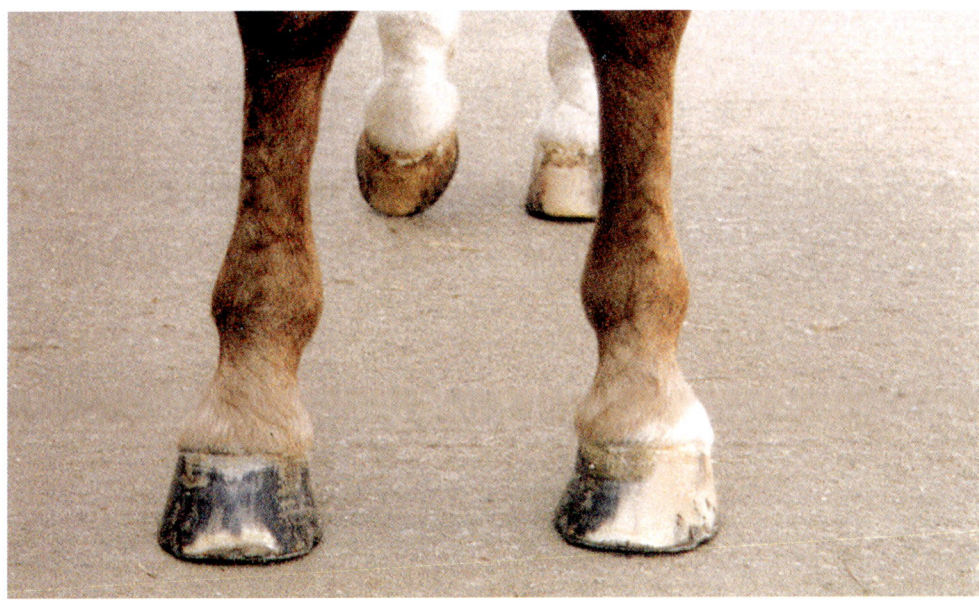

Fig. 6.8 Before remedial shoeing this horse looks pigeon-toed but it is merely an artefact of hoof capsule deviation.

ately see if that horse has any angular limb deformities in the joints in his lower limb because that portion of the leg relating to the deformity will not hang straight down. In this dressage horse you can see that his leg is straight when you hang it forwards. However, Fig. 6.8 shows this horse's front legs before he was remedially shod and you can see that he looks as if he is pigeon-toed – i.e. he has medial deviations in both front feet.

This pigeon-toed appearance is merely an artefact of his hoof capsule deviation. In other words, his legs are straight – it is the hoof capsule that is bent.

Another major misconception with regards to farriery is that the horse must be made to break over the centre of the toe. Again that is all well and good if the toe is actually in the right place, which in the horse in Fig. 6.8 it clearly is not.

Fig. 6.9 shows where the horse was breaking over prior to remedial farriery. Note how his previous farrier had slightly squared off what he considered to be the toe in an attempt to get him to break over the centre of a very deviated hoof capsule, believing that to be the correct approach.

The horse will break over that point on the toe which is suitable for his own conformation. To force him to do anything else will merely create abnormal forces through his limbs, which will eventually lead to breakdown.

However, this horse's conformation shows that he would break over the centre of the toe if the toe were in the correct place. Fig. 6.10 shows him breaking over after his remedial farriery. You could be forgiven for thinking that he has completely changed his point of breakover but in fact he is breaking

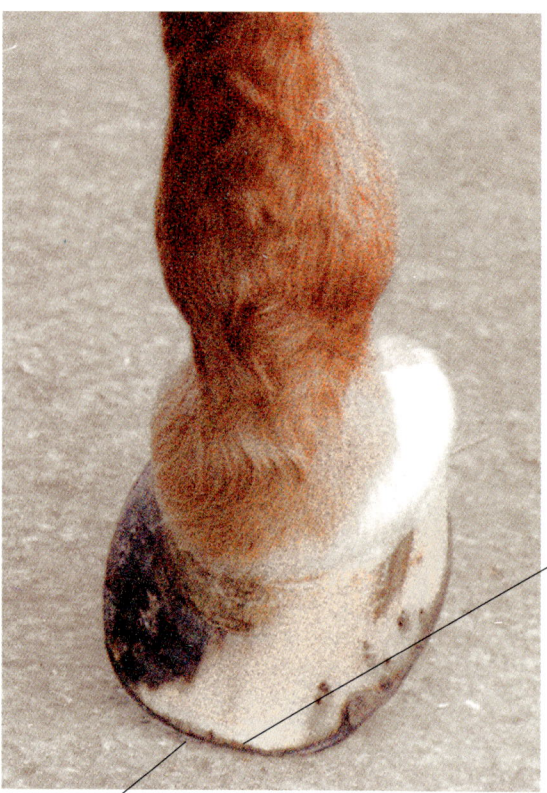

Fig. 6.9 The previous farrier had squared off what he considered to be the toe in an attempt to force the horse to break over there. This picture shows the horse's conformationally determined point of breakover. To force him to breakover anywhere else will have a detrimental effect. In fact because of the fact that his hoof capsule is deviated medially, his preferred point of breakover is actually where the centre of his toe should be.

■ horse's preferred point of breakover

■ slightly squared-off toe in an attempt to force horse to break over here

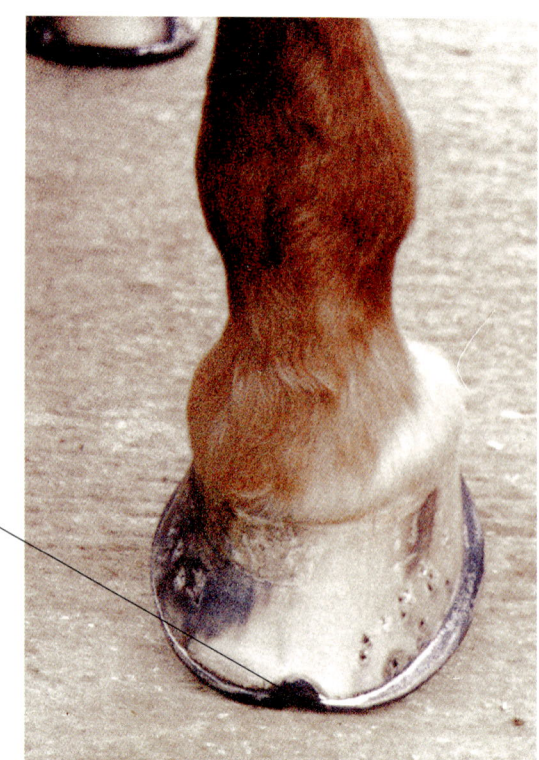

this point of breakover is exactly the same as in Fig. 6.9 ■

Fig. 6.10 Post remedial shoeing. Although the point of breakover is exactly the same as shown in Fig. 6.9, the horse has been trimmed and shod with complete mediolateral balance.

over in exactly the same point on the foot as in Fig. 6.9. Because the foot has been correctly dressed and shod with complete medio-lateral balance and support he can be seen to be breaking over that point in his foot where the toe would be if the hoof capsule were not distorted.

Because it may be difficult for you to assess where your horse is breaking over when he is on the move there is an easy way of assessing his breakover point whilst he is standing still as follows.

Assessing the breakover point

- Lift the leg as shown in Fig. 6.6.
- When the horse is completely relaxed lower the leg gently towards the ground.
- The first point of the toe to touch the ground is the preferred point of breakover for your horse – which may or not be the centre of the toe. (See Fig. 6.11.)

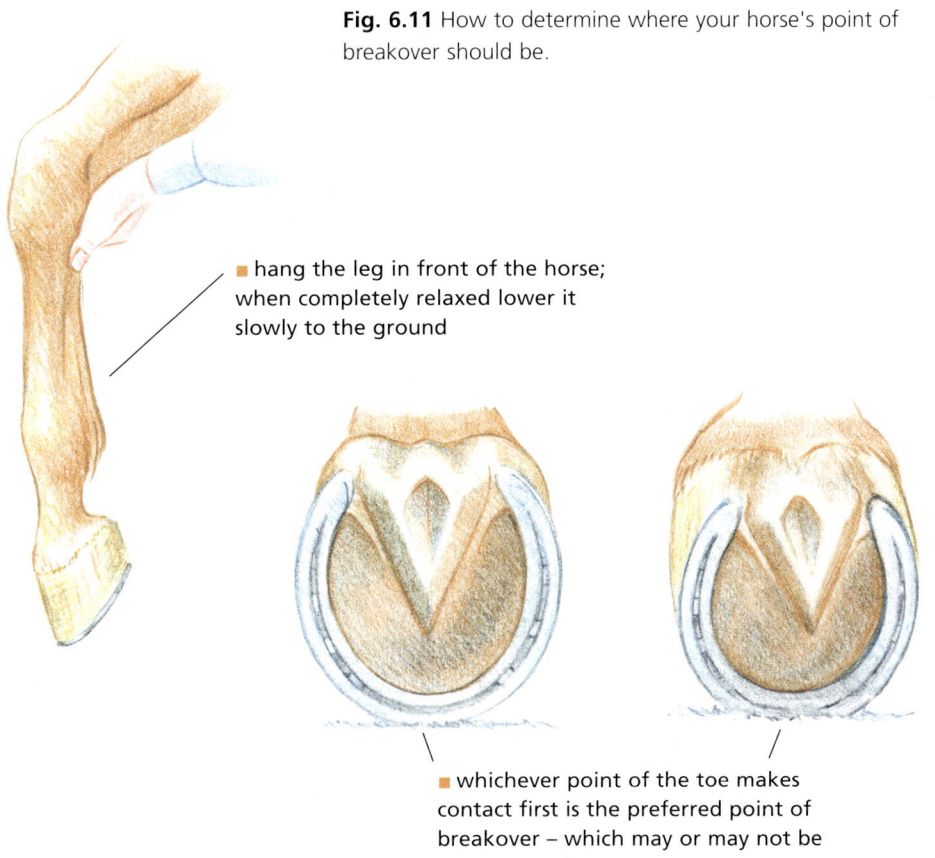

Fig. 6.11 How to determine where your horse's point of breakover should be.

■ hang the leg in front of the horse; when completely relaxed lower it slowly to the ground

■ whichever point of the toe makes contact first is the preferred point of breakover – which may or may not be the centre of the toe

Just by looking at this one dressage horse (in Figs. 6.4 –6.10) we can see how detrimental medio-lateral imbalances can be in the long term. These imbalances are then made worse because deformation of the hoof capsule produces artefacts which can make the unwary believe that the horse has a limb deviation. Again, as with many of the horses who sustain back problems because of foot imbalance, horses with hoof capsule deformation are often discarded because of ill-conceived judgments that they have conformation defects and/or move badly. But simply by picking the limb up and sighting down it can immediately tell you whether you have a limb deformity about which you can do little, or a hoof-capsule deviation about which you may be able to do a lot – albeit probably over a lengthy period of time. The dressage horse whose remedial farriery we have discussed above and who had been lame for many months previously, was back in work only two months after those photographs were taken. It will take, however, many more months – perhaps even years – of remedial farriery to get his feet back into a correct shape.

Medio-lateral imbalances can have very serious effects upon a horse's movement, soundness and performance ability. They are probably the major cause of shoeing-related injury and disease. Further, the vast majority of horses who fail to perform to their full potential (the so-called 'poor performance syndrome') are thought likely to be suffering from chronic bouts of subtle foot soreness as opposed to overt clinical lameness. And yet in the vast majority of cases medio-lateral balance can easily be ascertained with the use of a T-square.

Of course there is a very small minority of horses to whom the application of a T-square would not be useful, for example in the horse with multiple angular deviations in a limb – the horse with 'Z' legs (see Chapter 8). However, this type of horse is unlikely to be suitable as a sports horse whichever way it was shod!

Hoof-capsule deviations can also be occasioned by dorso-palmar imbalances and these are mainly related to collapsed and under-run heels.

Take, for example, the horse in Figs 6.12 and 6.13. This horse did not have sufficient weightbearing at the heels, which were collapsing because they could not cope with the forces being transmitted down the leg (remember the example of the Bauhaus chair in Chapter 3).

The white line in Fig. 6.12 approximates where the perpendicular line from the centre of the coffin joint would be, and you will recall that there should be equal amounts of weightbearing support both in front and behind that line. You can see that there is only half the amount of support that there should be towards the back of the foot. Therefore this portion of the foot cannot withstand the forces it is being subjected to and it buckles under.

Fig. 6.14 (page 76) shows how this foot looks after it has been correctly shod. You may be alarmed at the amount of shoe stretching back behind the heel but when you think about the forces being experienced through the leg, where this shoe ends is where the foot should be ending. Years of inadequate support at the heels has caused this much distortion to the heels. You only need to

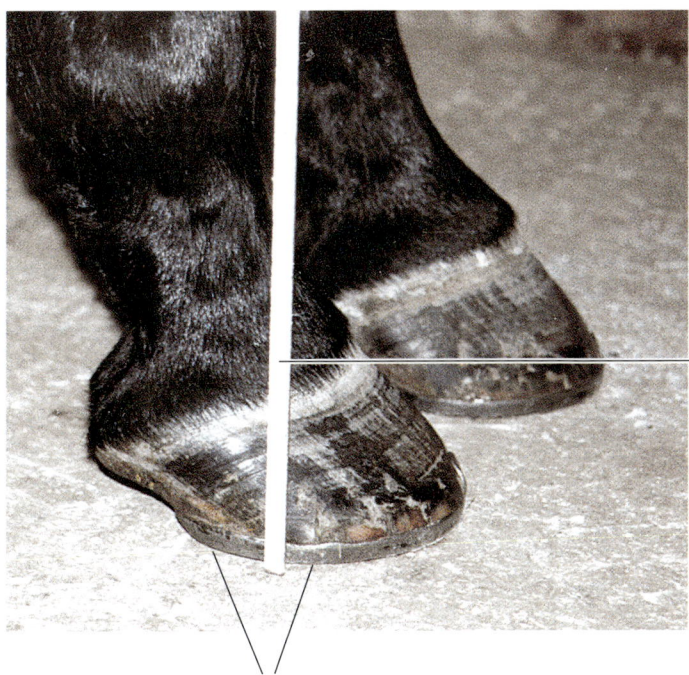

Fig. 6.12 Collapsed and under-run heels caused by chronic dorso-palmar imbalance.

■ this line is an approximately perpendicular line dropped from the centre of rotation of the coffin joint

■ weightbearing surface should be equal either side of the line; in this horse there is 50% less support at the back of the foot

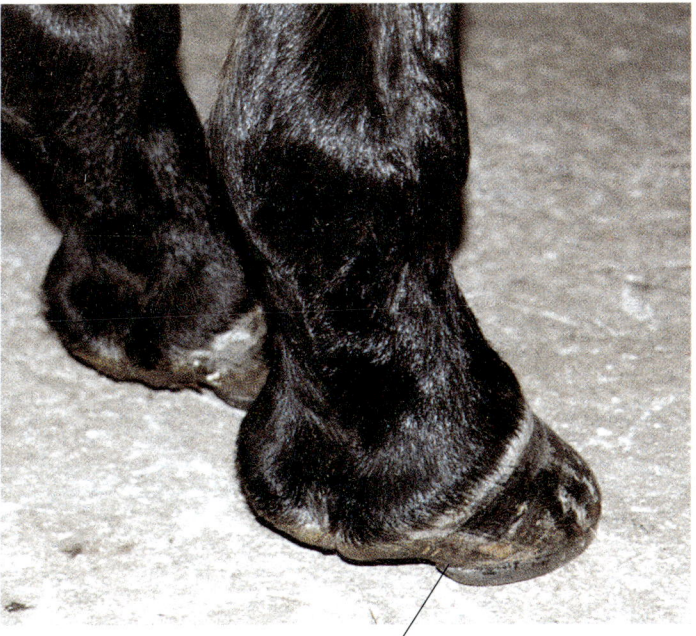

Fig. 6.13 Same horse viewed from the rear.

■ note how the heels have completely buckled under this horse

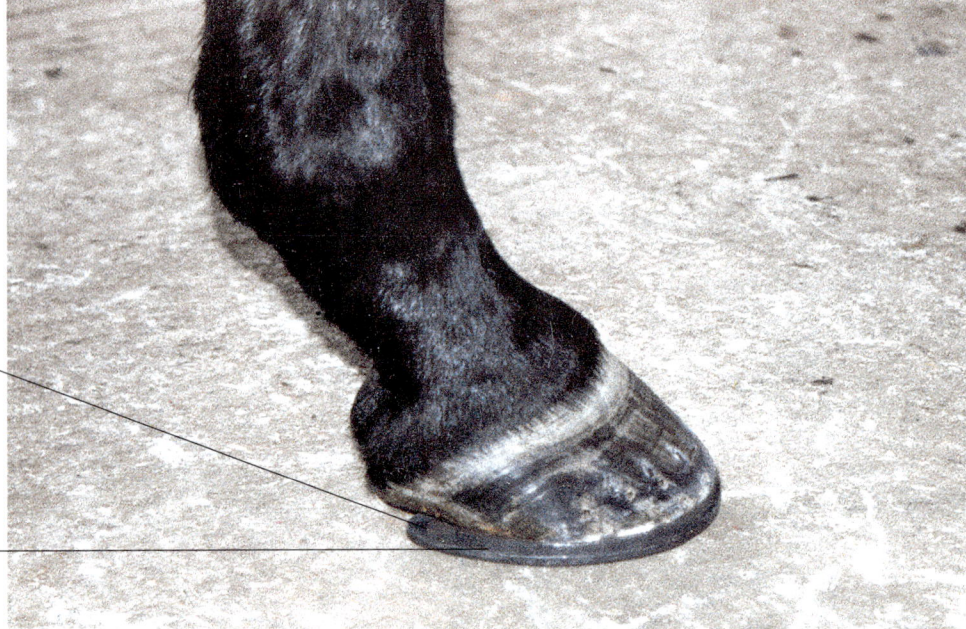

shoe finishes here; this is the point where the heel of the horse should be and where it started off before poor shoeing caused it collapse ■

heel of the horse is here ■

Fig. 6.14 After remedial shoeing. Note how far the shoe extends back under the heels to give them support. This is where the heels of the foot were before years of poor shoeing allowed them to collapse under the foot.

compare the shoe that was removed from this horse with the shoe that was put on (Fig. 6.15) to appreciate how much hoof capsule distortion there was.

To a certain extent it may not only be the farrier who is at fault here – the

Fig. 6.15 The shoe on the left is the one taken off the horse in Figs 6.12–14; it was replaced with the shoe on the right. Observe how much more there was for this horse to stand on, thus dissipating the forces over a much greater area and giving him much needed support.

owner may bear some of the responsibility. Most people feel that if a shoe is extending back beyond the heels it will easily be pulled off and so the farrier is blamed if the horse loses a shoe. Therefore to keep his client happy the farrier will shoe the horse shorter than he perhaps feels is correct. As the abnormal forces bear down on the heels and the heels collapse further under the horse, the farrier has to shoe the horse shorter and shorter.

Owners must realise the simple fact that **horses with balanced feet rarely pull shoes off from the heels**. If horses with balanced feet do lose a shoe then it is much more likely that they forge them off from the toe when they become fatigued. The obvious exception is a horse jumping out of sticky mud where elevation of the front feet is retarded and the hind feet may come in and pull the front shoe off from the heels. However, surely it is much better to lose a couple of hours' hunting as a result of a lost shoe than a couple of months lost because of a lameness caused by imbalanced feet? The worst case scenario is that you could lose a good horse entirely!

This is not a problem confined to front feet. Although it is much more prevalent in front feet because they are supporting more of the weight of the horse, the heels on the hind feet can collapse just as dramatically if they are not given enough length at the heels. The horse in Figs 6.16 and 6.17 is a case in point, and the bulbs of the heels on this horse are virtually touching the ground (the front feet of this horse were no better). Note how, after remedial shoeing, the branches of the shoe extend backwards and outwards to where the heels of the foot should be.

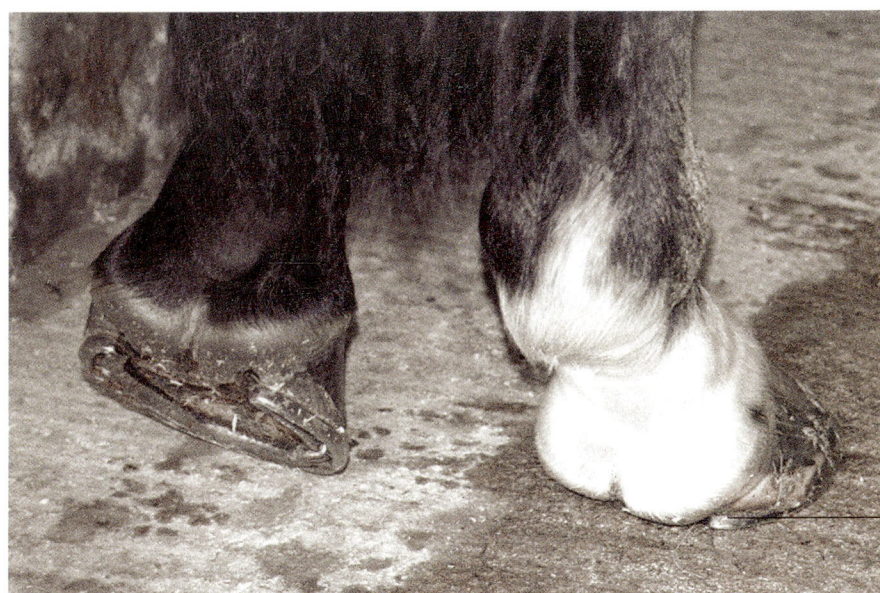

■ shoe gives no support and heels have collapsed and rolled under

Fig. 6.16 Collapsed heels in hind feet. Note how the bulbs of the heels are nearly touching the floor.

Fig. 6.17 After remedial farriery the heels of the shoe extend to where the heels of the foot should be.

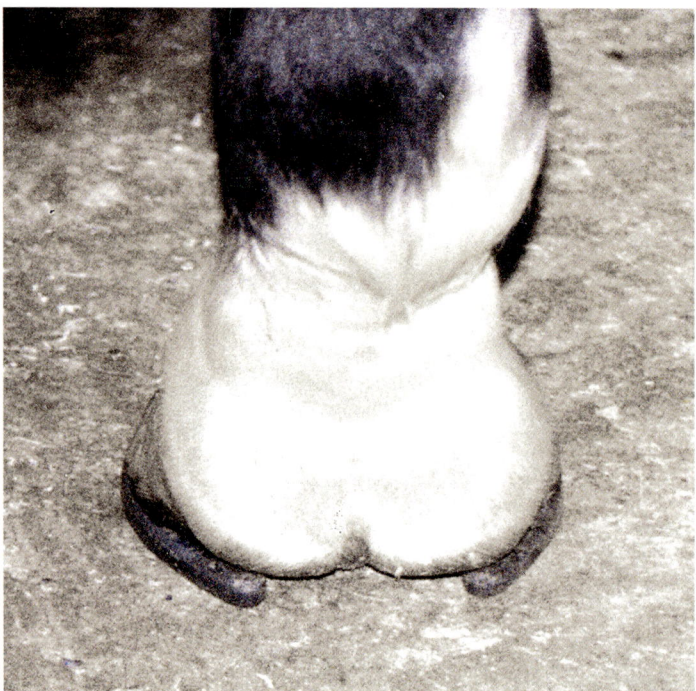

Fig. 6.18 again shows a horse with a front foot hoof capsule distortion caused by shoes being fitted too short. Note how the foot has deformed forwards as the weight of the horse has caused the heels and bars to collapse. After corrective farriery (Fig. 6.19) the foot has resumed a more correct shape. However, the

Fig. 6.18 This foot has deformed forwards as a result of lack of support at the heels.

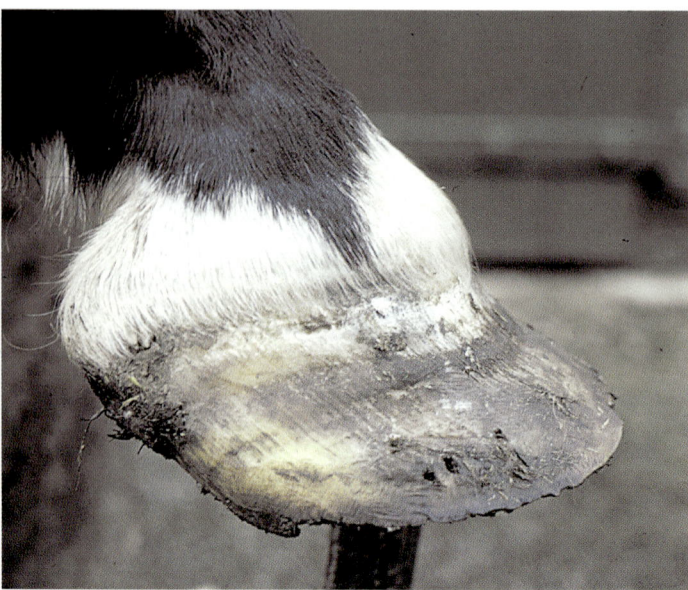

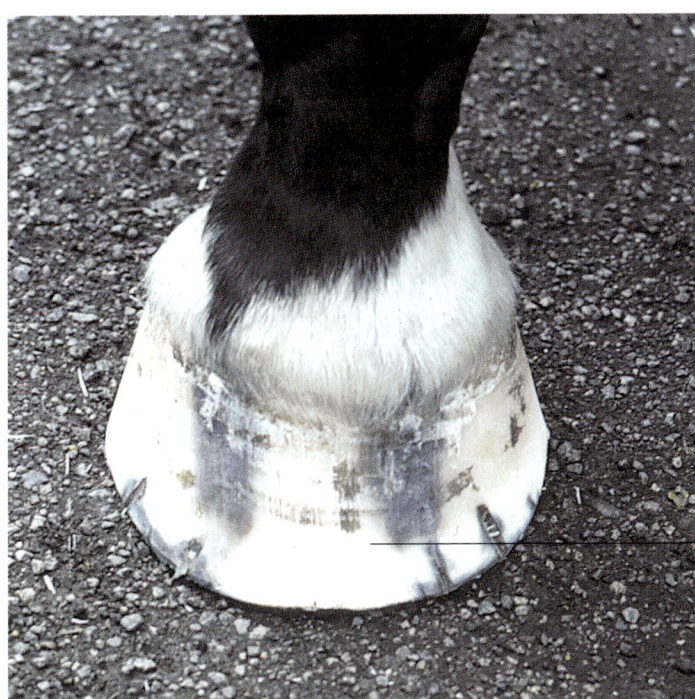

Fig. 6.19 Corrective trimming of the foot in Fig. 6.18 restores the foot to a more normal shape

■ the flare has been removed from the front of the foot

full extent of the damaged caused to this horse is evidenced by the solar view in Fig. 6.20. Note how the heels and bars have collapsed, how the foot is wider than it is long, how the frog is over-developed as the foot has spread and the sole has lost its concavity. You can also see how the sole is separating from the

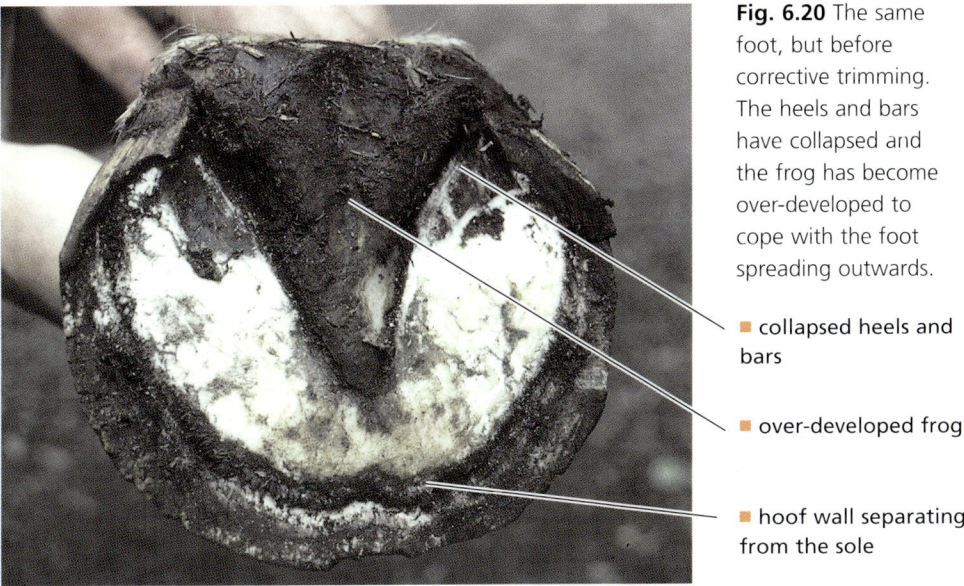

Fig. 6.20 The same foot, but before corrective trimming. The heels and bars have collapsed and the frog has become over-developed to cope with the foot spreading outwards.

■ collapsed heels and bars

■ over-developed frog

■ hoof wall separating from the sole

Fig. 6.21 After corrective trimming, the foot is a more natural shape and ready to accept a shoe.

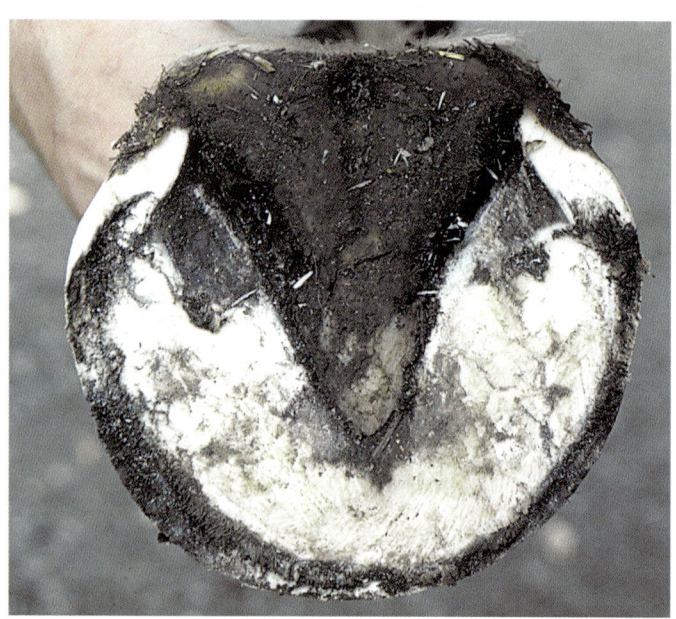

hoof wall. After trimming (Fig. 6.21) the foot is already in a much better shape and is ready to accept a shoe.

All the horses profiled in this chapter will be in danger of pulling their own shoes off – even in the stable they could pull a shoe off just by getting up or lying down. Therefore they will all have to live for twenty-four hours a day in overreach boots to give them the best possible opportunity to keep their shoes on. When they are ridden, the rider will have to alter their schooling to ensure that shoes are not pulled off. But this is essential if these horses and others like them are to recover a normal foot shape. It could take months or years – particularly for collapsed heels – to return to normal.

It is therefore vital for you to ensure that your horse does not get into this chronic state. If you continually assess your horse then you should spot these problems long before they become major ones. Make sure that you discuss your concerns with your farrier – any farrier worth his salt will be more than pleased to discuss your horse with you and tell you why he is shoeing your horse like he is (especially if you give him a cup of coffee).

CHAPTER 7

Flat Feet and Hoof Cracks

There are, of course, many deviations to normal foot conformation that are not strictly hoof capsule distortions brought about by chronic foot imbalance. There are, for example, deviations caused by weak horn, chronic pain (either in the foot or elsewhere), and the hoof capsule can crack either as a result of poor hoof quality or abnormal forces. There are ways in which the skilled farrier can trim and shoe these horses to make them function to their biomechanical optimum.

For the past 300 years we have been trying to breed horses with small feet for no better reason than our forefathers believed that large feet in horses were 'common'. The Thoroughbred particularly is now renowned for weak, small feet, and foot problems are common in racehorses. British native horses have been crossed with Thoroughbreds to lighten them and, as such, weak feet have been genetically introduced to those breeds. Surely there can be nothing more disastrous than a Thoroughbred x Irish Draught which ends up with an Irish Draught body supported by Thoroughbred feet? But there are many such horses around because native breeds crossed with Thoroughbreds produce some of the finest sports horses in the world. What can be more frustrating than having an athletically outstanding horse who suffers recurring lameness because of weak feet?

Flat feet

Horses can be born with flat, splayed feet or they can acquire them. Either way they can be a nightmare for the owner and the farrier alike. Flat feet are defined as being those whose sole has no concavity – the sole of the foot is flat. If the weight of the horse is more than the feet can support, the walls spread out (splay) and can separate from the sole.

In Chapter 2 we explained that to resist the forces acting through the foot during locomotion, the hoof capsule must alter shape by spreading outwards. If

Fig. 7.1 A heavy-topped horse with weak feet.

the foot is flat or splayed it has lost the ability to alter shape in this way. As a result the foot loses all its shock-absorbing capacity and horses become more susceptible to concussion-related injury. To try and cope with the spreading of the foot the frog becomes large and over-developed. In some horses the sensitive and insensitive laminae start to separate at the bottom of the hoof as the weight of the horse bears down on its weak feet, forcing the horn tubules outwards in the bottom half of the foot. This must feel like someone continually trying to rip your toenails off, and horses suffering from this plight, not unnaturally, demonstrate pain. These horses may commonly be called 'footy'.

These weak-footed horses create something of a paradox in farriery terms. Unlike with collapsing heels where the farrier shoes the horse shorter and shorter as the heels buckle under, as flat feet splay out more and more the farrier feels he has to shoe the foot wider and wider. Eventually it comes to the stage where the laminae are separating and the sole is separating from the foot. Really what the farrier should be doing is trying to tighten them up – pull them back in. This is not easy and requires great skill, not only from the farrier but also from the owner who has to have the management skills and dedication to look after these weak feet in between farriery appointments.

The horse in Fig. 7.1 is a case in point – a heavy-topped horse on weak feet. This horse was a six-year-old who had been with his present owner for two years. During that time he had very rarely been sound. X-rays revealed nothing wrong and the owner's vet was stumped; meanwhile the owner was at her wits' end.

You can see the shape of this horse's front feet prior to remedial farriery in Fig. 7.2. The hoof does not have the inverted ice-cream cone shape that one would want to see – the angle at the top of the hoof is more acute than the angle in the bottom half of the foot. This is because the foot is splaying out as the horn tubules comprising the hoof wall are being crushed and deformed outwards and are now not strong enough to support the weight of the horse. Remember the analogy of the bundle of drinking straws – if they are straight, they are strong; if they are crushed, they are weak.

The foot has become too wide and the foot is failing to function correctly. Every time the horse puts weight on the foot tiny amounts of separation occur in the laminae causing pain. What needs to be done is to 'tighten up' the foot

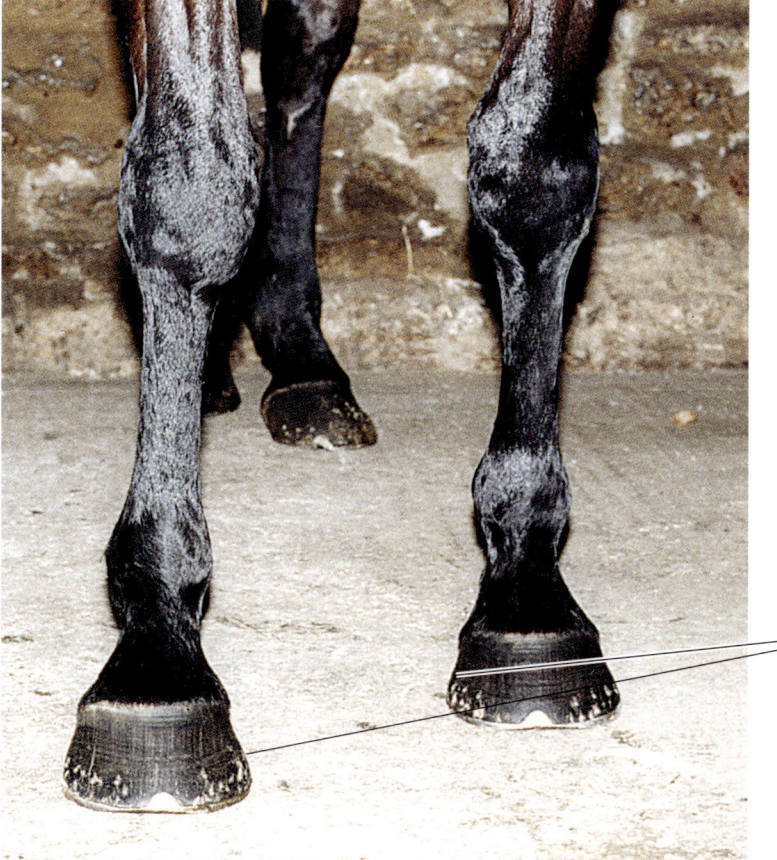

Fig. 7.2 Note how the angle of the hoof wall just below the coronet is at a different angle from the hoof wall lower down. This is because the feet cannot withstand the weight of the horse and the hoof wall is splaying out.

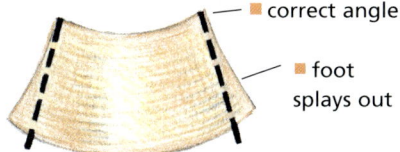

■ correct angle

■ foot splays out

■ the angle of the hoof wall is different at the bottom from that at the top

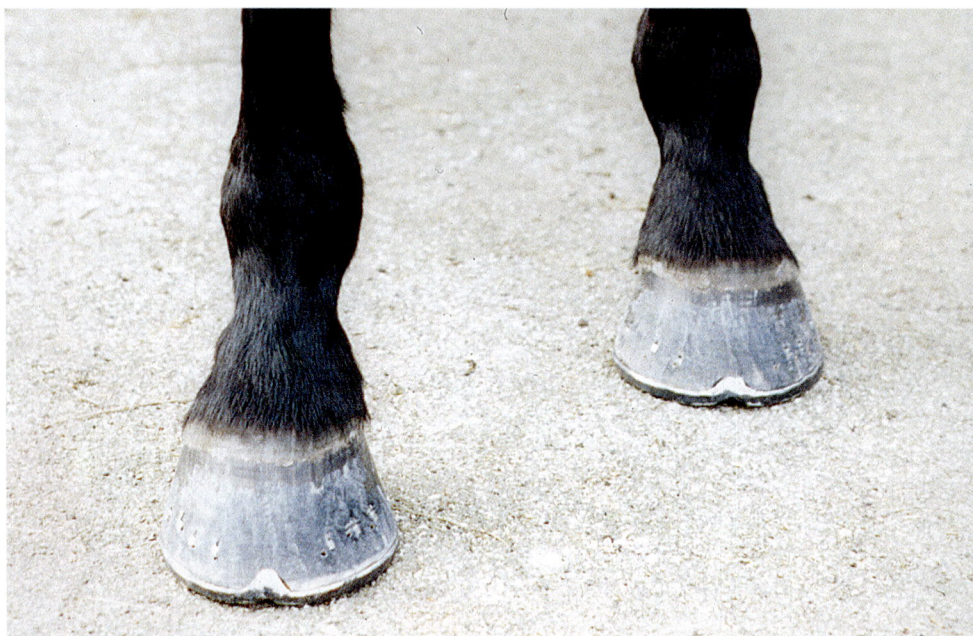

Fig. 7.3 After farriery the walls are at a constant angle from the coronet to the ground surface. The hoof now has an appropriate inverted ice-cream cone shape and can start to function correctly.

to encourage the horn tubules to straighten and return the foot to a proper function. Fig. 7.3 shows this horse immediately after remedial farriery.

To a certain extent, one problem has been corrected but another has arisen. Taking this much wall off the foot of a horse is an extremely skilled job because the horn left is very thin and driving nails into it to hold a shoe on is very difficult. Further, because the hoof wall is now so thin it represents a very difficult management problem for the owner. Without scrupulous attention to the management of these feet on a daily basis the hoof wall could break down. It is vital, therefore, that these feet receive the greatest of care, and we recommend the application of a hoof dressing (eucalyptus oil with 3% iodoform by volume) to keep them as strong as possible. This can be administered by using a syringe to inject a small amount into old and new nail holes and then applying it direct to the weak areas of the hoof wall. Eucalyptus oil and iodoform is an old remedy (it is mentioned in the first edition of the Horace Hayes' *Veterinary Notes for Horseowners*) but there is nothing like it for holding weak feet together until the stronger horn grows down. You can have it made up by your veterinary surgeon – it can be quite expensive, but a little goes a very long way.

The horse shown in Figs 7.1–7.3 was in light work within six weeks and after three months the owner was finally able to enjoy her horse. However, a horse with such conformation will always require the most meticulous foot care and farriery. One should not take on such a horse lightly.

A more graphic example is the horse pictured in Fig. 7.4. A combination of weak feet and poor farriery had combined to give this little Thoroughbred feet that were so deformed that he could barely stand up straight. Note the overlong toes, the broken back hoof/pastern axis, and the collapsed heels. In addition to all this, Fig. 7.5 shows the solar aspect of the foot with the collapsed heels, the crushed bars and, worst of all, an almost complete separation of the sole from the wall where the foot had spread out so much that the sole could not keep up. As evidence of this the frog is severely over-developed in an attempt to allow the sole to remain in contact with the walls.

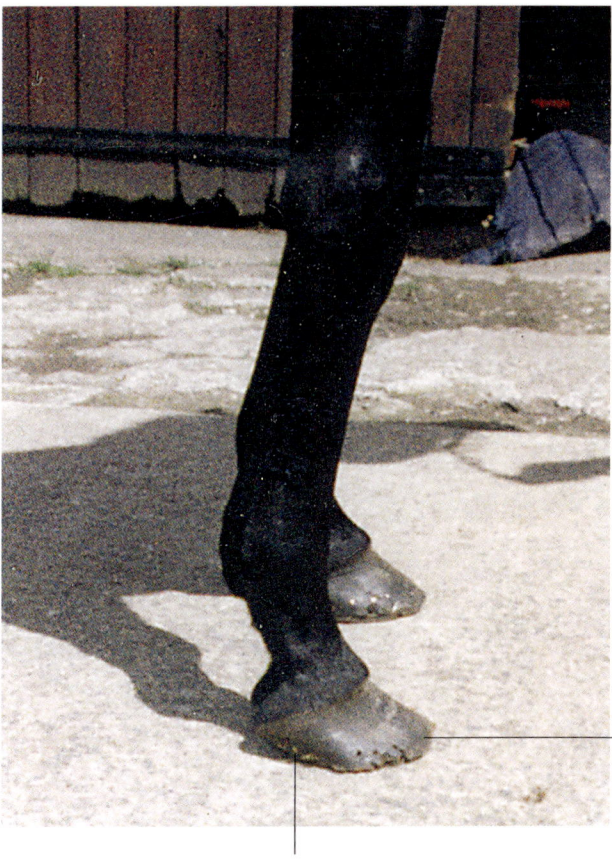

Fig. 7.4 A combination of weak feet and poor farriery have combined to give this Thoroughbred feet that were so deformed that he could barely stand up. He looks very badly over at the knee but this is more as a result of his poor feet than his conformation.

■ overlong toes

■ collapsed heels

Even when looking at this foot from the front as it is weightbearing, the separation of the sole from the foot is evident (Fig. 7.6). Not surprisingly, this horse was lame and must have been in some pain.

This type of foot creates enormous problems for the farrier and it should only be tackled by an extremely skilled farrier because there is little or nothing of the hoof wall upon which a shoe can be nailed. After remedial farriery,

Fig. 7.5 A glance at the solar surface shows how the sole is separating from the wall and how the frog has become large and overdeveloped in an attempt to keep pace with the spreading foot. Note also how the heels have completely collapsed under the foot.

collapsed heels ■

overdeveloped frog ■

separation of sole from hoof wall ■

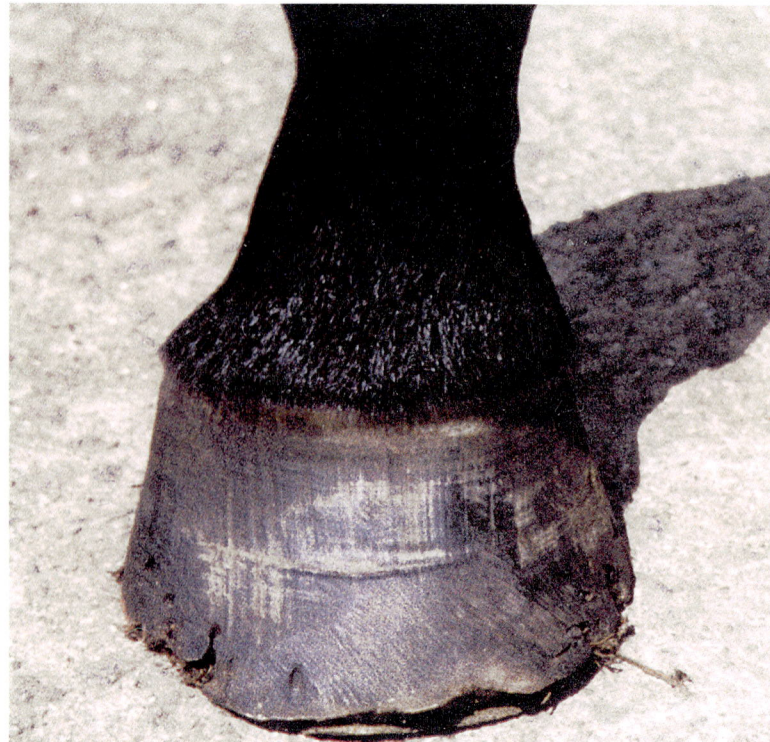

Fig. 7.6 Even when viewed from the front the separation of the sole from the hoof wall is evident.

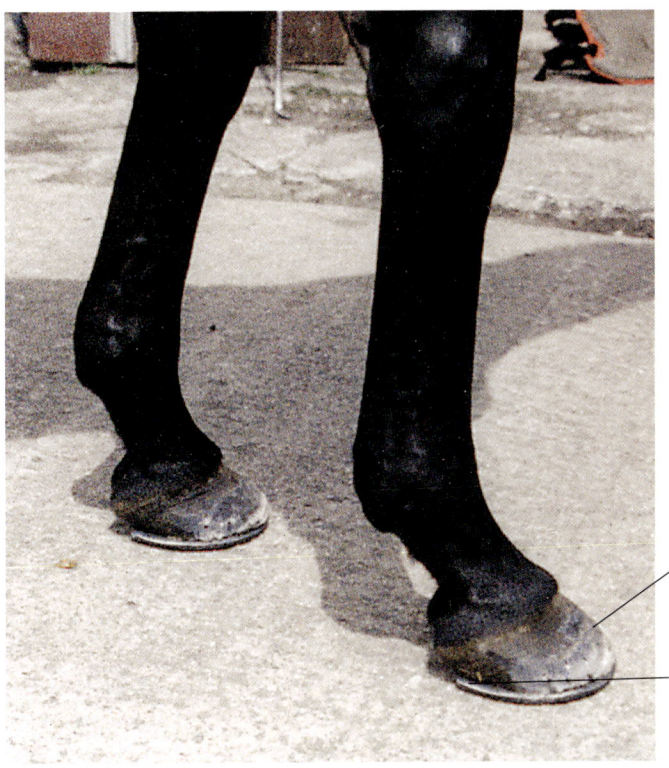

Fig. 7.7 He is clearly much more comfortable after corrective farriery. He can stand up straight. The toe has been taken back, the hoof/pastern axis is straight and the heels of the shoe have been taken back to support the fetlock.

■ toe has been taken back and the hoof/pastern axis is straight

■ the shoe has been extended at the heels to give support to the fetlock

■ shoe brought right back and fitted wide to give support to collapsed heels

■ nails have to be driven in where there is enough hoof wall to accept them

Fig. 7.8 The solar view after farriery. Compare with Fig. 7.5.

Fig. 7.9 The front view after farriery. The toe has been taken back but it has been protected and supported by the front of the shoe extending to where the toe should be.

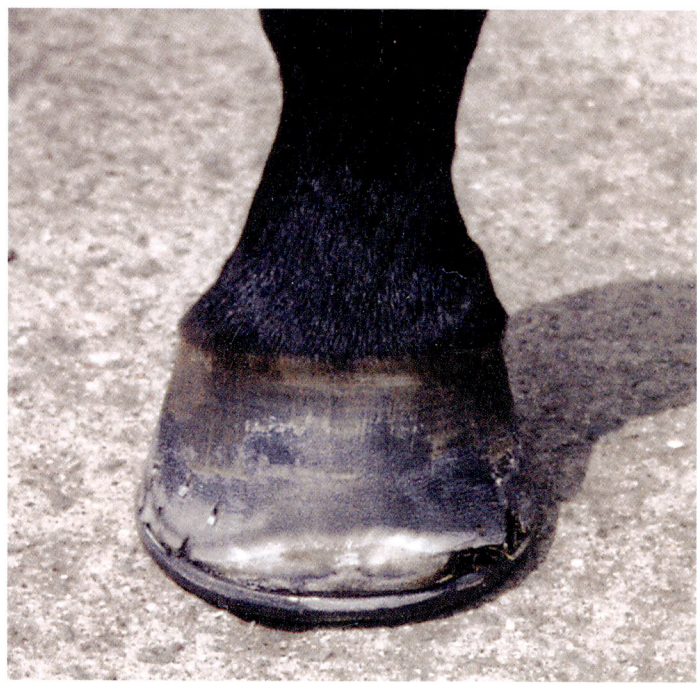

however, this horse was looking much better (Figs 7.7–7.9).

To fully appreciate the difference between the shoe that was previously fitted and the remedial shoe, Fig. 7.10 shows them one on top of the other. Note how

'before' shoe ■

'after' shoe ■

Fig. 7.10 The 'before' (top) and 'after' (underneath) shoe. Note how much more support will be derived from the 'after' shoe.

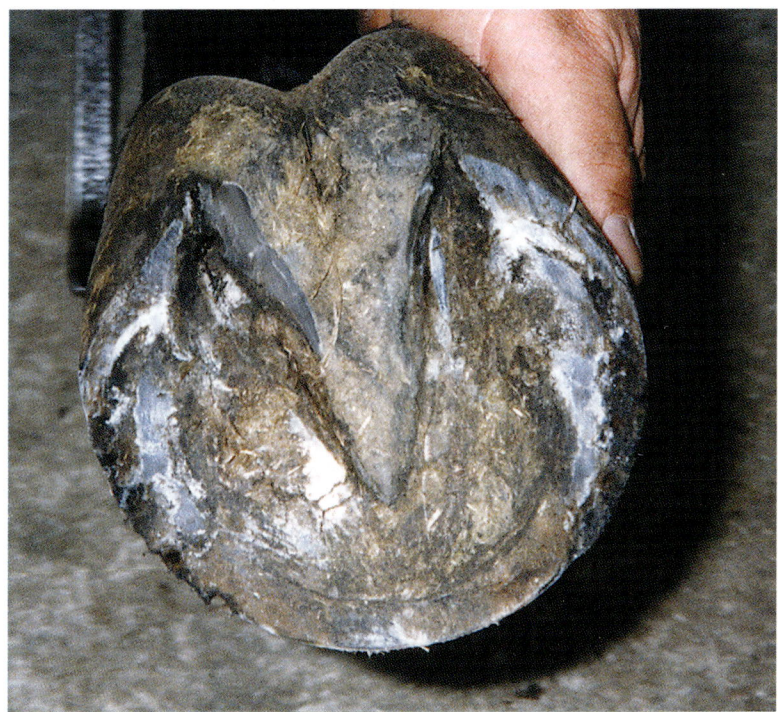

Fig. 7.11 The same horse only two treatments later. Compare with Fig. 7.5.

the broad-webbed remedial shoe give the horse much more to stand on and thus distributes the weight over a greater surface. Fig. 7.11 shows the solar surface of the foot of this horse after only two remedial farriery sessions – compare this picture with Fig. 7.5.

Horses with weak feet such as these need as much help from the farrier as possible. These feet must be regarded as a long-term management problem, not only to return them to their optimum (which will take about eighteen months) but also because they will never be adequate to support the horse.

Hoof cracks

Another major problem for farrier and horse owners alike is the hoof that cracks. Most cracks are superficial – they do not penetrate the whole hoof wall. These superficial cracks can be dealt with relatively easily; the most important thing to remember is that they have to be cut out or else they will simply perpetuate. This is because, as the hoof wall deforms when it is weightbearing, the edges of the cracks move against each other and the crack becomes longer. Figs 7.12–7.16 demonstrate how these superficial cracks should be cleaned out and supported. In this particular case the horse was shod with a half-bar shoe with the inside heel floated off, thus enabling the forces to be taken off the inside quarter and allowing the hoof to grow down normally.

Fig. 7.12.This horse's foot has a long-standing superficial crack on the lateral quarter. The crack is most likely caused by chronic foot imbalance added to poor hoof quality. The growth rings around the top of the foot also indicate the possibility of dietary influence.

superficial crack ■ —

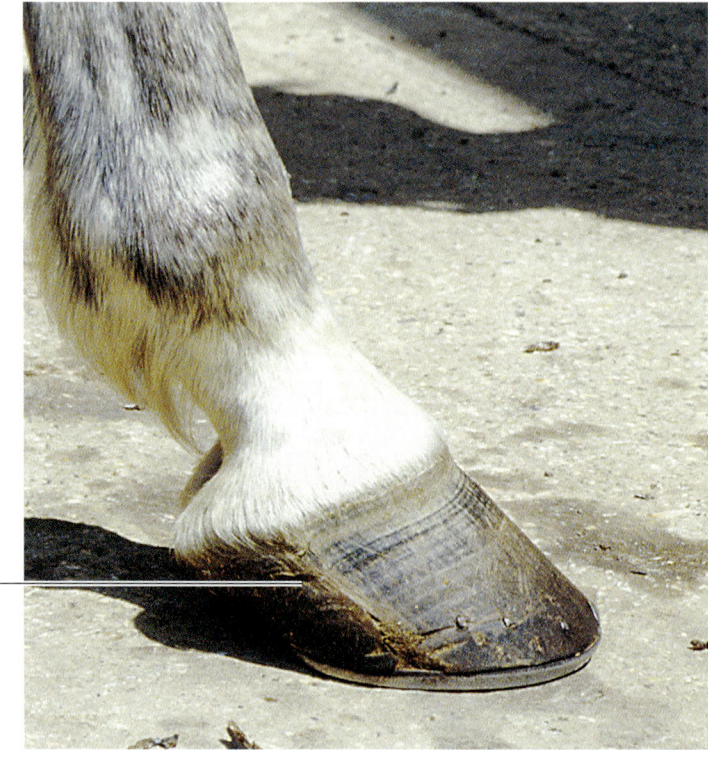

Fig. 7.13. The growth rings around the top of the hoof capsule can be seen more clearly.

superficial crack ■ —

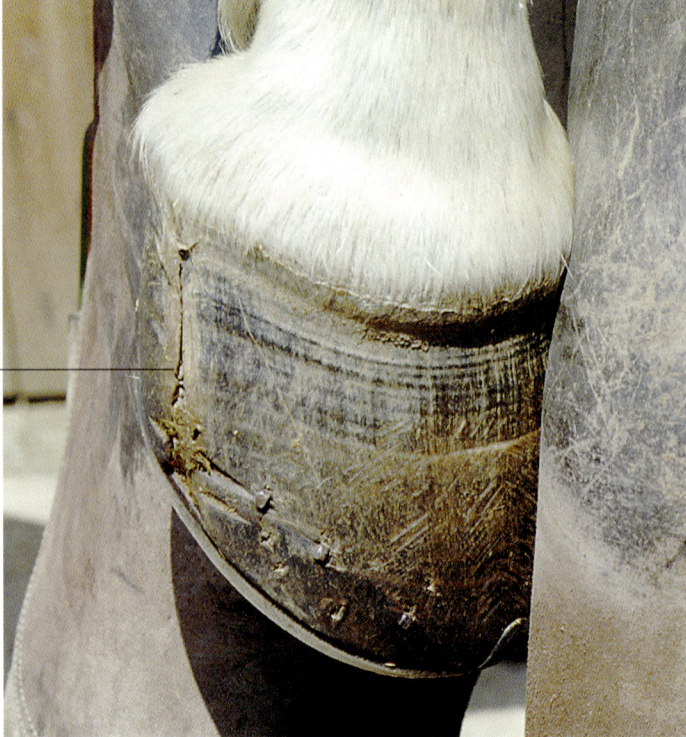

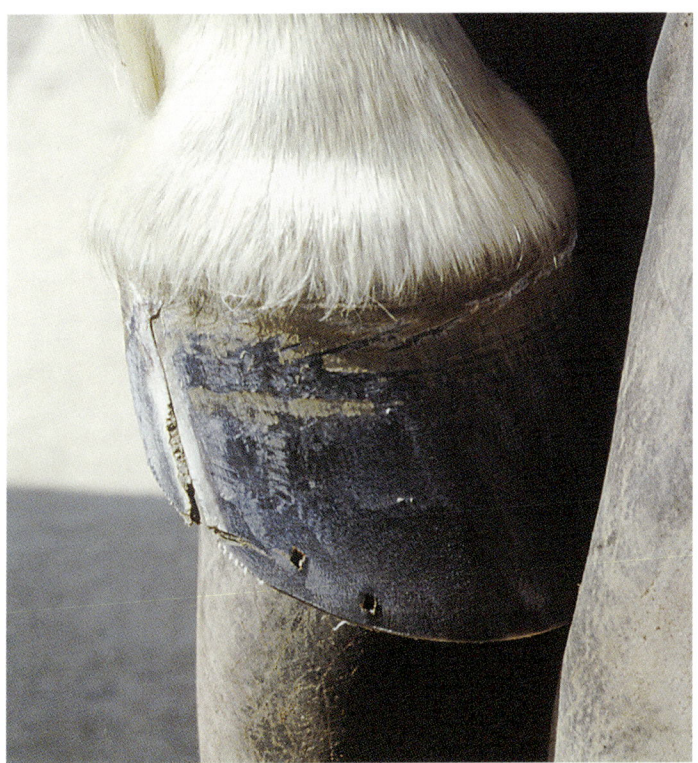

Fig. 7.14 After the shoe is removed, all the loose hoof wall is removed to prevent the edges of the crack rubbing together.

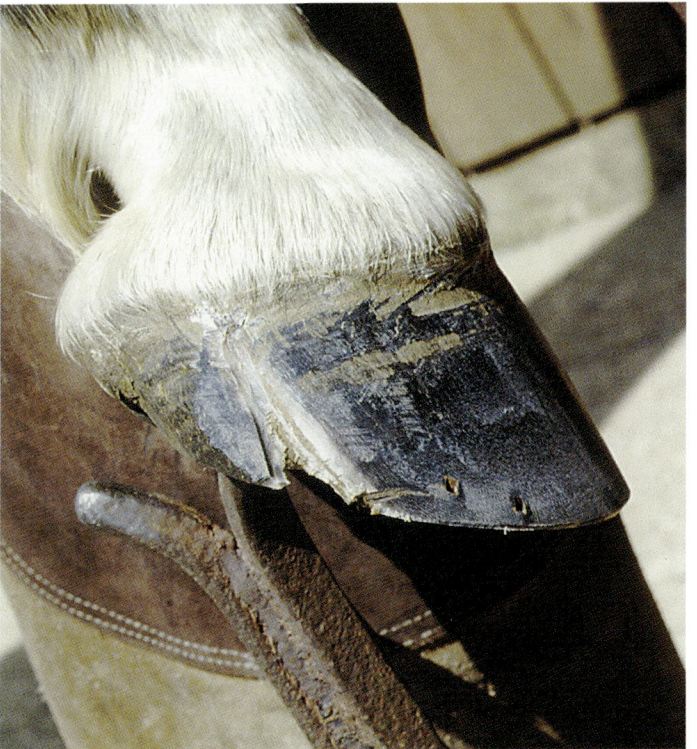

Fig. 7.15 Full view of the crack after it has been cleaned up. See how the edges cannot now rub against each other and perpetuate the cracking. (Note: This crack doesn't need special dressing. It is superficial and does not involve the sensitive laminae.)

Fig. 7.16 A half-bar shoe is fitted and the heel 'floated' off the branch of the shoe This enables the forces to be redirected onto the frog. This will allow the hoof to grow down normally.

By far the most serious cracks are those caused by chronic foot imbalances such as has developed in the right forefoot of the horse in Fig. 7.17.

Fig. 7.17 A serious full-thickness crack which has developed on a foot with chronic imbalance. The hoof capsule is being distorted to the inside by a medio-lateral imbalance.

upright outside wall and hoof capsule deviating to the inside ■ —

full thickness crack ■ —

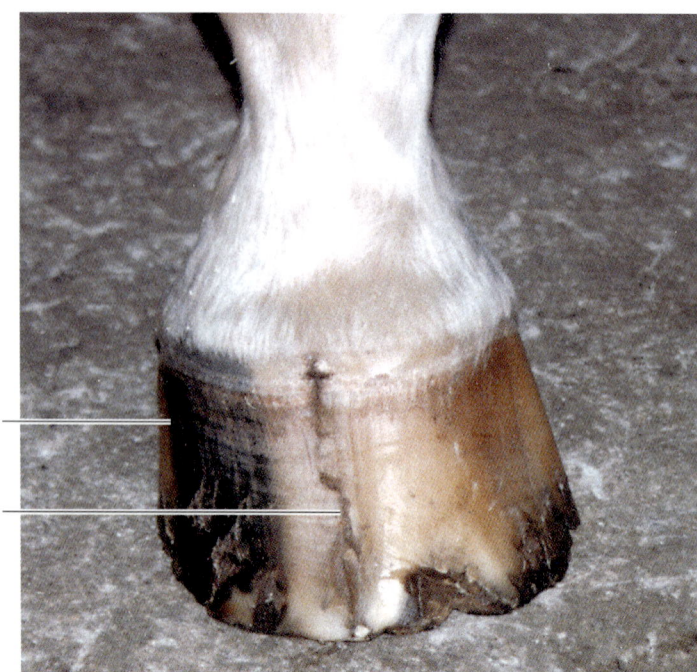

This particular horse had a chronic medio-lateral imbalance which was forcing a distortion of the hoof capsule to the inside. However, at the same time a chronic dorso-palmar imbalance was forcing the heels underneath the horse (Fig. 7.18). In mechanical terms what is happening to this horse is as follows. The medio-lateral imbalance has sheared his heels making the foot structure very unstable. The hoof capsule has started to deviate and the heels are under-run because there has been no heel support. The outside heel is being forced towards the inside and is moving up the limb. Every time the horse puts weight on this foot he creates a shearing force at the toe (the heels have already sheared) but because the weight of the horse is being suspended from the inside of the hoof, this shearing force is greater inside the hoof capsule and at the coronet band. This breakdown of tissue occurs from the inside out and the first time that the owner will realise that anything is amiss is when the wall becomes so weak that the front literally bursts open from top to bottom. Effectively the hoof is now in two halves and very unstable. The horse immediately becomes lame and the potential for infection to enter the sensitive structures of the foot is high. Such a state of affairs needs radical treatment

The first thing that had to be done with this horse was to ensure that his medio-lateral balance was corrected.

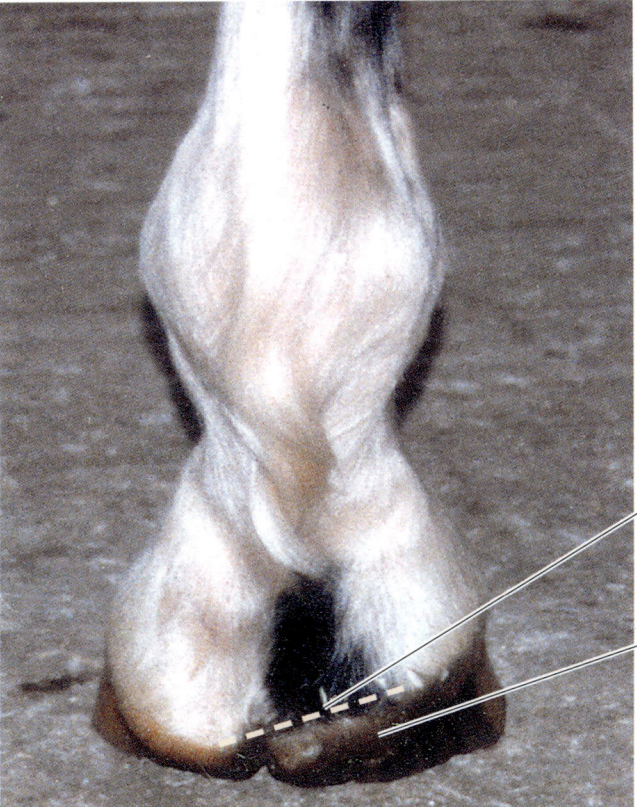

Fig. 7.18 At the same time the heels are sheared and the outside wall has collapsed underneath the foot

■ bulbs of heel unlevel

■ outside heel has collapsed underneath the horse and, because the heels have sheared as a result of the medio-lateral imbalance, the hoof wall is migrating towards the inside

Secondly, the crack needed be cleaned of all loose tissue (Fig. 7.19) so that the edges did not rub together. Thirdly, special screws were inserted at either side of the crack (Fig. 7.20) then threaded together with wire (Fig. 7.21).

Fig. 7.19 After correction of medio-lateral balance, the next stage is to clean the crack of all dead and loose tissue.

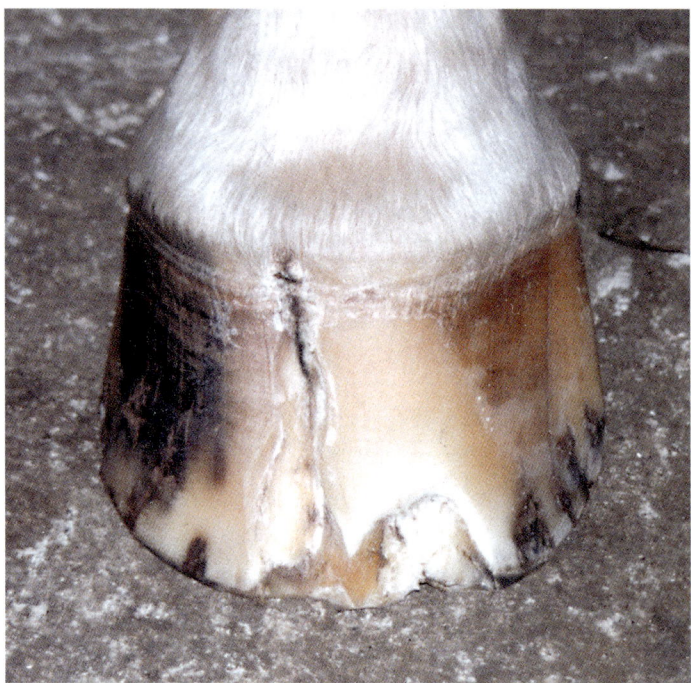

Fig. 7.20 Special screws are inserted into either side of the crack.

screws driven through the outer part of the hoof ■◄

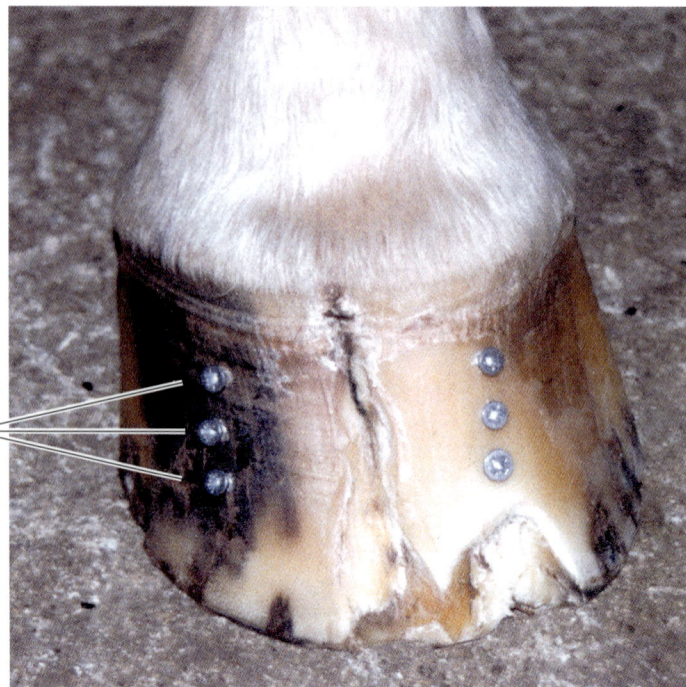

A shoe was then applied, ensuring that there were equal amounts of weight-bearing on either side of the line of force, and the screws and wires were bonded over and covered with acrylic (Fig. 7.22).

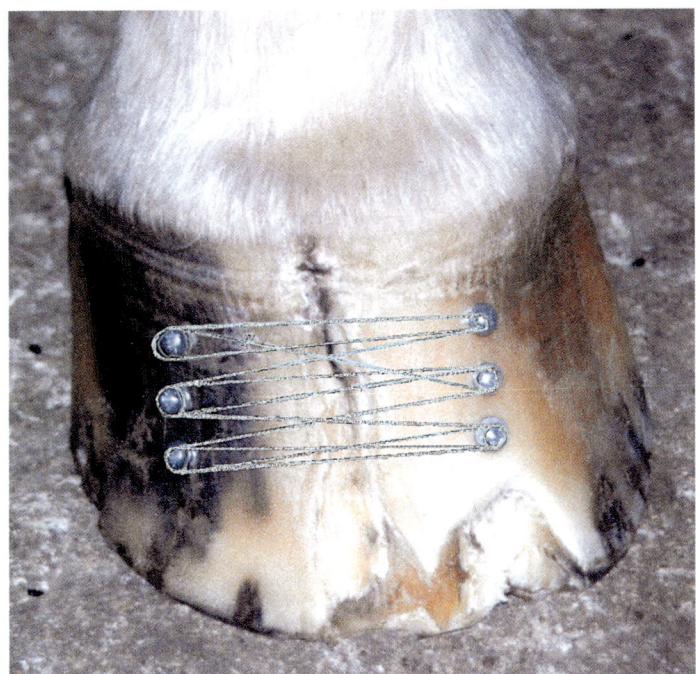

Fig. 7.21 The screws are threaded together with wire.

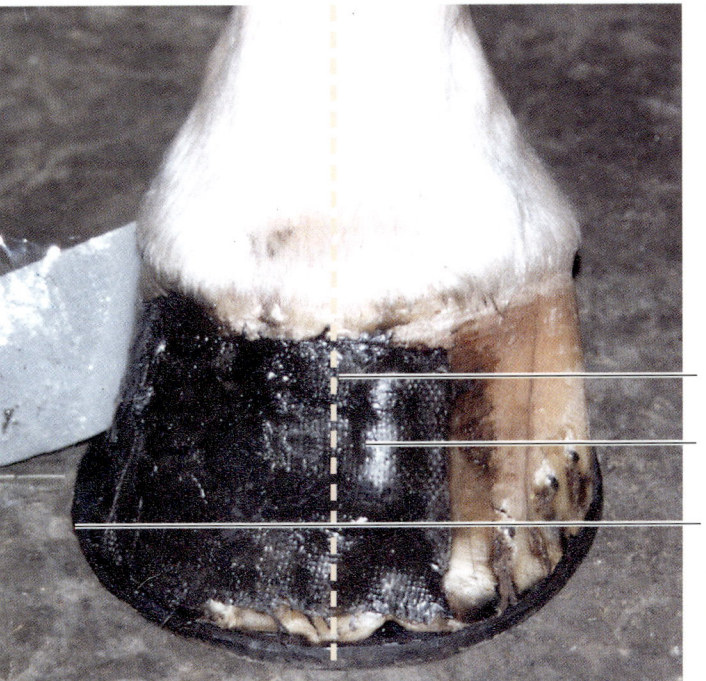

Fig. 7.22 Finally the shoe is applied – a lateral extension ensures equal amount of weightbearing either side of the centre line – and acrylic bonding and tape is applied over the screws and wire.

■ centre line down limb

■ acrylic bonding

■ lateral extension ensures equal weight-bearing either side of line of force

The left forefoot of this horse was in an equally parlous state but was caught just before the abnormal forces created by the imbalance could cause quite so devastating a problem, although a small superficial crack can be seen (Fig 7.23). A similar process was carried out on this foot ensuring that the medio-

Fig. 7.23 The left forefoot of the same horse shows a developing crack but this is not yet full thickness and can be treated conservatively. Again a lateral extension is provided to give equal weightbearing either side of the centre line.

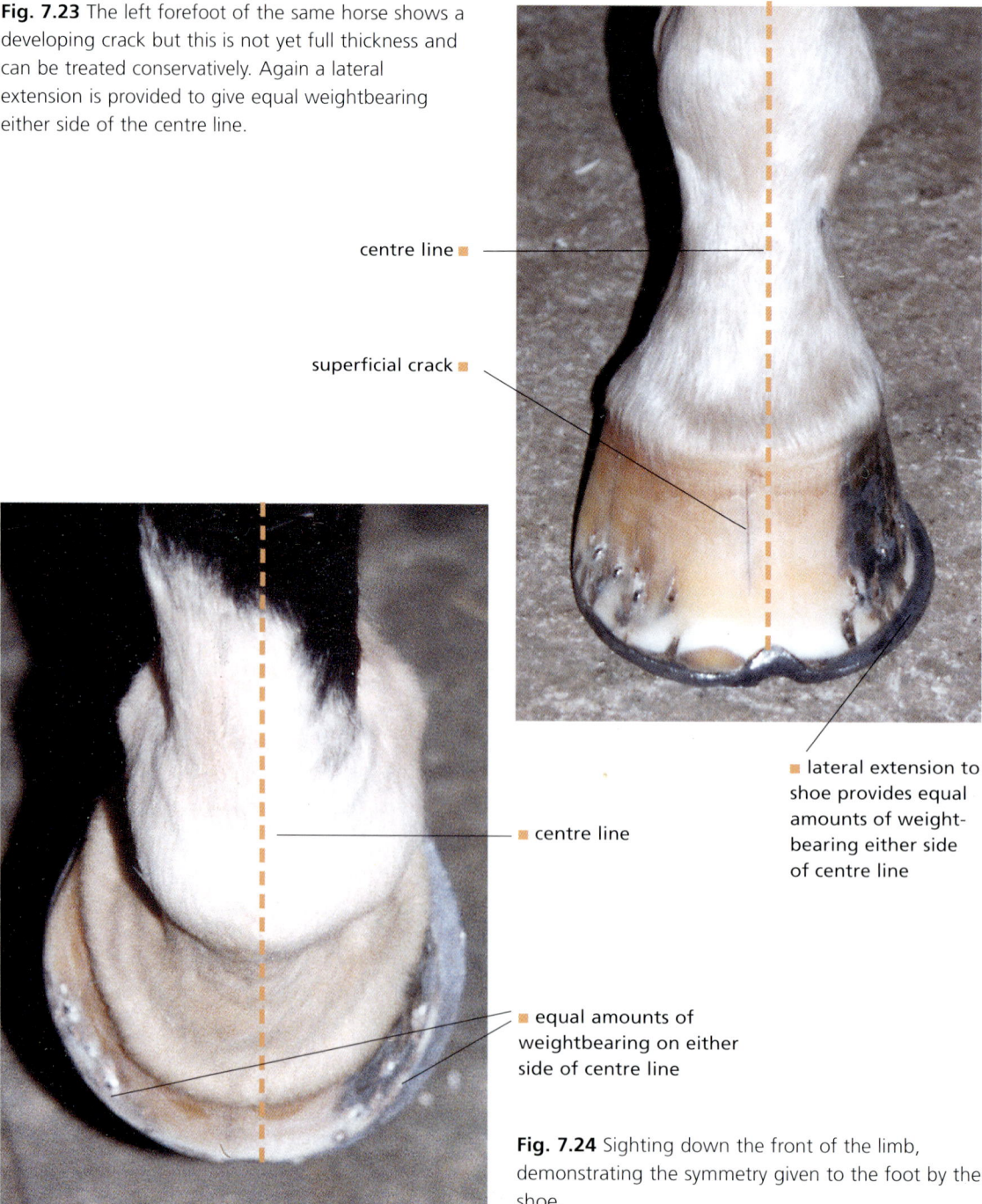

centre line ■

superficial crack ■

■ lateral extension to shoe provides equal amounts of weight-bearing either side of centre line

■ centre line

■ equal amounts of weightbearing on either side of centre line

Fig. 7.24 Sighting down the front of the limb, demonstrating the symmetry given to the foot by the shoe.

lateral balance was true to the T-square, that there were equal amounts of weightbearing on either side of the central line, and that there was sufficient support at the heels (Fig. 7.24 and 7.25). Like the right fore, the left fore of this horse required a straight-bar shoe to stabilise it (Fig. 7.26).

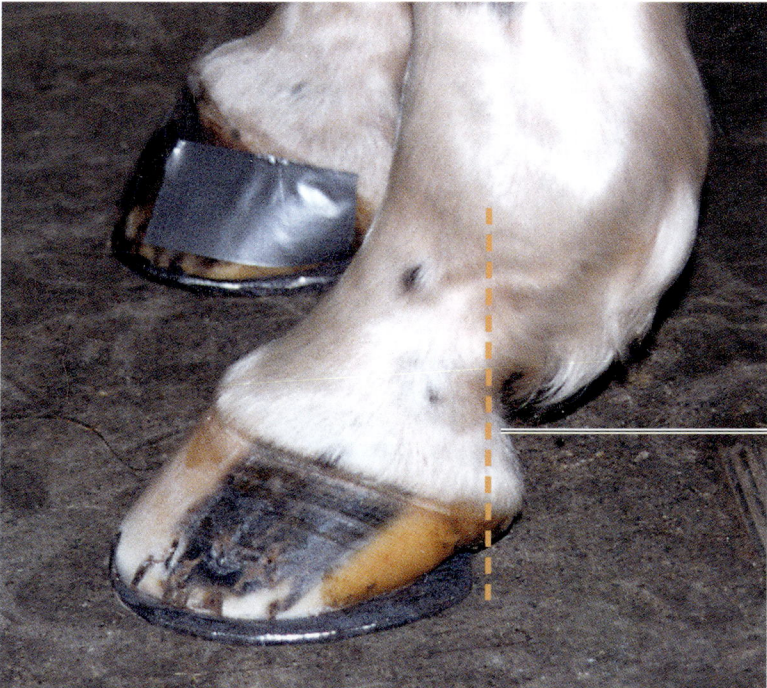

Fig. 7.25 The dorso-palmar imbalance is corrected by supporting the fetlock with the heels of the shoe.

■ perpendicular line from centre of fetlock joint brushes last weightbearing aspect of heels, providing straight hoof/pastern axis and support for heels and fetlock

Fig. 7.26 This horse needed a straight bar shoe to stabilise his sheared heels.

Again, skilful farriery can remedy what may seem to be the most devastating of problems in the horse, whether they have been caused by poor foot structure and/or poor farriery. It is vitally important that you treat your horse's feet with the same care and attention that you lavish on all other aspects of his management. Begin to learn about and appreciate your horse's individual hoof characteristics so that you can nip any problems in the bud before they get to the stage where he becomes lame. Remember, by the time these devastating problems have occurred it may well take up to two years to get him right again, during which time your competitive ambitions may have been thwarted, and your horse will have endured pain and suffering as a result.

CHAPTER 8

Optical Illusions in Farriery

Throughout the course of this book we have emphasised the need to closely observe your horse. This is because his muscular development and locomotion can reveal all there is to know about his mechanical function or dysfunction. However, it is not enough to restrict your observation to 'Is he sound or is he lame?' In the absence of physical trauma it may be a long road from sound to lame with many stages of dysfunction in between. Therefore your question should instead be 'Is he functional or is he dysfunctional?'

There are times, though, when our eyes deceive us and we misinterpret what we are actually seeing. For example, the following three figures demonstrate optical illusions.

In the 'T' shape in Fig. 8.1 the vertical bar looks longer than the horizontal bar when in fact they are both the same length. In Fig. 8.2 the person at the

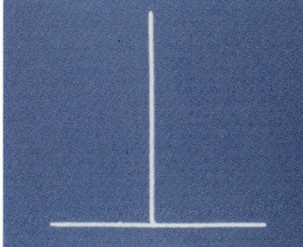

Fig. 8.1 Which is longer – the vertical bar or the horizontal bar?

Fig. 8.2 Which figure is the larger?

Fig. 8.3 Are the two central horizontal bars bent or straight?

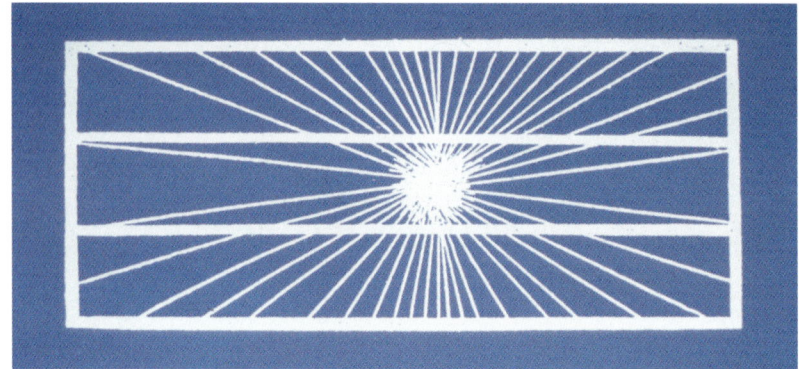

front looks considerably smaller than the figure at the back when they are actually the same size. It is the background shrinking that makes the figure at the back look much bigger than it is. In Fig. 8.3 the two central horizontal bars look bent when in fact they are parallel to each other and to the top and bottom bars.

The same sort of illusion can be demonstrated when looking at horses. Skilled farriery can be used either to fool the observer into thinking that bent legs are straight or to demonstrate that so-called 'conformation faults' were actually illusions created by poor farriery when the horse had no such fault. We have seen this demonstrated to some extent in previous chapters. Take, for example, the Grand Prix dressage horse in Chapter 6, who appeared to be pigeon-toed and break over the outside toe quarter. This horse had straight legs but the deviation of the hoof capsule to the inside made him look like he had

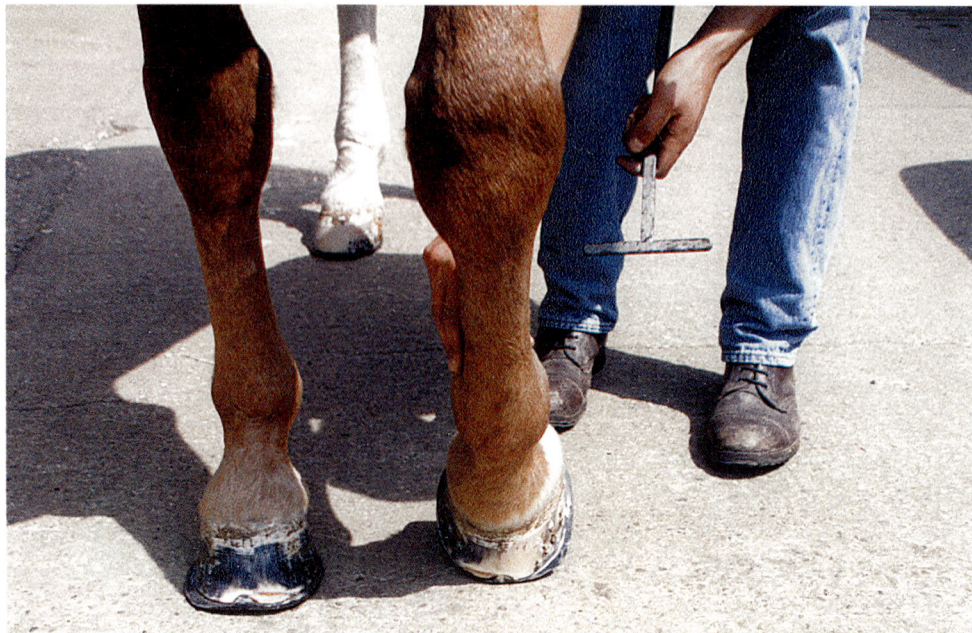

Fig. 8.4 The Grand Prix dressage horse (as seen in Chapter 6) still breaks over the centre of the toe.

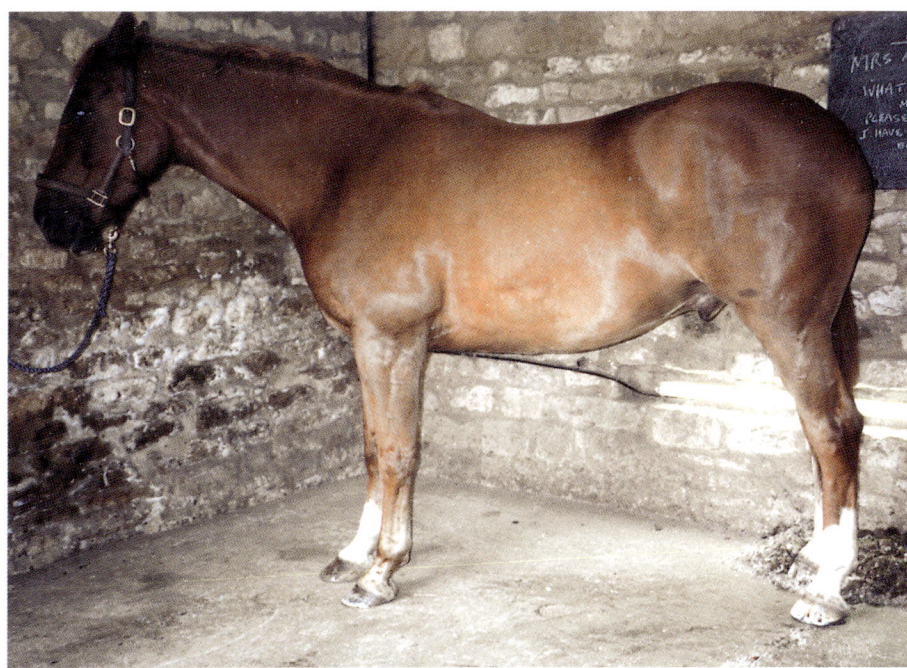

Fig. 8.5 Does this horse stand like this because of his conformation or because of his foot imbalance? (See Fig. 8.6 for answer.)

conformation faults. Fig. 8.4 shows that horse two months later demonstrating yet again that his legs are straight and that he does, in fact, break over the centre of the toe.

The horse in Fig. 8.5 looks camped in front. But this is merely an artefact created by the fact that his toes are overlong and his heels are collapsed thus

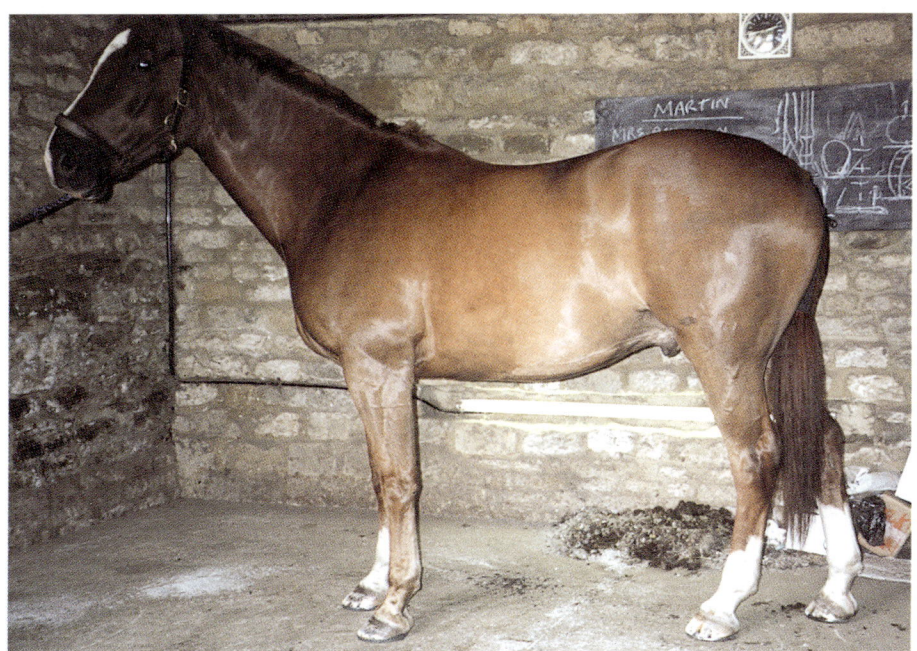

Fig. 8.6 After corrective shoeing he stands correctly.

Fig. 8.7 ...the front view shows that he has good limb conformation.

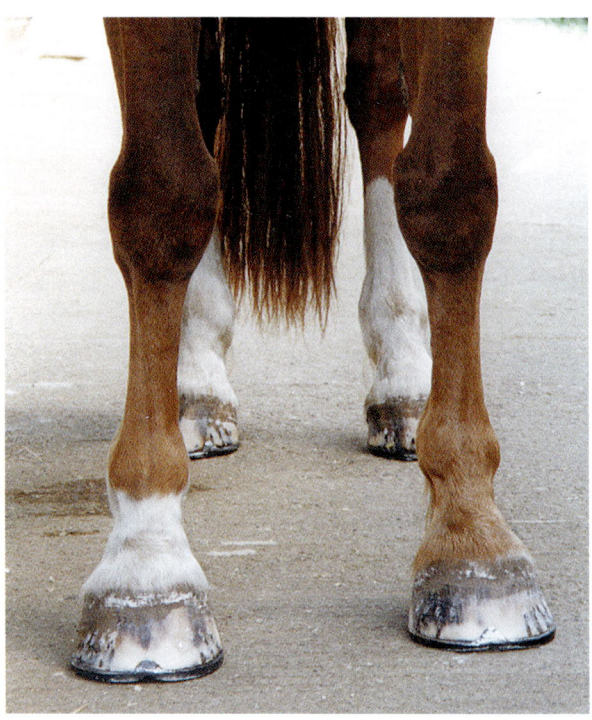

preventing him from standing correctly. Fig. 8.6 shows him standing normally after he has been correctly shod. Fig. 8.7 shows a view of this horse from the front demonstrating that he has good limb conformation.

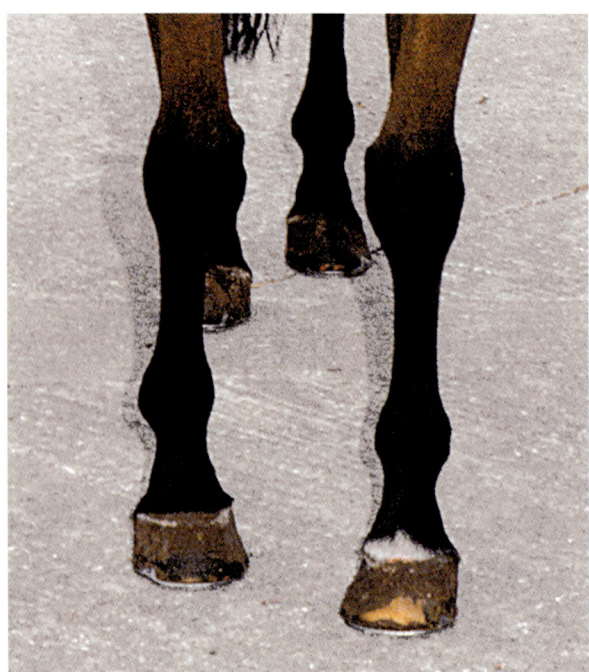

Fig. 8.8 Is this horse genuinely pigeon-toed – or has a medio-lateral imbalance created a hoof-capsule distortion which is forcing him to stand this way? To find out which, see Figs. 8.9 and 8.10.

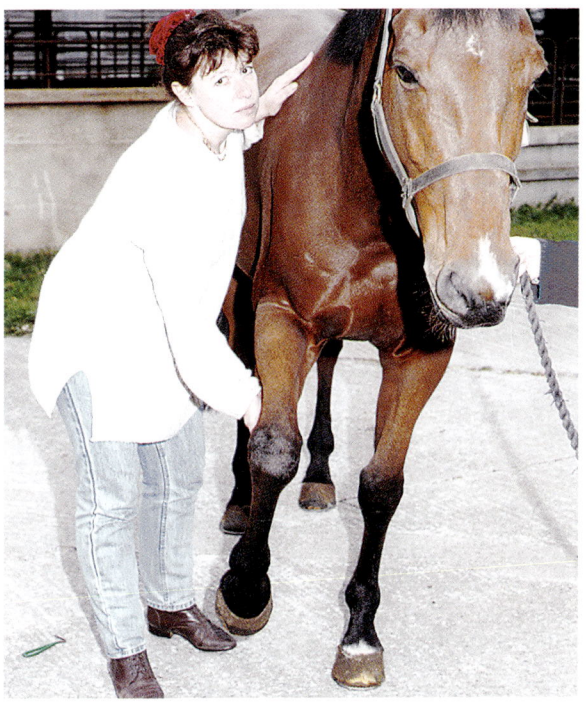

Fig. 8.9 Hanging this leg forwards demonstrates that it is mostly straight.

The horse in Fig. 8.8 appears to be pigeon-toed but this is an illusion created by his medio-lateral foot imbalance, which has not only created a distortion of the hoof capsule but also forced him to stand with his toes pointing in. To find

Fig. 8.10 Hanging this leg forwards also demonstrates that it is the hoof capsule which is distorted.

Fig. 8.11 Genuine toe-in conformation persists even when the limb is hung forwards. This horse really does have a pigeon-toe conformation.

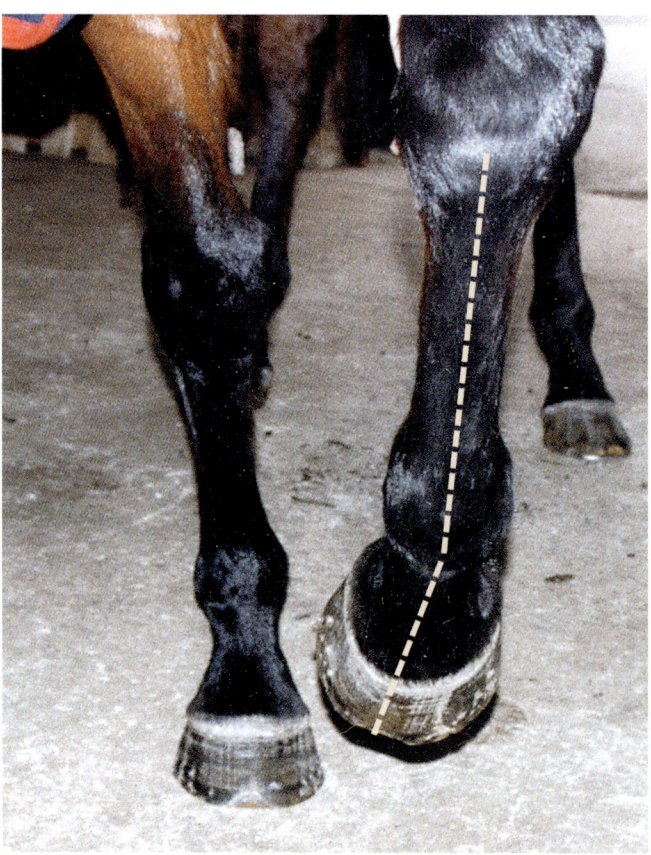

out whether you horse has bent or straight legs all you have to do is pick them up and hang them forwards (see Figs. 8.9 and 8.10). If the legs are straight but a chronic foot imbalance is making them stand in an abnormal manner, lifting the leg off the ground and taking the weight off the leg will allow it to hang in accordance with his natural conformation. The horse in Figs 8.8–8.10 actually has straight his legs; if he had a genuine toe-in conformation then the limbs would hang with the toes pointed in, as demonstrated by the horse in Fig. 8.11.

Good farriery practice can also make the horse with genuine conformation faults look correct. The Thoroughbred yearling in Fig. 8.12 has a number of serious limb problems. His left front limb deviates out from the knee but then rotates inwards from the fetlock down. The right forelimb rotates outwards from the knee down. Nothing can be done to straighten his legs surgically because X-rays show that the growth plates in the long bones have closed off. Anything that can be done for him now is purely cosmetic.

The sad thing about this horse is that if the owner had taken advice several months earlier, before the growth plates had closed, skilled farriery could have genuinely corrected these faults. The horse had been bred as an eventer and was by a very famous event sire. Consequently the potential value of this horse

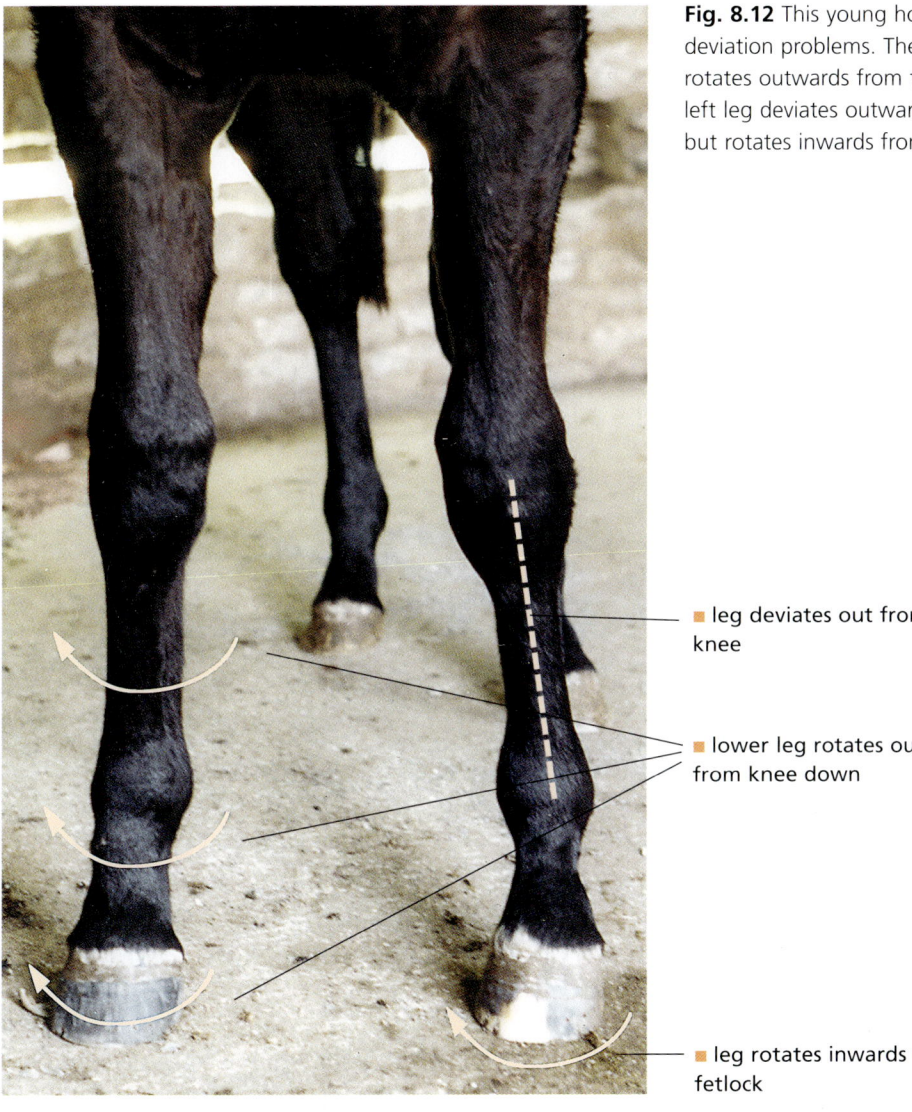

Fig. 8.12 This young horse has many limb deviation problems. The right lower leg rotates outwards from the knee down. The left leg deviates outwards from the knee but rotates inwards from the fetlock down.

■ leg deviates out from the knee

■ lower leg rotates outwards from knee down

■ leg rotates inwards from fetlock

could have been large, but instead the owner lost a valuable investment.

Fig. 8.13 (overleaf) shows the same horse after farriery. On first sight it looks as if his legs are now straight but this is an optical illusion. Certainly his farriery treatment made him more comfortable and able to stand a little better, but the underlying problem of his 'Z' legs remained (and sadly this horse was eventually destroyed because of these limb deformities).

It is therefore vitally important that youngstock – especially those who are bred for their performance potential – have their limbs evaluated and trimmed by a skilled farrier at regular intervals. There is no need for a horse to be lost like this. Some horses can go on to perform well despite their conformation problems and this is where the skilled farrier would be cheap at twice the price

Fig. 8.13 This is the same horse as in Fig. 8.12. As if by magic the legs appear straight, but this is purely an optical illusion created by Martin's expert farriery skills.

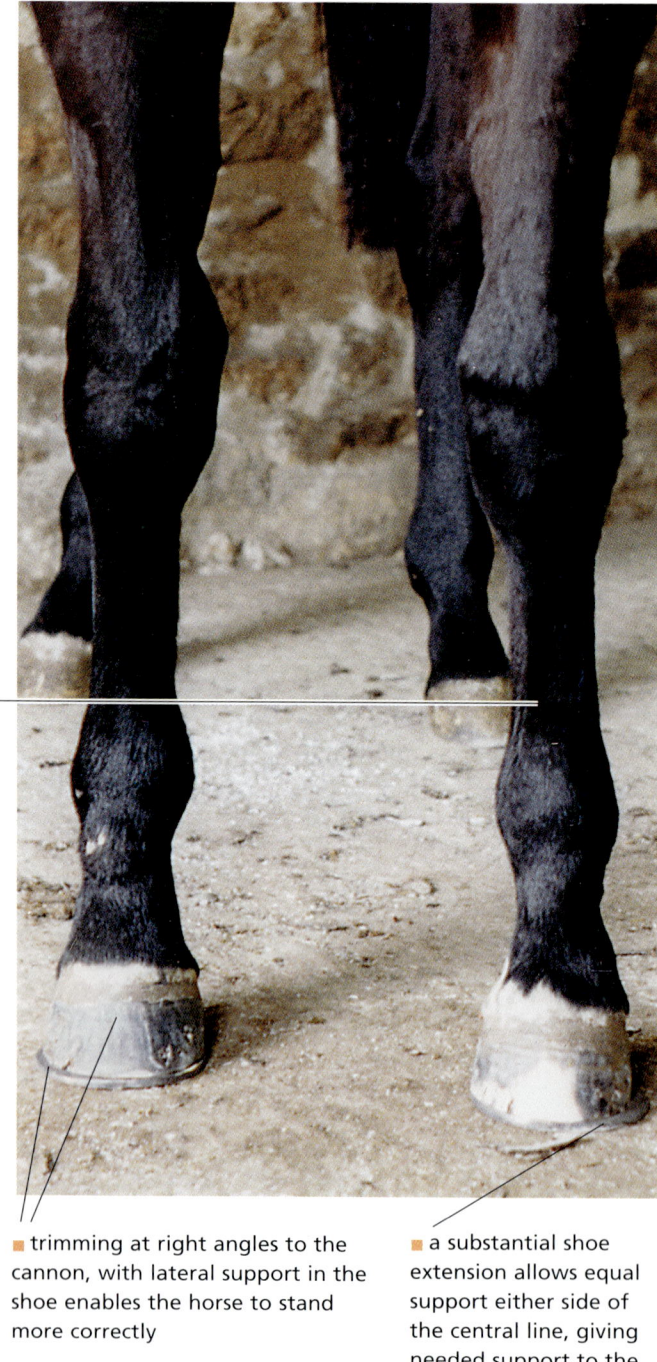

trimming the foot so that it is at right angles to the cannon bone has enabled the horse to stand under himself a little better and taken the strain off the knee, thus allowing it to 'straighten' ■

■ trimming at right angles to the cannon, with lateral support in the shoe enables the horse to stand more correctly

■ a substantial shoe extension allows equal support either side of the central line, giving needed support to the fetlock

– keeping our horses performing against the odds!

Fig. 8.14 shows a Hunt Master's horse who has the same 'Z' leg conformation in his right fore – albeit not quite so profound as in the previous horse. The

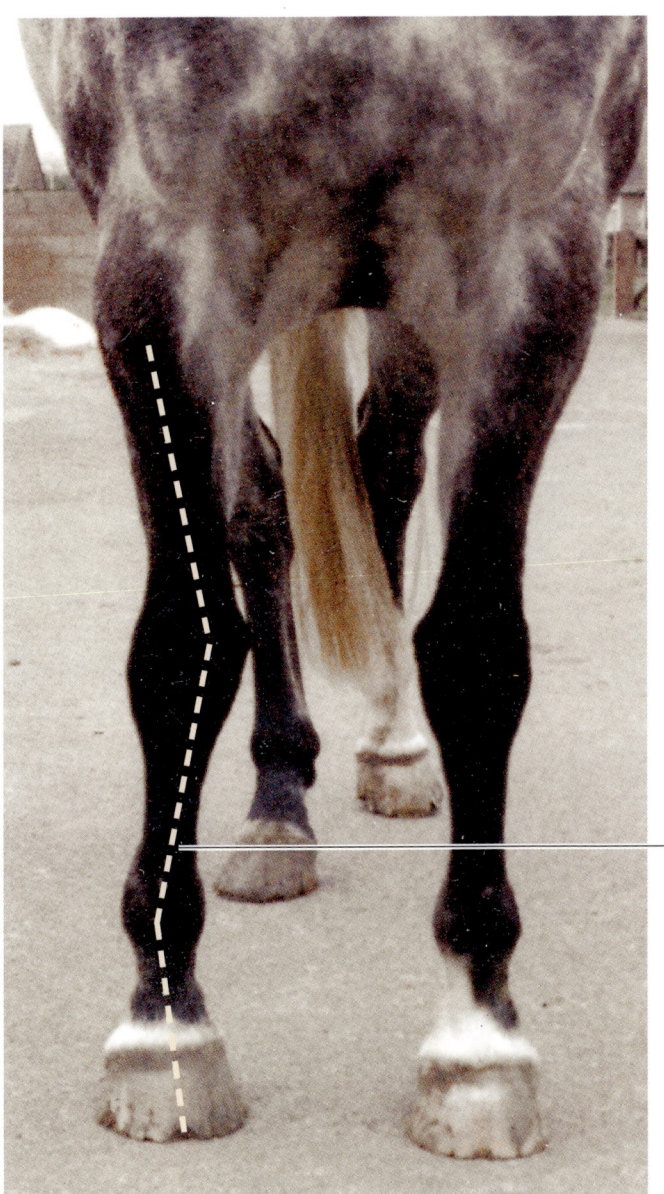

Fig. 8.14 A horse with 'Z' leg conformation. The leg deviates in from the shoulder, out from the knee and in from the fetlock.

■ the 'Z' leg conformation

medial deviation from the fetlock can be helped by applying the shoe so that the branches are at right angles to the long axis of the cannon bone. Effectively this means that although the foot is pointing inwards, the shoe is applied so that it faces directly forwards (Fig. 8.15). By doing this, and ensuring that the foot is trimmed at right angles to the long axis of the cannon bone (the T-square method), the placement and the breakover of the foot will correspond with the conformation above the fetlock. In this way the natural pendulum swing of the forelimb is not inhibited and the forces of locomotion will be

long axis of cannon
bone going straight
down through the toe
of the shoe ■

branches of the shoe at right
angles to long axis ■

line through centre
of frog points to
actual toe of horse as the foot
is deviated to the inside ■

Fig. 8.15 When the toe of the horse does not point towards the front it is important to apply the shoe so that it faces forwards. In this way the dynamic weightbearing on the foot is at its optimum and the horse can move forwards without additional abnormal forces being created.

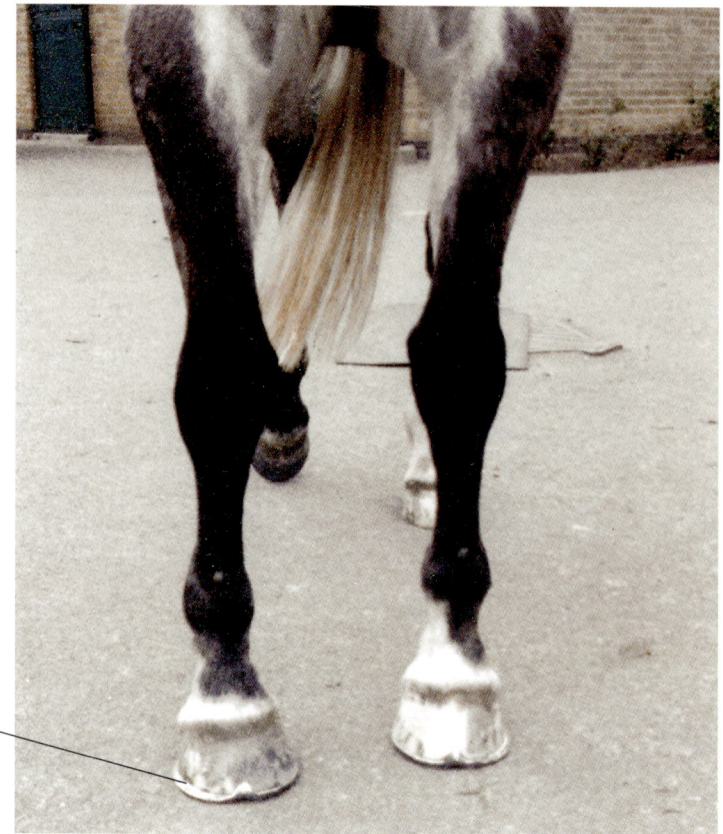

lateral extension ■

Fig. 8.16 The lateral extension to the shoe supports the fetlock.

transmitted more naturally. Thus the joints are not overstrained and the horse is able to perform.

Finally, the fetlock is supported by a lateral extension to the shoe (Fig. 8.16).

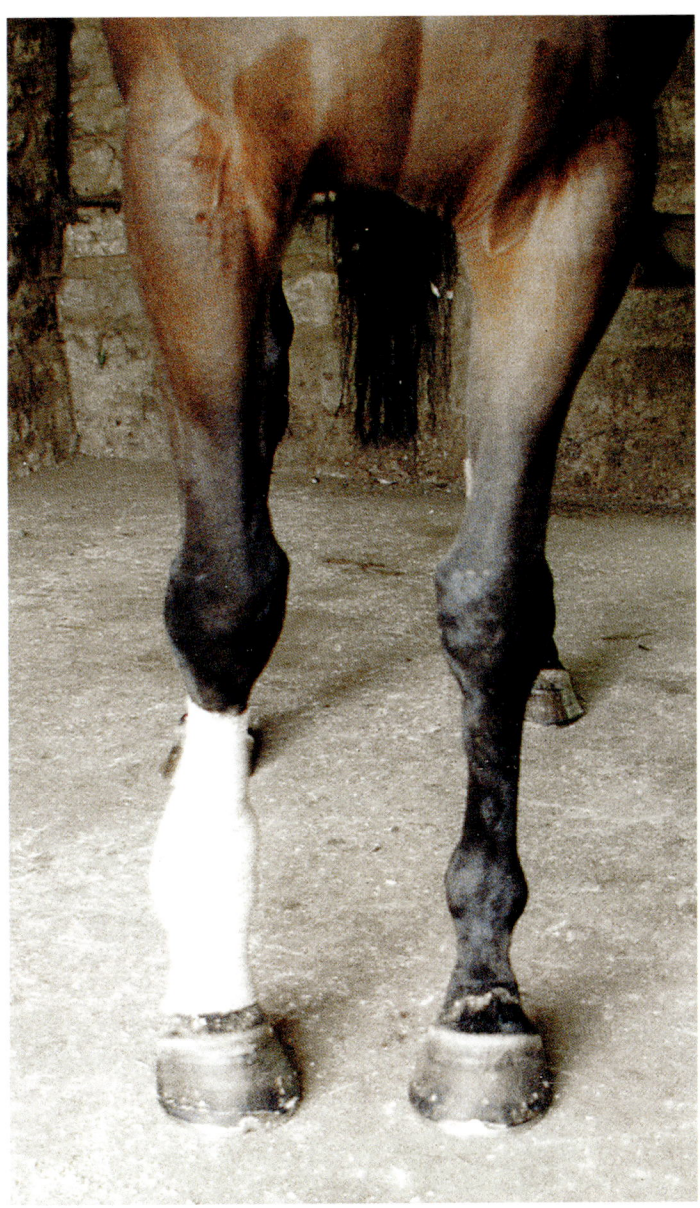

Fig. 8.17 The strain caused by this horse's conformation defect has resulted in injury.

A horse with a similar problem is seen in Figs 8.17–8.18. In this horse, however, the strain caused by his abnormal conformation has caused him to suffer fetlock problems. He is treated in exactly the same way as the previous horse with the shoe being applied so that the toe of the shoe faces the front and lateral support given for the fetlock (Fig. 8.19).

Fig. 8.18 ...his pigeon-toed conformation is plain to see.

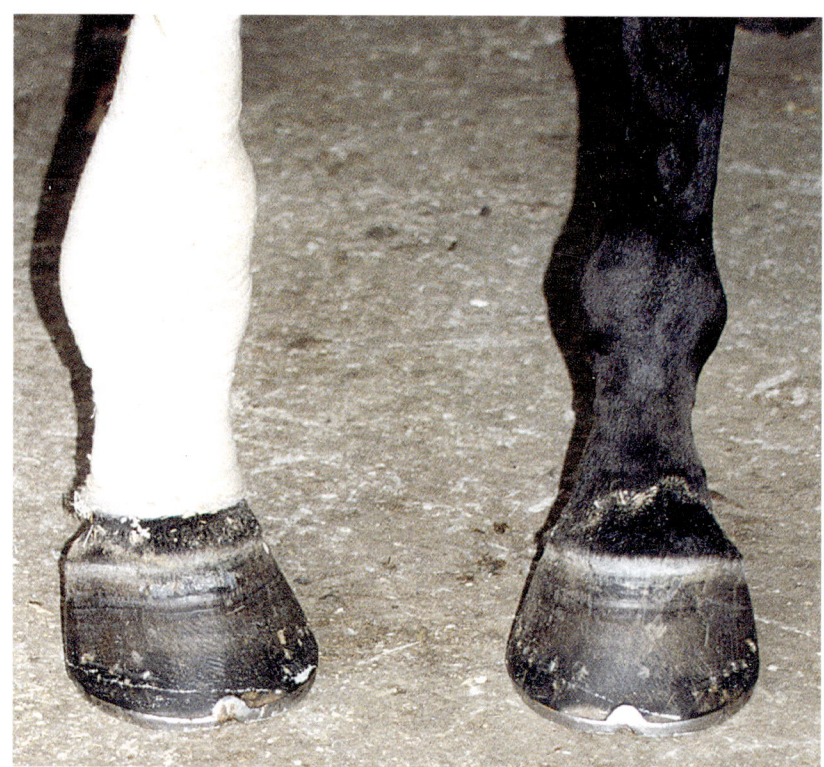

heels show that foot is turned in ◼

shoe applied so it is facing forwards ◼

line through centre of frog gives the position of the actual toe of foot ◼

chalk mark shows toe of shoe ◼

Fig. 8.19 He is shod in a similar manner to the previous horse in that the shoe is applied as if the foot faced the front. In this way as the horse puts his foot to the floor the heels of the shoe will be landing at the same time and will not cause additional rotational problems.

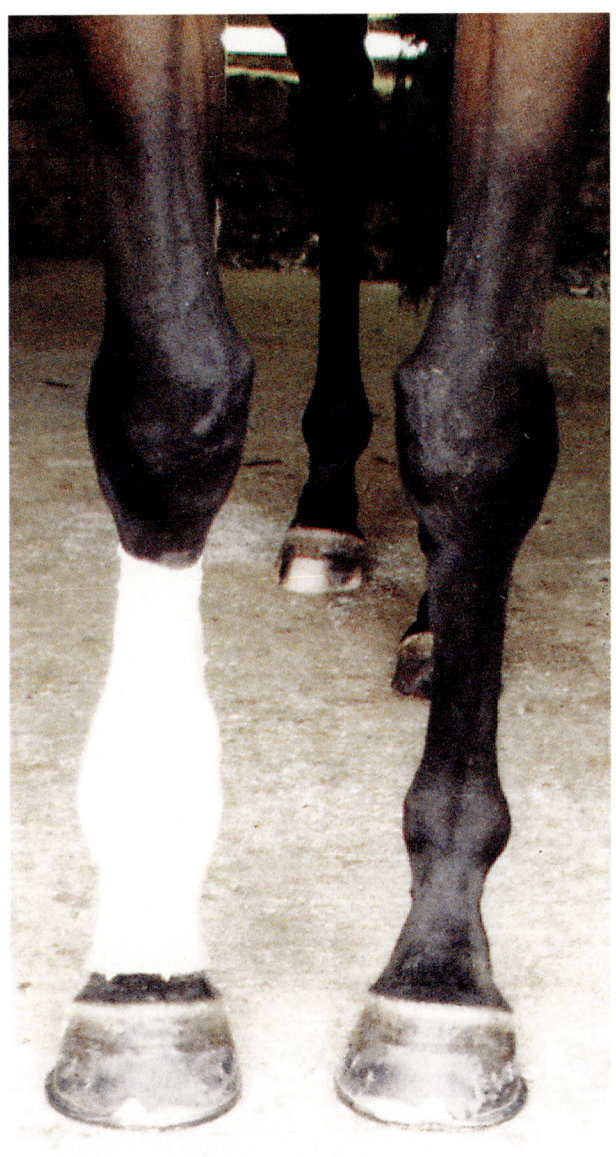

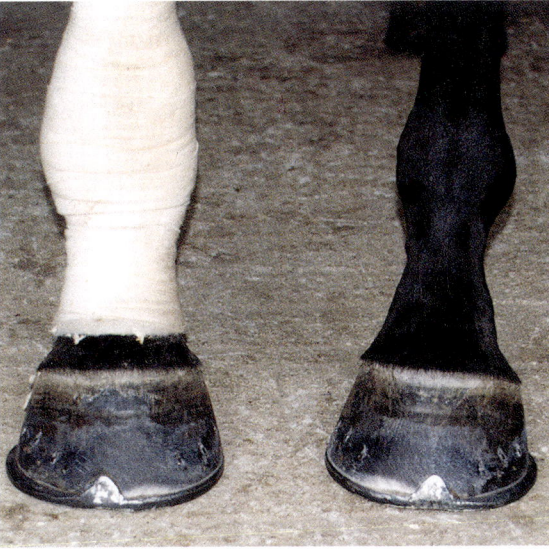

Fig. 8.20 Note the use of the lateral support. In this picture you can see where the toe clips were placed on the old shoes – on the centre of the toe. On the new shoes the toe clips are facing the front – again creating an optical illusion.

Fig. 8.21 The very pleasing effects. Again the horse still has his pigeon toes but he can stand and move more comfortably which gives the appearance of a straight leg.

The very pleasing effects are shown in Figs. 8.20 and 8.21. Again, it must be stressed that these horses still have all of their original conformation faults but remedial farriery has given them an optimum dynamic base off which they can perform to the best of their ability. By so doing, you can lessen the abnormal forces that the horse with poor conformation will experience and therefore give him every chance to stay sound.

CHAPTER 9

Diseased or Injured Feet

The concepts outlined in the earlier chapters apply equally to the diseased or injured horse and it is right that we should demonstrate why this is so.

Mismatched feet

One of the topics that we have not dealt with elsewhere is the horse with mismatched feet (Figs. 9.1 and 9.2). There are many causes of mismatched feet and generally your vet will need to x-ray the feet to find out exactly why they are not a pair. Very often, mismatched feet are seen in horses who had contracted tendons as foals. In these cases the pedal bones themselves will not be a pair and the mismatched feet are something that you will have to learn to live with, for if the pedal bones are not the same, the hoof capsules will never be the same.

Mismatched feet can also occur where there is some degenerative change inside the hoof capsule. For example, the horse with chronic pain in one foot will stand so that he takes less weight on that foot. As a result the hoof capsule will contract. Conversely, the other foot of the pair, because it is taking more weight than it should, can splay out and collapse at the heels. With this scenario diagnosis and treatment by your veterinary surgeon is imperative because if the horse is not taking weight on the contracted foot because of pain then remedial farriery can do little for him.

The general rule, however, when balancing and shoeing a horse with mismatched feet is that each foot should be shod in accordance with the conformation of its individual limb. In other words do not shoe them as a pair unless the conformation of the limbs is the same.

Injured/diseased feet

Injured horses need their feet in optimum balance so as to provide the peak conditions for recovery. The last thing that an injured horse needs is having to

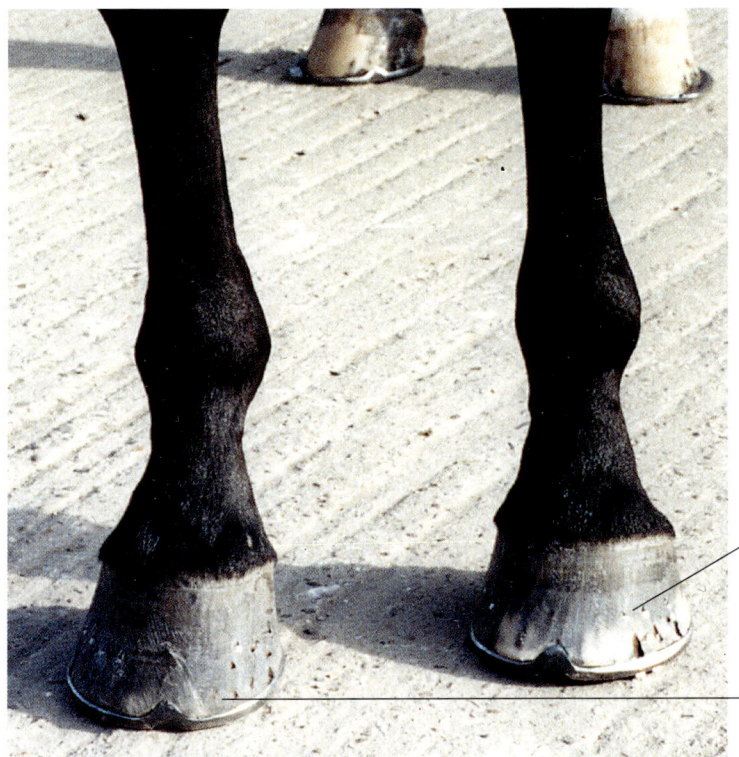

Figs. 9.1 and 9.2 A horse with mismatched feet. The right foot is upright and 'boxy' whilst the left foot is sloping with collapsed heels.

■ sloping, wide foot with collapsed heels

■ upright, boxy foot

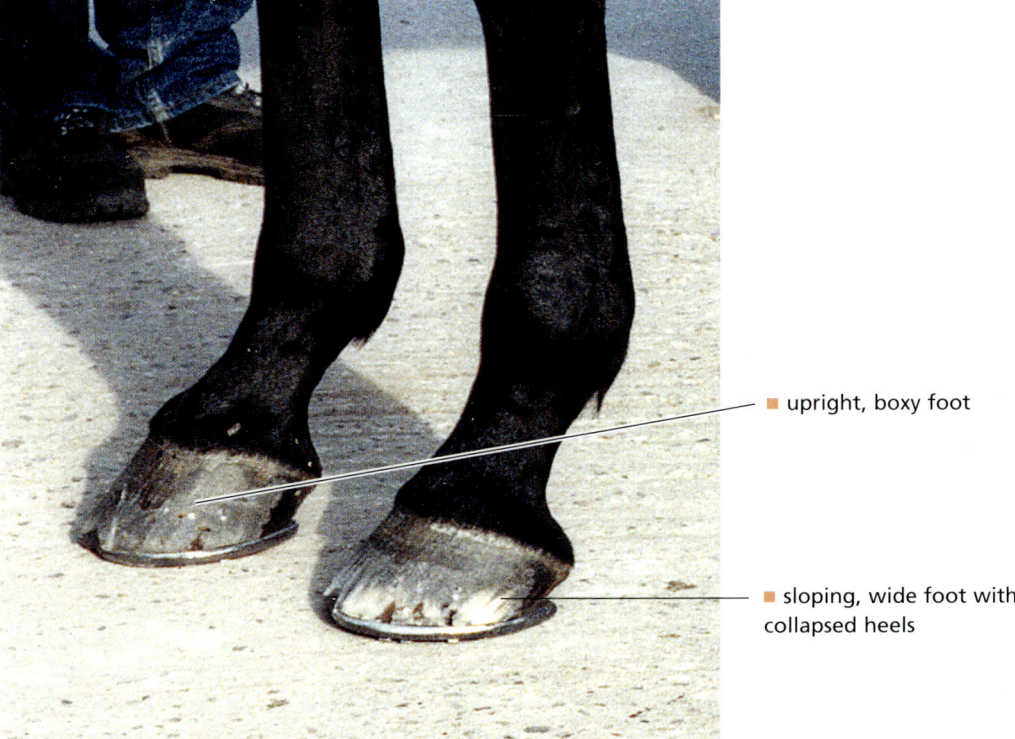

■ upright, boxy foot

■ sloping, wide foot with collapsed heels

cope with abnormal forces. The horse in Figs 9.3 and 9.4 was found in his field with the lateral bulb and lateral aspect of the frog of his left hind sliced away. Not only does this horse's medio-lateral balance have to be perfect to enable recovery to take place, but also the force being taken down the back of the leg has to be relieved as much as possible. In these circumstances the egg-bar shoe

Fig. 9.3 This horse was found in the field with this injury to the bulb of his heel.

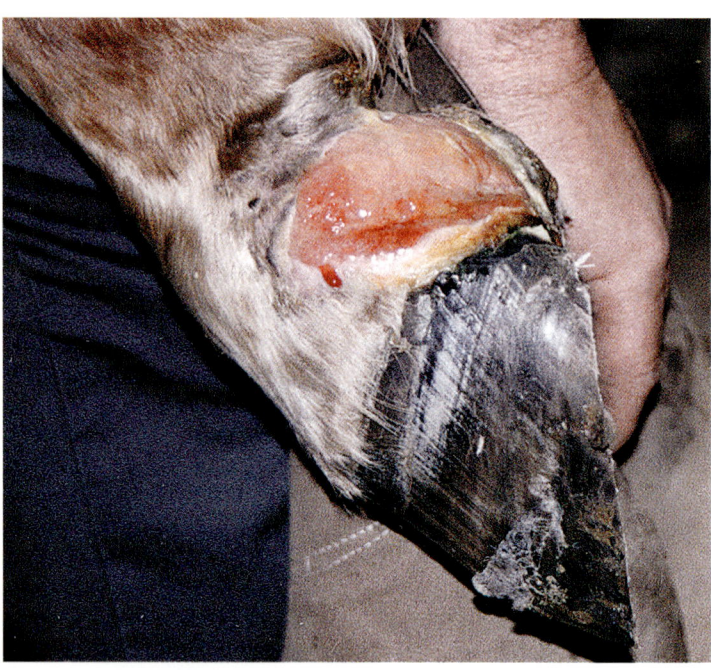

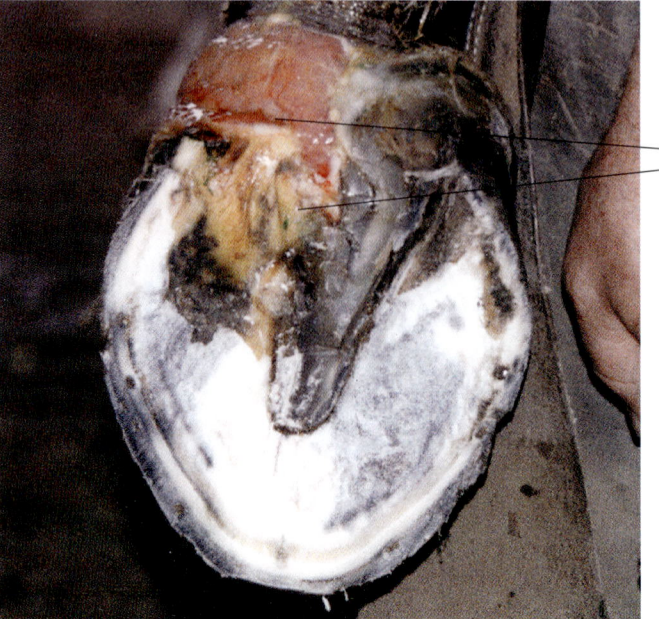

■ bulb of heel and frog sliced away

Fig. 9.4 Note how the bulb of the heel and part of the frog has been sliced away.

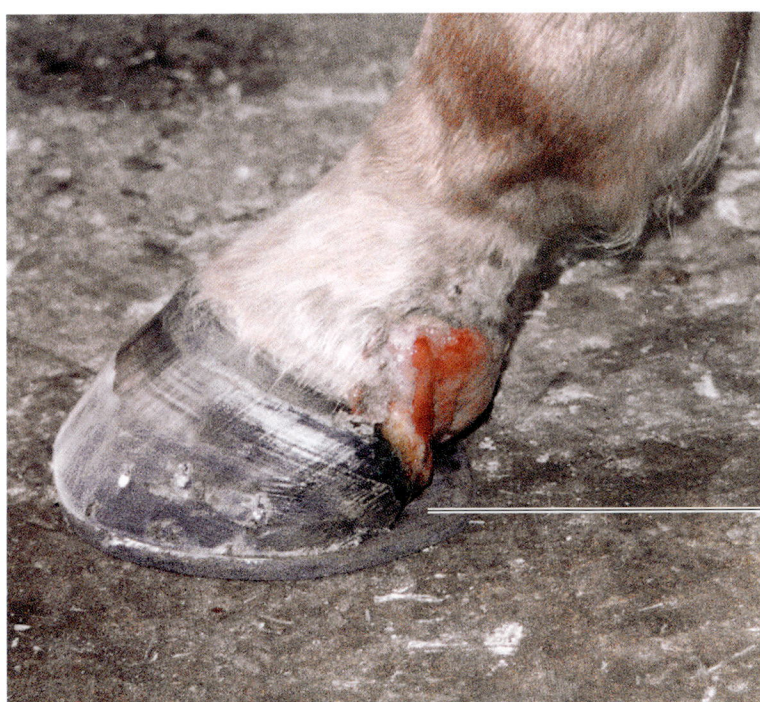

Fig. 9.5 The egg-bar shoe dissipates concussive forces from the injured heel allowing it to heal.

■ egg-bar shoe dissipating forces from injured area

is the shoe of choice because it can relieve forces down the back of the limb, and this foot had an egg-bar shoe applied (Fig. 9.5). As a result of this farriery treatment the foot was stable and the forces dissipated to provide optimal healing conditions. Further, all the structures above the missing heel were supported so that this injury did not suffer a knock-on effect brought about by altered movement patterns.

In a previous chapter we mentioned that there is nothing magical about bar shoes and navicular disease. It is vitally important that horses are shod for their conformation and not for the disease. Take, for example, the horse in Fig. 9.6 who is a ten-year-old Thoroughbred with all the classic symptoms of navicular disease, including radiographic changes (Fig. 9.7). He is moderately lame on both his forefeet.

This horse had problems over and above his navicular disease in that his owner was allowing the feet to become too long by not calling in the farrier at regular intervals, and also because the farrier (when he did come) was not helping the horse with the poor state of his farriery. Fig. 9.8 shows the solar view of the horse's foot in which you can see that the farrier has taken an ordinary machine-made shoe and attempted to weld a bar across the heels. The weld was so poor that it had fractured and the bar was wobbling around, causing the horse even more problems.

The main points to note about this horse, however, are that:

1. Despite the dreadful state of his feet, the heels are not sheared. Therefore he

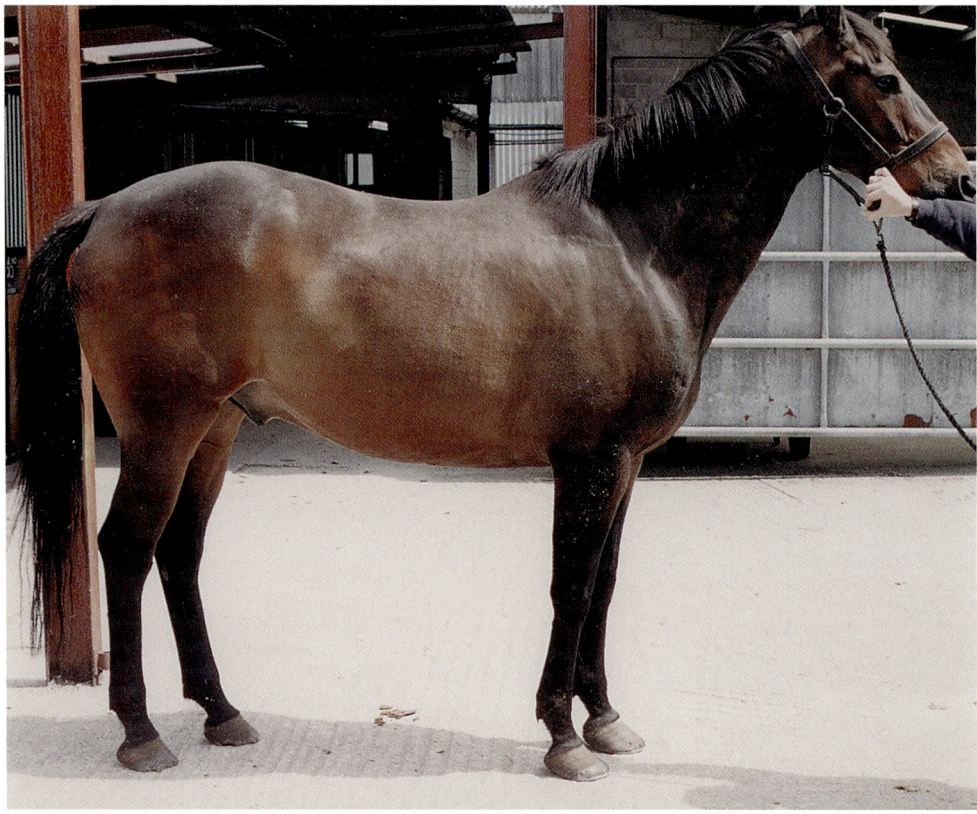

Fig. 9.6 (above) A horse with clinical signs of navicular disease. Note the overgrown feet with broken-back hoof/pastern axis.

the 'lollipop' shaped lesions which are characteristic of navicular disease; they are known as either nutrient foramina or synovial fossae ■

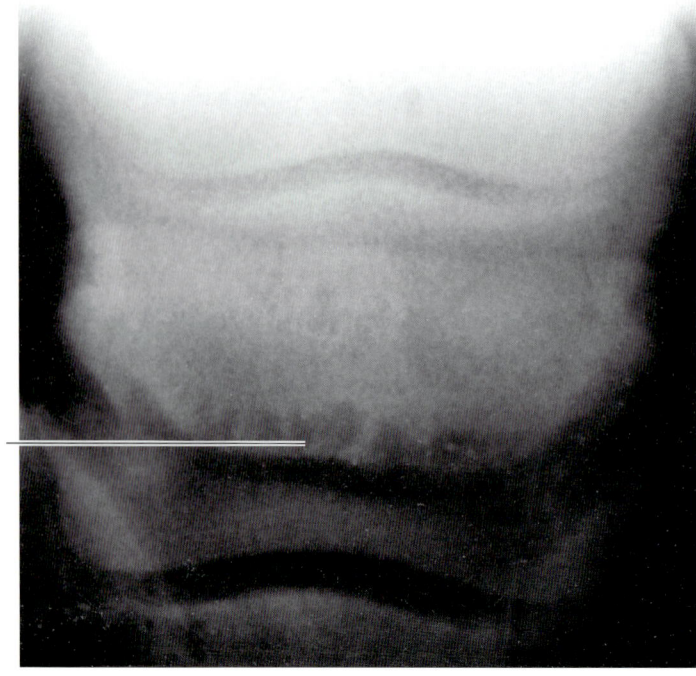

Fig. 9.7 Radiographic signs of navicular disease. The characteristic 'lollipop' shaped lesions can clearly be seen.

Fig. 9.8 The solar view of this horse's foot shows the poor state of its farriery.

has no need of a straight-bar shoe because the foot is stable.

2. His conformation shows that he does not have long sloping pasterns and his heels are not so under-run as to need egg-bar shoes.

3. The sole of his foot is not flat and the feet are not splayed out, so he has no need of a heart-bar shoe.

Therefore there is nothing in this horse's conformation or hoof-capsule shape (after it has been correctly trimmed) that indicated a need for any sort of bar shoe at all. The fact that he has navicular disease is neither here nor there. Putting any sort of bar shoe on him at all will be a complete waste of time because you will be doing nothing above what an ordinary, correctly forged, open-heeled shoe can, provided of course that he is trimmed so that he is in balance (Fig. 9.9).

Once this horse had been shod his level of lameness markedly diminished

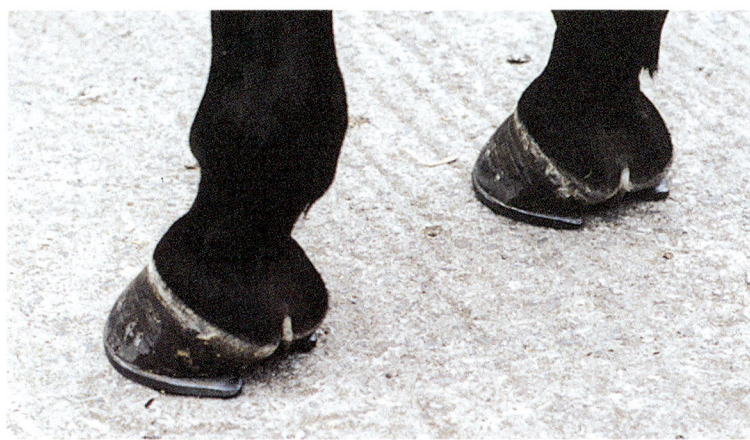

Fig. 9.9 This horse does not need a bar shoe. Just because he has navicular disease does not mean that the rules of good foot balance and shoeing advocated in this book should be ignored.

and his lameness score improved from an initial score of 3 (lameness is consistently observable at a trot under all circumstances) to a score of 1(lameness is difficult to observe, not consistently apparent regardless of circumstances, i.e. weight carrying, circling, inclines, hard surface, etc). So merely by shoeing the horse for his natural conformation and hoof-capsule shape his lameness was significantly improved and his pain was diminished to minimal levels.

Horses with navicular disease need egg-bar shoes only if they have long sloping pasterns or have substantially under-run heels. Interestingly many horses with navicular disease do have very under-run heels – it is thought to be one of the many predisposing factors to the disease. Perhaps, therefore, it is not surprising that egg-bar shoes and navicular disease have become synonymous. But as a point of principle if a horse has not got the conformation for a bar shoe then he shouldn't wear one.

CHAPTER **10**

Wedges, Pads, Studs and New Materials

Wedges and pads

Many things other than horseshoes seem to be applied to horses' feet in the so-called interests of getting the balance right. Many farriers feel that to correct a broken back hoof/pastern axis all you have to do is apply a heel wedge. See Fig. 10.1. However, **applying heel wedges is neither necessary nor advisable.**

The horse in Fig. 10.2 is a case in point. He has been shod with a plastic heel wedge between the shoe and the foot (Fig.10.3). The problem with heel wedges is that although they provide a very short-term solution in cases where the heels have collapsed, in the long term they create more problems because

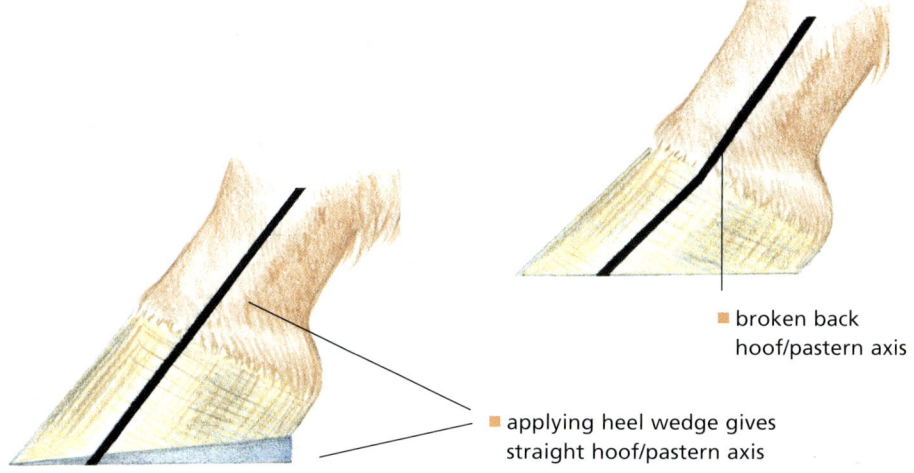

■ broken back hoof/pastern axis

■ applying heel wedge gives straight hoof/pastern axis

Fig. 10.1 The application of a heel wedge to correct a broken-back hoof/pastern axis. This is a poor remedy.

Fig. 10.2 This horse has been fitted with a heel wedge in an attempt to give him a correct hoof/pastern axis.

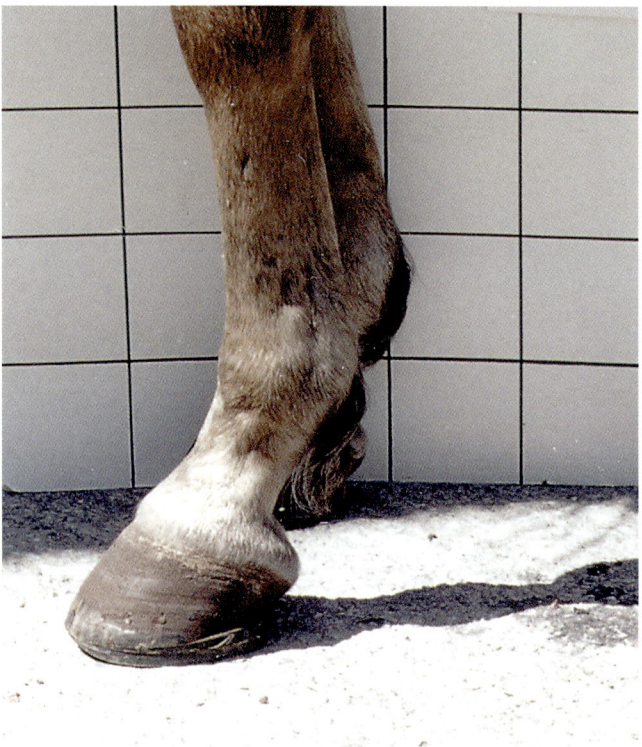

they act to crush the horn tubules at the heels even more. Therefore you create a vicious spiral – the heels are collapsed, heel wedges are applied, these crush the horn tubules at the heels, which leads to more collapse at the heels.

It is particularly unnecessary when the broken back hoof/pastern axis can be corrected just by applying the basic principles we have outlined throughout

Fig. 10.3 The shoe and heel wedge taken off the horse (left) and the new broad-webbed shoe without wedge which was applied (right).

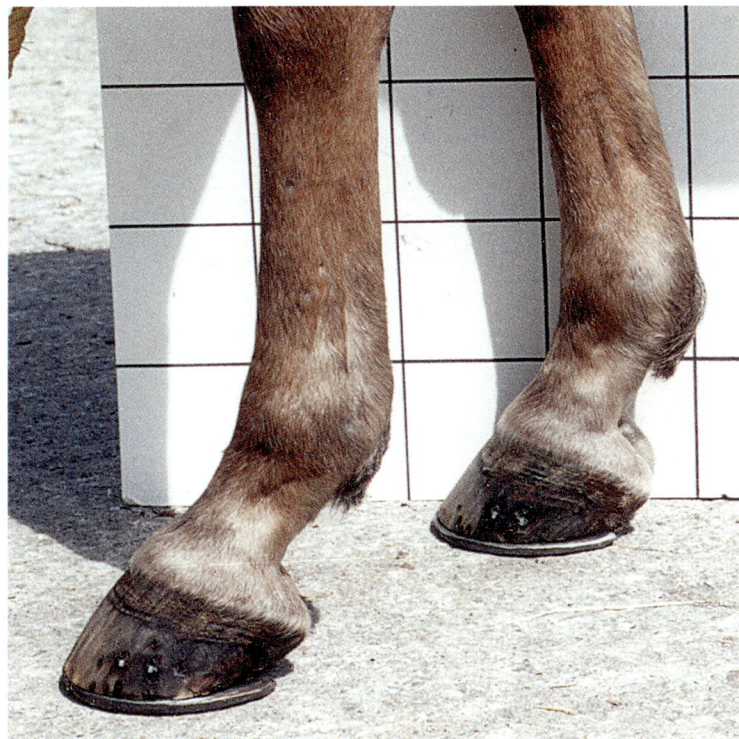

Fig. 10.4 The horse now has a correct hoof/pastern axis without the use of the wedge.

this book. Fig. 10.4 shows the same horse shod without the heel wedges and you can instantly see that he has no broken back hoof/pastern axis now, despite the fact he has no heel wedges. This is because a broad-webbed shoe with plenty of support at the heels has created support for the fetlock, which has lifted up, thus correcting the broken back axis.

Similar problems also occur with pads and there can be no real cause to use pads in any horse except perhaps if you have a horse with a punctured sole and you need to get round a cross-country course. In such cases you should have the pads applied just before you enter the start box and have them removed just after you cross the finishing line. Two of the main problems with pads is that you are likely to end up with bacterial/fungal infections in the frog, or the nails work loose because of the constant compression of the pad between the shoe and the foot.

Alternative shoe materials

Alternative materials for horseshoes seem to have become very fashionable. Plastic, aluminium and rubber horseshoes have been developed and their manufacturers have made many claims about how their product is the Holy Grail of farriery. Alternative materials for horseshoes are something that

Fig. 10.5 A major problem with aluminium shoes is that because the metal is so soft, the hoof capsule can be driven down into the metal. At the heels this can prevent the correct functioning of the foot.

groove created by heels being driven into the soft aluminium ■

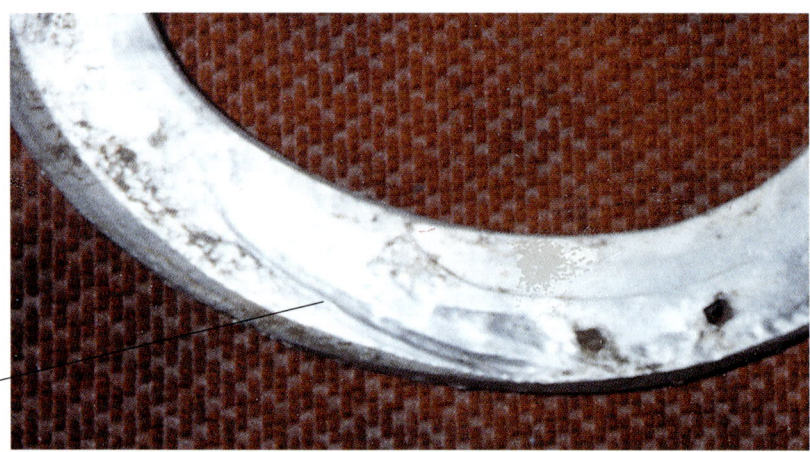

require much more research as to their effects on equine locomotion. You have only to go into your local sports superstore to see the myriad types of sports shoe for every type of human sporting endeavour, all biomechanically tested to provide optimal performance and minimise risk of concussive-related injury. And still the horse is putting up with the same old type of shoe that he has been putting up with for hundreds of years. Perhaps we should start thinking about 'Nike Airs' for horses.

While it is important to keep an open mind about alternative modern materials, the fundamental functions of the foot should not be overlooked. Some of the aluminium shoes, as well as the rubber shoes, have to be cold-shod. Although there is nothing inherently wrong with cold-shoeing, it must be borne in mind that a shoe that cannot be changed in shape must be applied to a foot that it fits exactly. The farrier then becomes a little like Prince Charming – searching for a foot to fit the shoe. Also rubber shoes cannot have bars or extensions welded to them and are perhaps therefore not as versatile as metal shoes in the correction of hoof capsule or conformation problems.

Aluminium shoes also present a problem in that the metal is softer than that of the normal horseshoe. To a certain extent it is the lightness of this soft metal that is at first appealing. It is presumed that putting a lighter shoe of a softer construction on the foot of the horse will reduce concussion, and that may well be the case – which is why racehorses are shod in racing plates of aluminium construction. However, aluminium shoes are worn away much more easily because of their softer composition. Secondly, and much more importantly, the force of the horse bearing down on the shoe can actually drive the hoof wall into the shoe itself.

Fig. 10.5 shows an aluminium shoe which has suffered this fate. Where the hoof wall has ground into the shoe a groove has been created, and the surrounding metal would have created painful ridges digging into the white line. Further, the heels would have stuck into the groove and been prevented from expanding, thus affecting the whole functioning of the foot.

Studs

The application of studs to shoes is a very contentious issue. The 'one stud or two?' argument is a perennial one and the fact is that there is no simple answer.

Although there are times when studs must necessarily be applied to the shoes of the performance horse, it is as well to remember that, like all other things that we apply to our horses' feet, they create biomechanical dilemmas. It is for the owner/rider to decide which of these dilemmas carries the least risk to their horse, bearing in mind the conformation of the horse, the type of competition, the level of competition, the skill of the horse and rider combination, and the relative risks of competing with or without studs.

In the following photographs we will demonstrate the effects of applying one or two studs. The fact that we have shown one stud applied to the front foot and two studs applied to the hind foot is not relevant – this was merely to demonstrate the effect of the studs.

Fig. 10.6 shows the solar aspect of the foot with one stud applied to the outside heel quarter. In a foot which has been balanced medio-laterally you can immediately appreciate that this will have the effect of creating an imbalance in that the foot will become 'outside high'. Of course, the whole point about a stud is that it will sink into the ground and create an anchor point to prevent the horse from slipping, but there are many times when the ground will not be so giving or when – perhaps out hunting – the horse will be moving

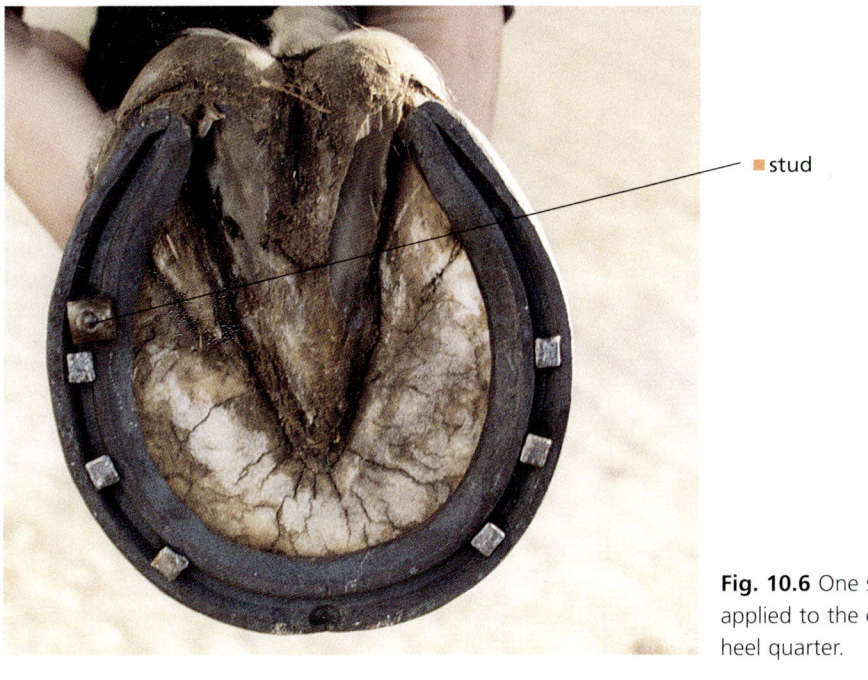

■ stud

Fig. 10.6 One stud applied to the outside heel quarter.

on hard road surfaces. Because studs are generally applied to horses who are doing fast work then the effects of this stud-created imbalance can be catastrophic.

Figs 10.7 and 10.8 show how a stud can affect the limb orientation. You may wonder why we have shown the horse standing on one front leg – the answer is simply that when the horse is moving he rarely has both front feet on the floor together! Viewed from the back, as in Fig. 10.9, the limb deviation is even more apparent.

Another problem with applying just one stud to the outside of the foot is that when the horse places his foot to the ground during locomotion the stud is the first part of the foot to make contact. The effect of this is that the inside part of the foot will still be moving for a fraction of a second after the stud has connected with the ground, and the inside part of the foot will spiral around to

Fig. 10.7 Note how one stud in the outside heel quarter has created a limb deviation at the fetlock – ripe for a chip fracture in any performance horse.

Fig. 10.8 You can see how the stud lifts the outside of the foot off the floor, making the foot outside high.

■ note how the fetlock joint is deviated medially, creating a compression of the joint on the outside aspect

■ the stud is lifting the outside of the foot off the floor

the outside, around the stud. Think about a pencil in a drawing compass – when the spike of the compass is stuck in the paper, the pencil swings around it. So on top of a stud-created medio-lateral imbalance, a torque is created around the stud, causing the whole limb to spiral around to the outside (Fig. 10.10). As a result of this spiralling of the limb, abnormal forces in the tendons and ligaments can lead to breakdown.

One of the benefits of having just one stud is that when the horse is not moving in a straight line at high speed in soft ground, the one stud allows the foot to swivel with the turns of the horse. This is particularly important when, for example, during a cross-country phase, the horse is jumping combination fences which require twists and turns in between.

The abnormal biomechanical effect created by one stud is the reason why road studs are a major causes of chronic hind-limb lameness. In our opinion road studs should never be applied to horses, despite – or particularly in view of – the fact that they are doing large amounts of road work. Anti-slip nails are by far the best approach.

■ stud

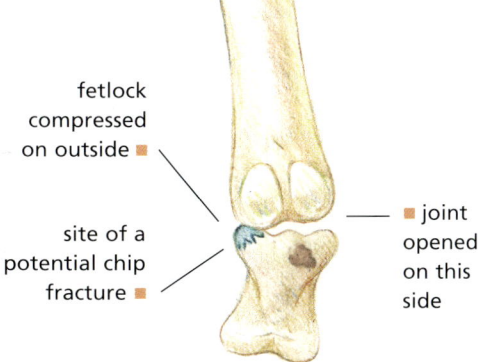

Fig. 10.9 The outside aspect of all the joints in the lower limb are compressed (see diagram) leading to potential for chip fractures.

fetlock compressed on outside ■

site of a potential chip fracture ■

■ joint opened on this side

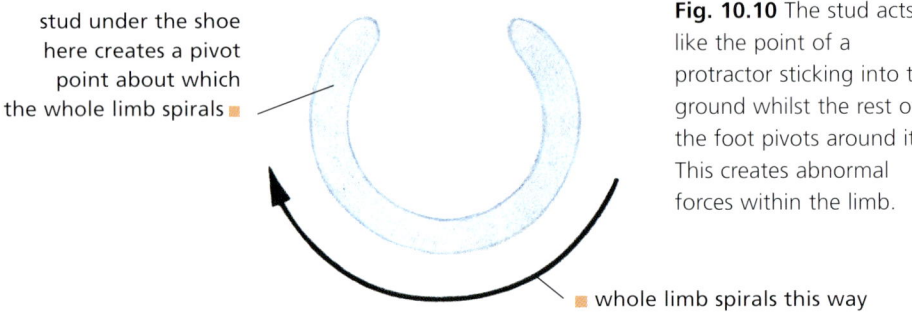

stud under the shoe here creates a pivot point about which the whole limb spirals ■

Fig. 10.10 The stud acts like the point of a protractor sticking into the ground whilst the rest of the foot pivots around it. This creates abnormal forces within the limb.

■ whole limb spirals this way

The alternative to having just one stud in the outside of the foot is to put one stud in each heel – Figs 10.11 and 10.12. Many texts will tell you that putting a stud in the inside aspect of a shoe is not recommended because they predispose to injury in the other hind limb because the inside stud can make contact if the horse brushes. Again this is very possibly correct but only if the feet are not in balance. If the feet are properly balanced and moving correctly there should be no contact between limb pairs.

The benefits of having a stud in each heel are that they do not create a medio-lateral imbalance and neither do they force the limb to spiral around the pivot point of the stud when the foot is placed to the floor. They are, however, not without their own problems in a biomechanical context.

Fig. 10.13 shows a pair of hind limbs in which one shoe is fitted with studs and the other one not. You can see from this picture how the heels of the foot are elevated by the studs, thus throwing the weight of the horse forwards and onto the toes. Again, this has the effect of completely unbalancing the horse.

The disadvantage of having two studs is that once the foot has been planted

Figs. 10.11-12 A stud applied to each heel.

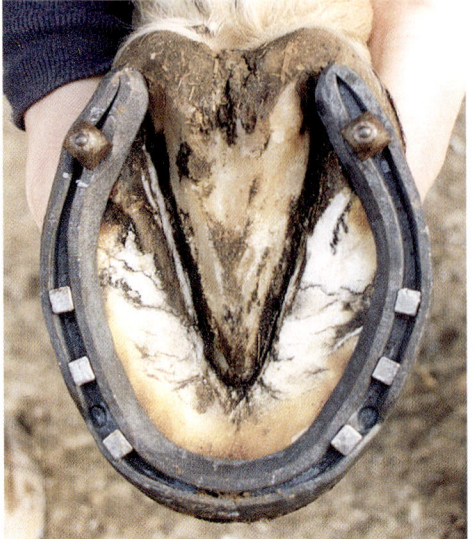
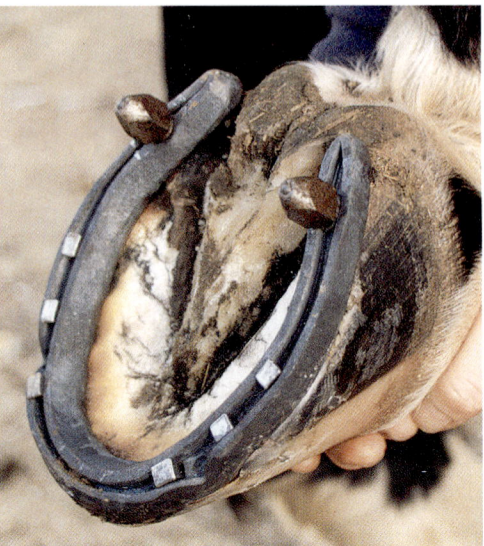

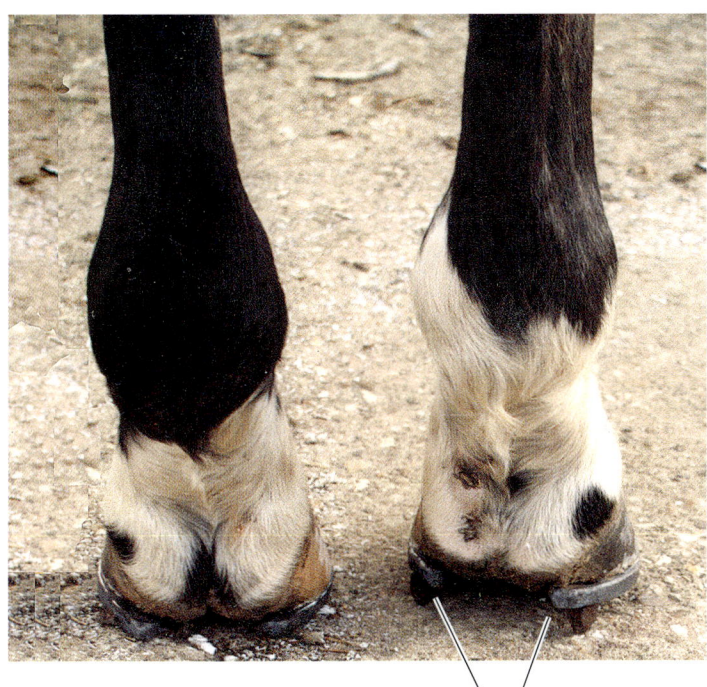

Fig. 10.13 The left shoe has no studs fitted; the right shoe has studs in the heels. Elevating the heels in this way throws the horse forward and unbalances him.

■ stud in each heel throwing the horse's weight forward

on the ground it is effectively fixed there and cannot undergo any rotation. If the horse is moving in a straight line this is not a problem. The problem arises when the horse has to negotiate tight turns – with the foot firmly fixed on the ground any turns will cause strain on the joints and ligaments, creating the potential for breakdown.

So there simply is no easy answer to the question 'One stud or two?' The best advice we can offer is that if you have a small 'whippety' type of horse and you are going to take the long and winding route through combination fences or if you are engaged in a sport which requires quick turns, you are probably best to stick with one stud. If you have a bigger horse with a bold rider who is going to take the straight route through combinations or if you take part in a sport which does not require tight turns then you are best advised to have two studs.

Unfortunately, despite this advice, the bold, straight horse is going to need to make tight turns at some stage, just as the quick, turning horse is going to have to move in straight lines. As we said at the outset – you have to make your own decisions as to which will cause the least problems to your horse, because there is no doubt that applying studs in the first place, however many there are, will cause disruption to normal locomotion.

CHAPTER 11

Farriery into the 21st Century

At present, research into equine locomotion lags far behind the scientific study of human locomotion. Unfortunately we cannot generally apply the human scientific advances to horses because humans rely on two legs and synergistic pairs of muscles for their locomotion whereas horses are quadrupeds with a greater reliance on elastic recoil energy to propel them forwards.

To enable us to develop new shoes and locomotor aids for horses we first need a complete understanding of the biomechanics of the horse and, more especially, of his feet. Our lack of understanding in this vitally important area is largely due to the fact that we have been unable to utilise the equipment that was devised for making quantitative assessments of human locomotion. This was because the equipment could not withstand the forces generated by horses. Further, locomotion laboratories for humans can be built on a considerably smaller scale than locomotion laboratories designed for horses, and consequently equine locomotion laboratories are extremely costly units to set up and equip.

However, there are a (very) few equine locomotion laboratories throughout the world and some researchers have used them to look at the role of the foot in equine locomotion[1]. Data collected have been able to increase our knowledge of how the horse moves, how he loads his limbs during the stance phase, and how he moves his limbs through the air, both when his feet are balanced and out of balance. This chapter looks at the knowledge we have gleaned from these studies and demonstrates how horse welfare can be improved by applying hi-tech advancements to the age-old skill of farriery.

To be able adequately to quantify equine locomotion we need to acquire a full understanding of both equine kinematics and kinetics. Expressed more simply, we need to know how the horse moves and what forces he generates to enable him to move. These studies are in their infancy but as we begin to understand how we can prevent injury and increase performance, studies in equine biomechanics are likely to sky-rocket.

Usually injury to a limb occurs whilst that limb is weightbearing and being subjected to forces with which it is not equipped to deal. What we need to know is: what are the normal forces to which the limb is subjected during locomotion? To assess this we need a method of demonstrating locomotor forces that is non-invasive and not damaging to the horse in any way. We need a method that does not alter the way in which the horse moves.

Some researchers have attempted to apply devices to metal shoes to measure the forces being applied to the shoe and, hence, to the foot. Fig. 11.1 shows one such device. However, it is generally considered that applying these 'force shoes' to horses' feet may in some way interfere with normal locomotion and represent a source of error in our search for limb loading characteristics.

The majority of studies today utilise a piece of equipment known as a 'force plate'. The force plate measures the duration, magnitude and direction of ground-reaction forces (GRF) as a function of time. Equine limb GRF can be divided into three orthogonal (directional) forces (see Fig. 11.3 overleaf) – the medio-lateral force (forces moving from left to right) known as **Fx**; the cranio-

Fig. 11.1 A force shoe. A force transducer is applied to each heel and the toe. Researchers can then ascertain where the foot is taking the greatest forces. (Both illustrations courtesy Professor Marc Ratzlaff, Washington State University.)

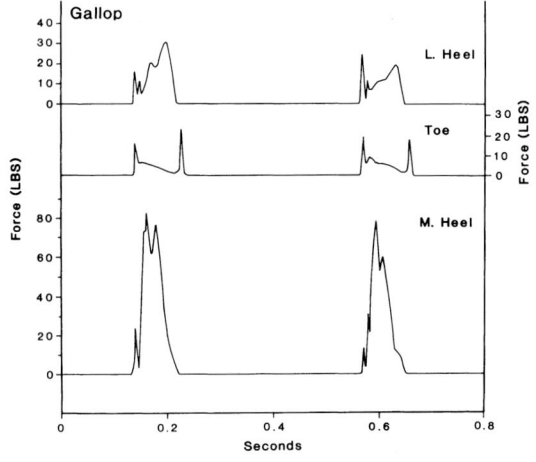

Fig. 11.2 The computer print-out from a force shoe of a galloping horse. Note that it is the medial heel which is experiencing the greatest forces.

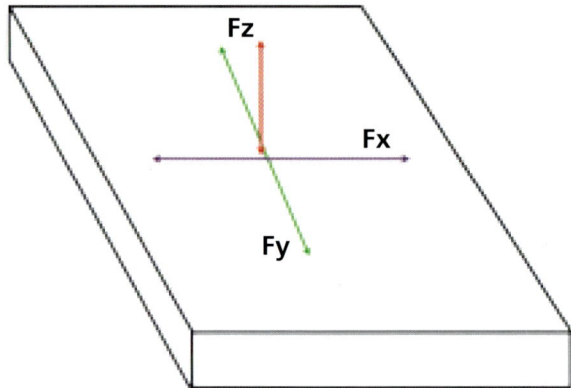

Fig. 11.3 A graphical representation of a force plate showing the three orthogonal components of force.

caudal force (forces moving from front to back) known as **Fy**; and the vertical force (forces being transmitted down through the limb) known as **Fz**.

The force plate is a kind of aluminium 'sandwich', in the middle of which, at each corner, is a piezo-electric crystal. When a force is applied to this crystal it changes shape and, in so doing, gives off an electric charge which is time and rate dependent. This electric charge can be digitised and logged onto a computer and analysed. Fig. 11.4 shows a picture of the most commonly used force plate for quantifying equine GRF patterns – a Kistler 9286, measuring 60 x 90 cms.

Fig. 11.4 A Kistler force plate commonly used for quantifying equine ground reaction force patterns.

The force plate is bolted to a steel frame embedded in 1cm³ of concrete and disguised by a piece of rubber matting (Fig. 11.5). The horse is trotted over the force plate and the forces generated when his foot hits the plate are calculated by computer.

When the data have been collected the computer can generate graphs to show how the forces are being applied to the plate. Fig. 11.6 shows how the three orthogonal components of force are applied by the horse shown in Fig. 11.5.

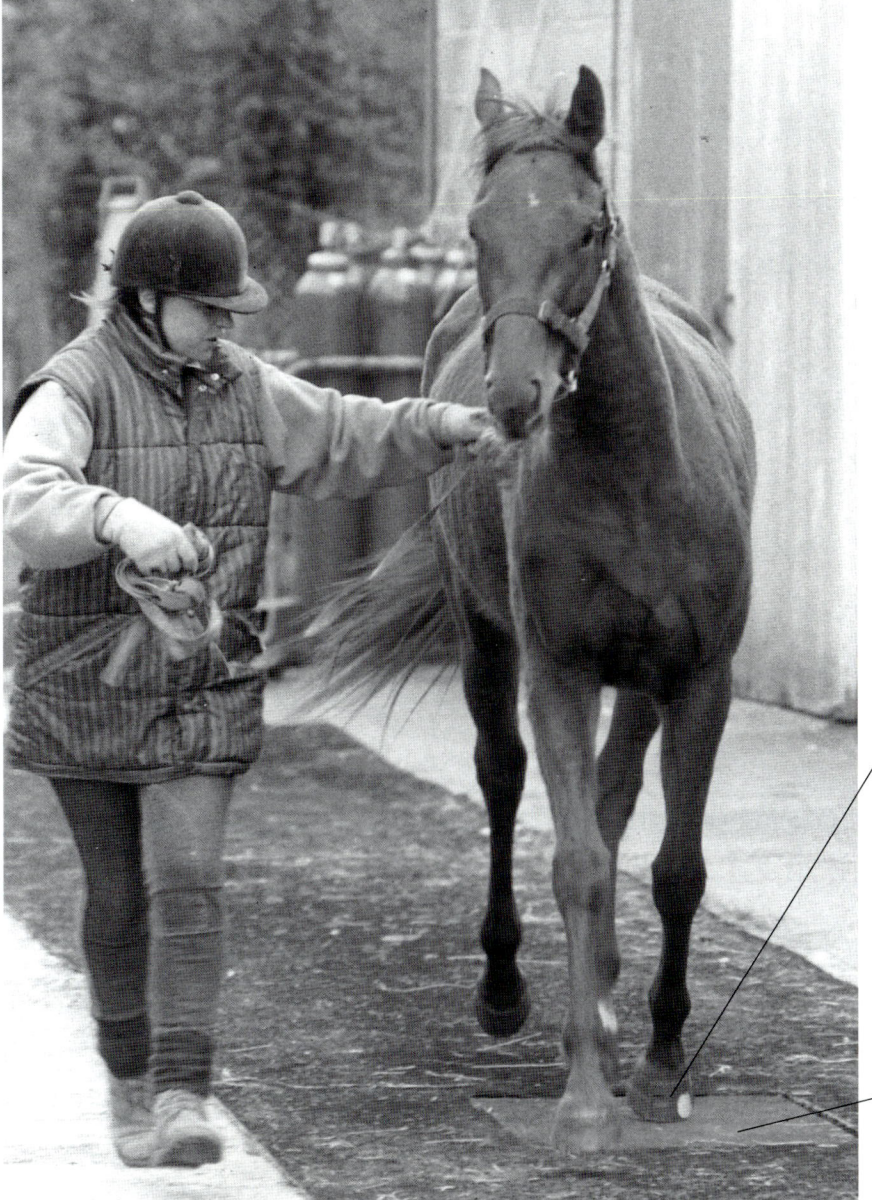

Fig. 11.5 The force plate in situ.

■ horse's foot lands on the force plate and the forces generated are digitised and sent via an underground cable to a computer in an adjacent building; the force plate takes 500 individual readings per second and a lot of data are generated

■ force plate set into a rubber matting runway; the top of the plate is disguised by a similar piece of matting

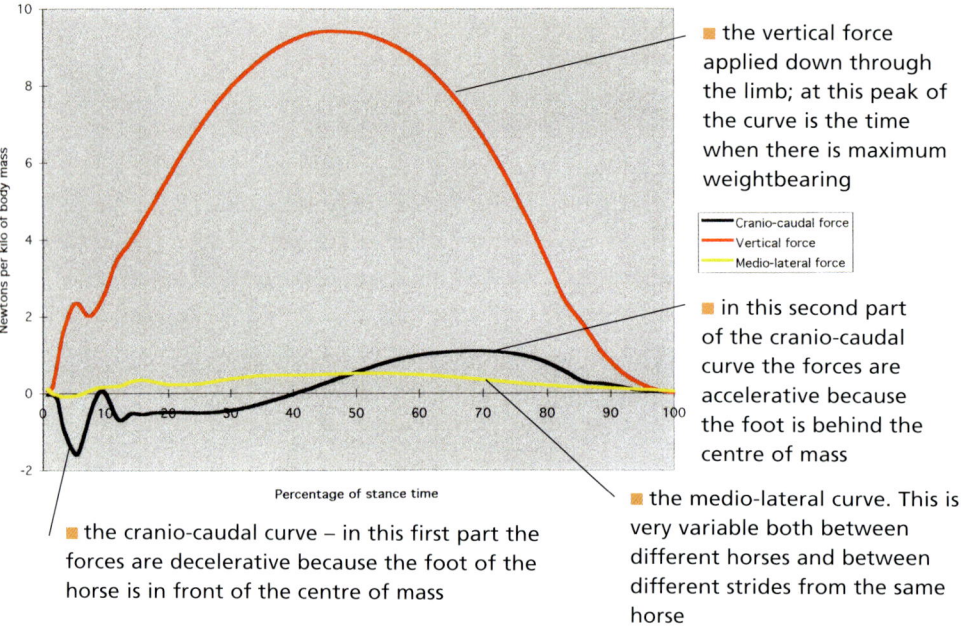

■ the vertical force applied down through the limb; at this peak of the curve is the time when there is maximum weightbearing

■ in this second part of the cranio-caudal curve the forces are accelerative because the foot is behind the centre of mass

■ the medio-lateral curve. This is very variable both between different horses and between different strides from the same horse

■ the cranio-caudal curve – in this first part the forces are decelerative because the foot of the horse is in front of the centre of mass

Fig. 11.6 A graph of the ground-reaction force patterns of a typical Thoroughbred horse at the trot.

From the point of view of farriery and foot balance, the computer can use the data generated by the force plate and can show where the point of force was being applied. The point of force represents the point on the surface of the force plate where the force would act if it were considered to have a single point of application. Consider the weight (and thus the force) that you are applying to your foot as you walk. Of course, whilst your foot is flat on the floor the entire sole of your foot is in contact with the ground and is bearing weight, but as you move the weight is concentrated more to the back or the front of the foot. The point of force, very simply, is the position of the majority of weight averaged out. Fig. 11.7 demonstrates this very visually, showing the differences between balanced and imbalanced feet.

By using this piece of scientific equipment, therefore, we can fine-tune the balance of horse's feet in much the same way as your local garage can fine-tune the balance of your car wheels. At the present time, this type of analysis can only be carried out at specially equipped sites with skilled technicians and scientists analysing the results, but the farrier of the future may have a type of force mat that he can simply lay on the floor outside your stables and collect this data for himself. In this way the horses of the future will not be subjected to the damage created by abnormal forces arising from foot imbalances because his feet will always be trimmed to ensure the minimum of concussion-related injuries.

Of course, for the majority of your horse's stride, the foot is in the air and it is just as important to ensure that not only is he loading the limb correctly, but

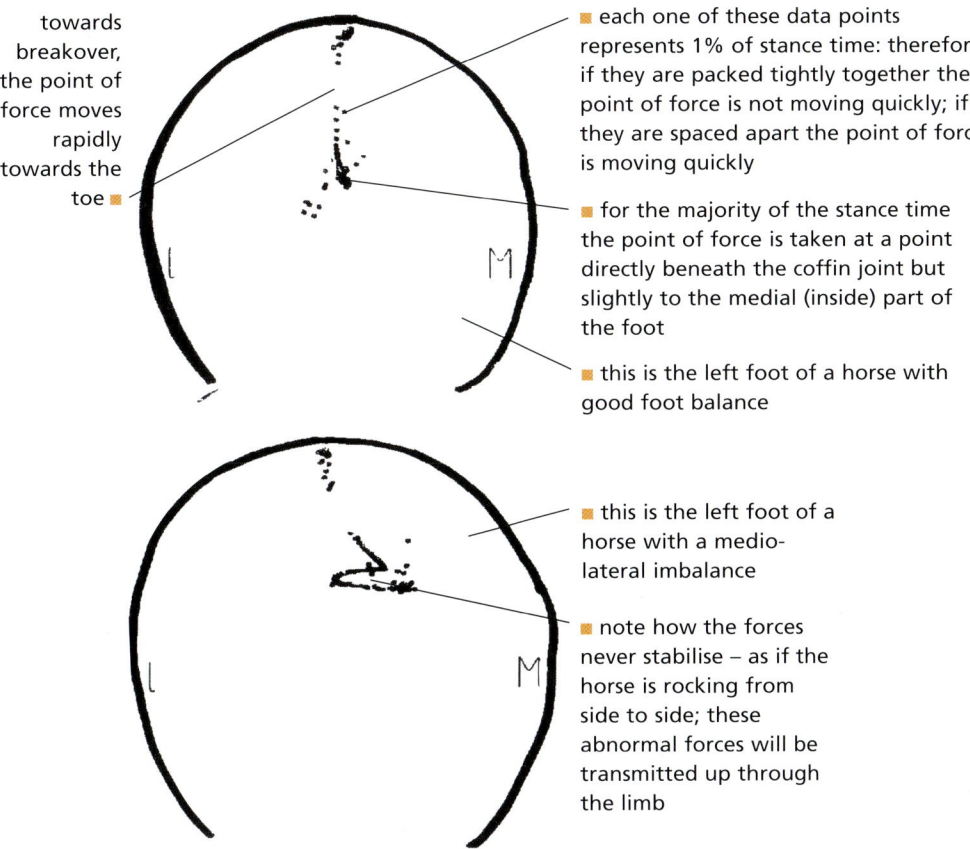

towards breakover, the point of force moves rapidly towards the toe ■

■ each one of these data points represents 1% of stance time: therefore if they are packed tightly together the point of force is not moving quickly; if they are spaced apart the point of force is moving quickly

■ for the majority of the stance time the point of force is taken at a point directly beneath the coffin joint but slightly to the medial (inside) part of the foot

■ this is the left foot of a horse with good foot balance

■ this is the left foot of a horse with a medio-lateral imbalance

■ note how the forces never stabilise – as if the horse is rocking from side to side; these abnormal forces will be transmitted up through the limb

Fig. 11.7 A comparison of the point of force under the left front foot of a horse with balanced feet (top) and imbalanced feet (bottom).

also he is not moving the foot through the air in such a way as to cause interference with another limb. We need to assess his kinematics by quantifying his limb movement.

The kinematic analysis of equine locomotion began in 1887 when the American photographer Muybridge demonstrated that photography could serve as a tool for capturing the accurate information needed to characterise the kinematics of the equine limb[2].

Modern kinematic investigations invariably utilise visual recording systems coupled with the referencing of anatomical landmarks. The problems associated with kinematic investigation of horses are that they are generally very large animals and fast moving. Therefore, the only way to capture realistic data is either for the data collection camera to move alongside the horse mounted on a vehicle (which can be dangerous, is subject to the vagaries of the weather and very rarely produces reproducible data) or for the camera to be stationary and have the horse moving on a treadmill. The second option is by far the most appropriate for collecting useful data, although again at the present time collection of this sort of kinematic data can only take place in properly equipped locomotion laboratories.

Some people believe that making horses run on a treadmill is cruel and unnecessary but generally, after a few initially wobbly steps, horses tend to enjoy the experience. Fig. 11.8 shows a horse being exercised on a high-speed equine treadmill in an equine locomotion laboratory.

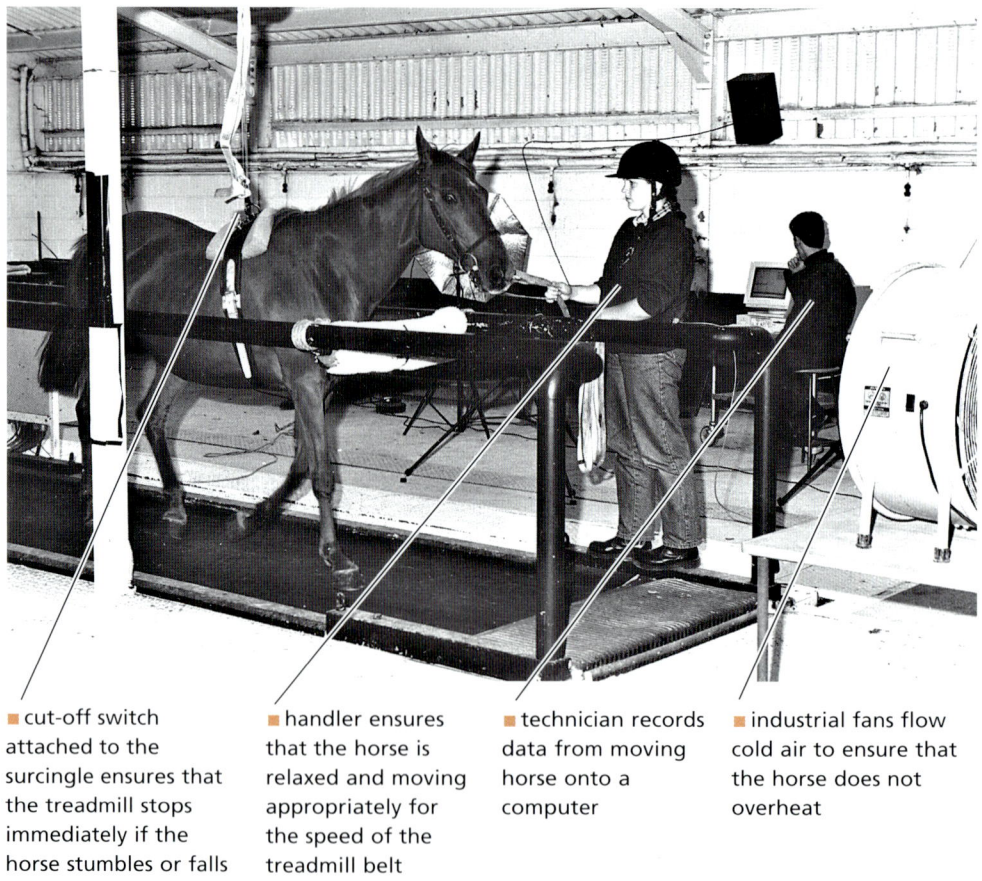

■ cut-off switch attached to the surcingle ensures that the treadmill stops immediately if the horse stumbles or falls

■ handler ensures that the horse is relaxed and moving appropriately for the speed of the treadmill belt

■ technician records data from moving horse onto a computer

■ industrial fans flow cold air to ensure that the horse does not overheat

Fig. 11.8 A horse trotting on a treadmill in an equine locomotion laboratory.

The horse on the treadmill can now be kept at a constant pre-selected speed and horses who are used to the treadmill move in a relaxed and even manner – ideal for analysing the way they move.

Having found a way of getting the horse to move in a manner appropriate for reproducible data collection, the problem now is one of how to collect and analyse the data. Most kinematic stride variables and joint angles can be obtained from a two-dimensional analysis utilising one camera placed at right angles to the horse. Deviations from the direction of movement or out-of-plane movement of the limbs cannot, however, be detected. Three-dimensional analysis is more desirable to obtain meaningful data but it is a far more complex task. Three-dimensional measurement of movement is reduced to the detection of the trajectories of several points that identify the position of the body segments in space. Active (those which emit some form of energy) or passive (light reflecting) markers are attached to palpable and repeatable musculo-skeletal landmarks. Those markers are then tracked by a marker detector device and their spatial locations determined by a computer.

Many studies of equine kinematics have utilised the MacReflex motion analysis system (MacReflex 2.5, Qualysis, Sweden) which locates the position in space of passive reflective markers attached to skeletal landmarks on the horse. The system uses either one camera for two-dimensional data collection, or two or more cameras for three-dimensional data collection, in conjunction with video processors. The electronic shutter on the camera exposes a frame for 0.8 milliseconds ensuring reduction of the effect of ambient light and capture of fast-moving objects. Further the camera contains an optical filter which cuts off the visible part of the light spectrum, thus suppressing ambient light. An infra-red flash within the camera housing illuminates the scene in the field of view in synchronism with the electronic shutter and the reflective markers reflect most of the light back into the cameras. As other objects within the field of view reflect light in different directions, this ensures that the reflective markers will stand out by comparison.

The video processor detects the markers in space and calculates the central point of each marker by scanning the picture from top to bottom, left to right to locate the brightness of the marker against the background blackness. By detection of the location of the change from black to white and white to black, subsequent central point locations can be calculated.

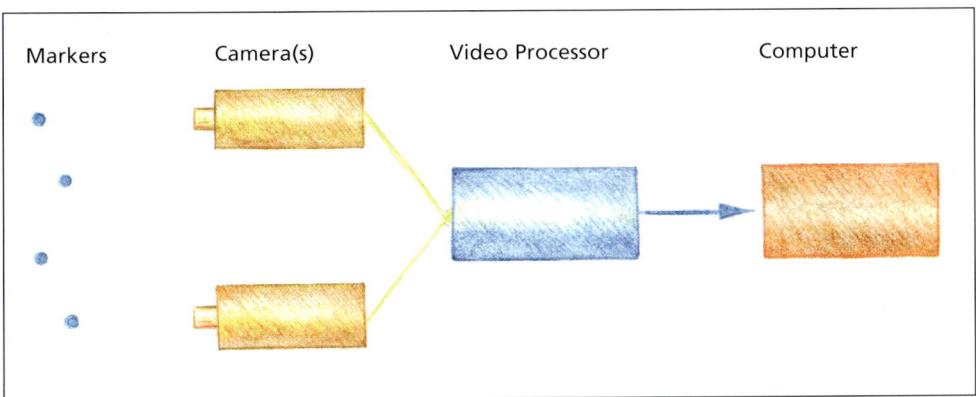

Markers　　　Camera(s)　　　Video Processor　　　Computer

Fig. 11.9 General arrangement of the MacReflex motion analysis system

The software package with the system calculates motion analysis quantities such as joint angles or the position of a marker in space.

Fig. 11.10 shows a horse with the markers attached, and Fig. 11.11 gives an impression of how the system works.

the horse is exercising on the treadmill ■

reflective markers (of the type used in outdoor sportswear) are attached to skeletal landmarks on the horse; the system camera(s) will track these markers, digitise the information, and store it onto a computer ■

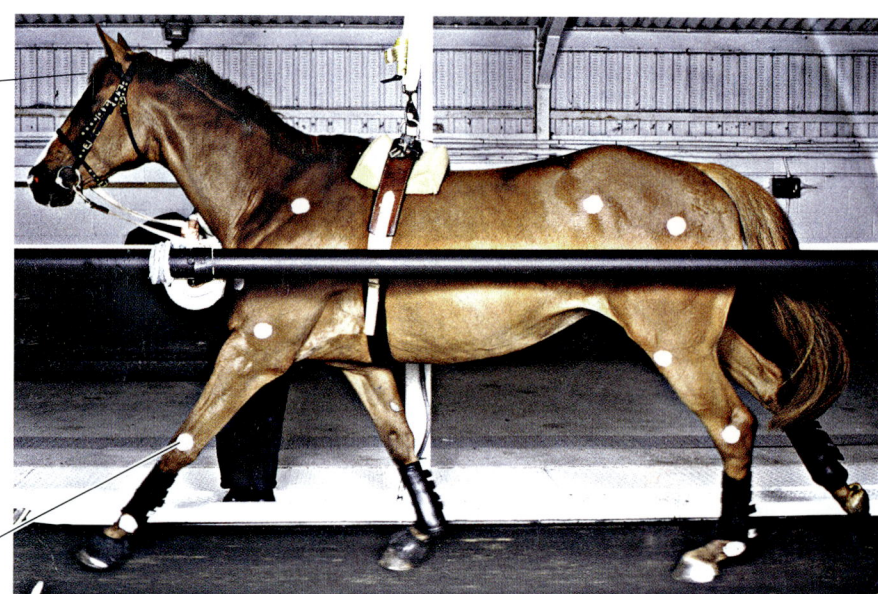

Fig. 11.10 Reflective markers applied to palpable skeletal landmarks on the horse can be tracked by the MacReflex system. (Courtesy Terri Richmond, University of Bristol.)

Fig. 11.11 Time-lapse photography gives an impression of how the markers move through space as the horse moves on the treadmill (Courtesy Terri Richmond, University of Bristol.)

The computer, having tracked those markers, can then give print-outs to demonstrate such things as left/right asymmetry of movement. Take, for example, the following three illustrations – Figs 11.12, 11.13 and 11.14. These are the MacReflex print-outs for the same horse, taken from the same few strides with the horse trotting at a speed of 4 metres per second on the tread-

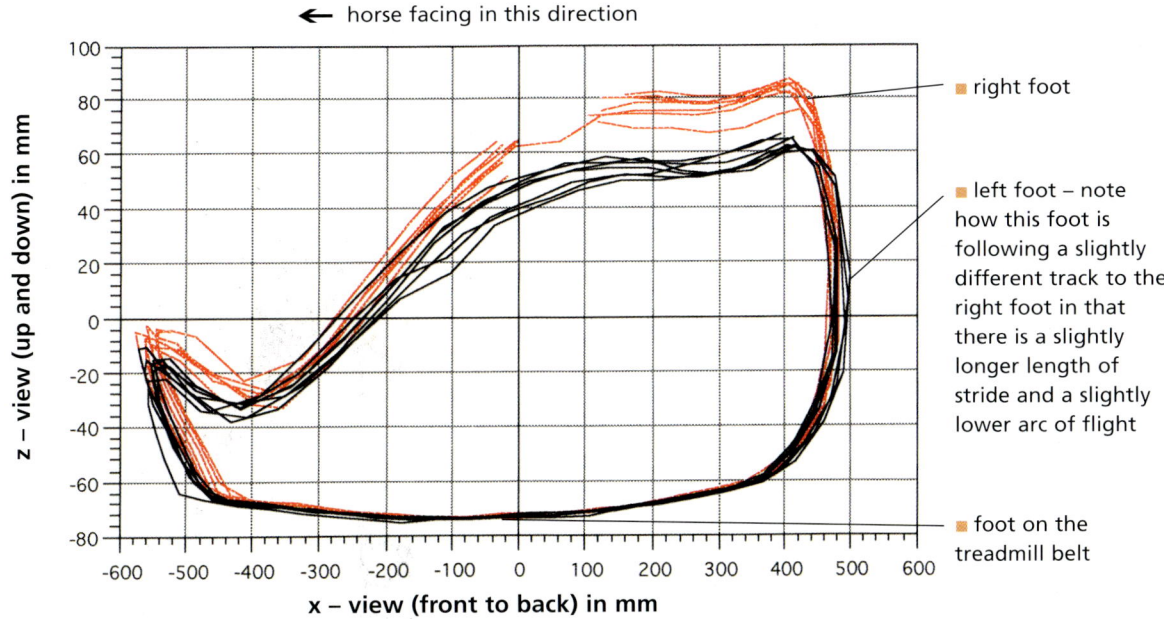

Fig. 11.12 MacReflex print out of the tracks made by the markers attached to the left and right feet of a horse trotting on a treadmill. Note that the axes are in millimetres and so the asymmetry of movement demonstrated is so small that it would be impossible to detect just by observation.

mill. In Fig. 11.12 the computer has calculated the arc of flight looking at right angles to the horse.

In Fig. 11.13 the asymmetry is not quite so obvious. What is interesting to

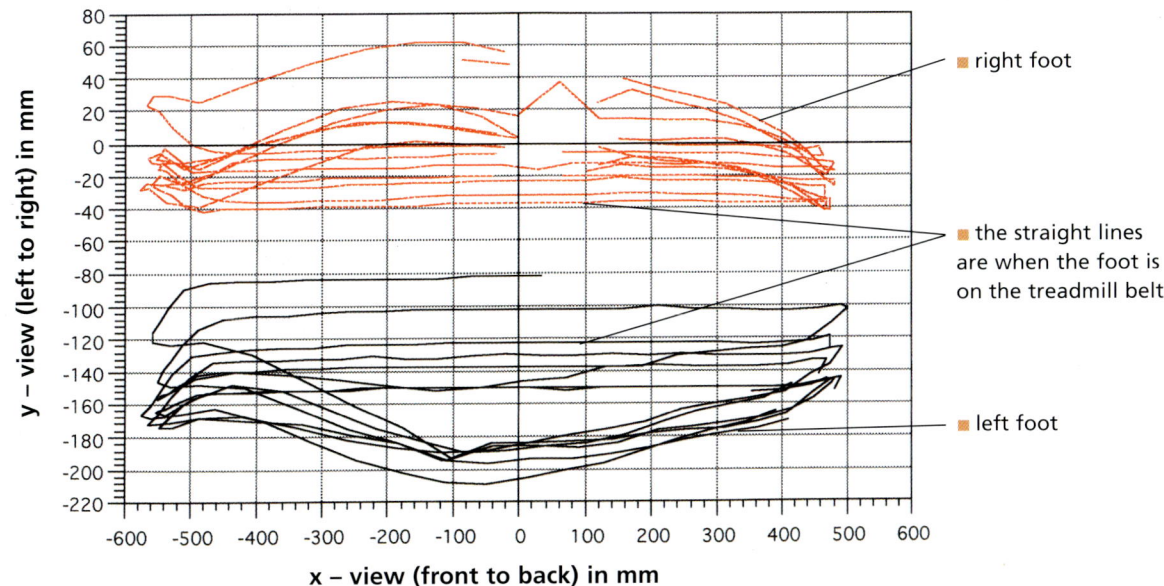

Fig. 11.13 The same horse and exactly the same strides as in Fig. 11.12 only the computer has calculated the arc of flight as if you were looking down from the withers.

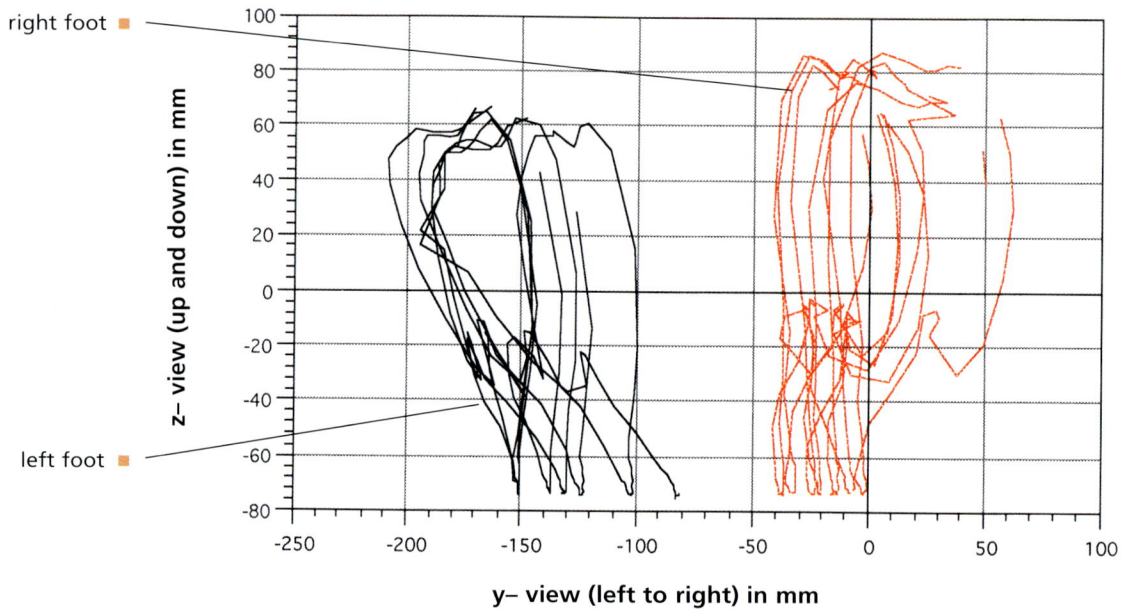

right foot ■

left foot ■

Fig. 11.14 The same horse and the same strides as shown in Figs. 11.12 and 11.13 only the computer has calculated the arc of flight of the feet as if you were standing behind the horse. Note how marked the asymmetry of action is in this plane.

note from this figure, however, is that the limb does not act like a perfect pendulum – it does not swing backwards and forwards in the same plane – but the horse swings the foot to the outside when it is in the air.

In Fig. 11.14 the computer has calculated the arc of flight from behind the horse. Note how marked the asymmetry has now become, even though the axes are still calculated in millimetres and you would not be able to see this just by looking at the horse yourself.

It is important to understand that although this horse is quite clearly moving asymmetrically, he is not clinically lame. In fact, to the eye, he is perfectly sound. So does it really matter that he is moving asymmetrically? The answer is 'Yes it does'. In human athletes asymmetry of movement between left and right limbs is highly correlated to injury. Initial work with horses also shows a high correlation of asymmetry of function to athletic injury. It is therefore likely that if this horse were to be put into hard work he would be more than likely to sustain a locomotor-related injury. Using this system it could be possible to fine-tune the balance of this horse's feet so that he was moving more symmetrically and, thus, would be less susceptible to injury.

This system is expensive to purchase and needs highly skilled technicians and equine scientists to operate it; as such it is available only to a very small minority of owners. However, as scientific advances are made it may be possible for the farrier of the future to have some form of system that can give him accurate data as to how the horse he is about to shoe is moving his limbs and whether any asymmetries need to be corrected.

Thus tomorrow's farrier is just as likely to pull a portable computer out of his van as an anvil. Hopefully by that time we will recognise farriers for what they really are – one of the primary health carers for our horses. Shoeing will no longer be regarded as a necessary evil but vital for performance and soundness – and the expression 'no foot, no horse' will be a thing of the past.

References for Chapter 11
1. Williams, G.E. (1996), 'The role of the foot in equine locomotion', PhD thesis, University of Bristol, England.
2. Muybridge, E. (1887), *Animals in Motion*, ed Brown, L.S., Dover Publications, New York, USA.

Useful Addresses

Gail Williams BA(Hons) PhD
Senior Lecturer in Equine Studies
De Montfort University
Caythorpe Court
Caythorpe
Grantham
Lincolnshire
NG32 3EP
e-mail – gew@dmu.ac.uk

Martin Deacon FWCF
Hill Farm
Ilston on the HIll
Leicestershire
LE7 9EG
tel: 01162 596700

Worshipful Company of Farriers
19 Queen Street
Chipperfield
Kings Langley
Herts
WD4 9BT
tel: 01923 260747

Farriers' T-squares can be obtained from:
Stromsholm
8 James Way
Marshall Court
Denbigh West
Bletchley
Milton Keynes
MK1 1SU
tel: 01525 237477

Index

Page numbers in **bold type** refer to illustrations.